BOMB SCARE

BOMB SCARE

The *HISTORY and* FUTURE *of*
NUCLEAR WEAPONS
With a New Afterword

JOSEPH CIRINCIONE

COLUMBIA UNIVERSITY PRESS   NEW YORK

COLUMBIA UNIVERSITY PRESS
Publishers Since 1893
NEW YORK   CHICHESTER, WEST SUSSEX

Library of Congress Cataloging-in-Publication Data

Cirincione, Joseph.
Bomb scare : the history and future of nuclear weapons / Joseph Cirincione.
    p. cm.
ISBN 978-0-231-13510-8 (cloth : alk. paper)—ISBN 978-0-231-13511-5 (pbk. : alk.
    paper) — ISBN 978-0-231-50940-4 (e-book)
1. Nuclear weapons—History. 2. Nuclear nonproliferation. 3. Nuclear arms
control. I. Title.

U264.C57 2007
355.02'17—dc22   2006029174

Columbia University Press books are printed on permanent and
durable acid-free paper.
This book is printed on paper with recycled content.

Printed in the United States of America
c 10 9 8
p 10 9 8 7

CONTENTS

FIGURES AND TABLES

PREFACE

From the beginning, nuclear weapons have both terrified and fascinated us. Fear of the bomb motivated the first atomic program; the allure of the bomb's power later propelled national leaders to build ever-larger arsenals. Today, fear of a nuclear attack by terrorists or another country has made nuclear proliferation the number one security threat facing the United States and many other nations. Yet several countries still maintain extensive nuclear arsenals developed for another era, develop plans for new weapons, and postulate new nuclear missions. Leaders in several other nations—motivated by their own perceived security needs as well as by a desire for symbols of power and status—covet the weapons now denied them.

This is a book about those weapons. More specifically, it is about how and why nuclear weapons have multiplied, and what can be done to slow, stop, and reverse their spread. This discussion makes one very important assumption: the proliferation of nuclear weapons is undesirable.

This assumption is far from universal. Since the early days of the nuclear age, there has been a vigorous debate among scholars and policy makers on this issue. Nuclear optimists contend that nuclear weapons are beneficial, that their presence enhances international stability, and that their spread is inevitable. Nuclear pessimists warn that nuclear arsenals create instability, that the risk of nuclear weapon use—either by intention or accident—is too great to accept, and that there is nothing inevitable about nuclear proliferation.[1]

The optimists embrace the theory of nuclear deterrence, which holds that fear of a devastating nuclear counterstrike prevents states from attacking other nuclear states. Because of mutual deterrence, they argue, nuclear weapons prevent war between nuclear nations. Their presence enhances stability by discouraging rash or aggressive action. There is some compelling evidence to support this view. From 1900 to 1950, for example, one hundred million people died in wars. From 1951 to 2000, only some twenty million people suffered that same fate.[2] "Well-managed proliferation," some say, with perhaps double the number of today's nuclear-armed states, would extend the benefits of nuclear deterrence to many areas of the world, helping to keep the peace in Europe, Asia, and elsewhere.[3]

The pessimists disagree. They believe that "we lucked out" during the Cold War, when the two nuclear superpowers stood "eyeball to eyeball," in former secretary of state Dean Rusk's famous description of the Cuban Missile Crisis.[4] The spread of nuclear weapons, they argue, reduces real security. States are not always rational actors, for example. State leaders may act irrationally and initiate a nuclear strike. Nor are states monolithic. Substate actors with their own agendas, such as military commanders, may ignore orders and trigger a nuclear attack. Even with stable governments, they argue, the risk of an accidental launch is great because of technical failure, breakdown of command and control, bad intelligence, or false assumptions. Finally, the proliferation of nuclear weapons and their related technologies increases the risk of nuclear terrorism. Osama bin Laden has declared it a "religious duty" to acquire nuclear, biological, and chemical weapons; the multiplication of state arsenals and facilities would give him more possible sources of supply.[5]

While presenting both sides of the debate, this book clearly aligns with the nuclear pessimists. Though no nuclear weapons have been used in war since August 1945, no one can guarantee that this good fortune will continue. There have been too many close calls in the past sixty years to warrant such optimism. The physical, economic, and political consequences of a nuclear explosion in any major city would be far beyond anything seen since World War II. The physical damage from the blast, heat, and radiation of a nuclear weapon would be enormous. A small atomic weapon of 20 kilotons (similar to those used on Hiroshima and Nagasaki) would destroy or damage most buildings in a modern city and kill almost everyone within a 10-square-mile area, while a modern 1-megaton hydrogen bomb would kill most people within 150 to 600 square miles, depending on the ferocity of the firestorms created by the explosion. Radioactive fallout from the blast would kill thousands of others.

Profound societal damage would also occur. Physicist Charles Ferguson and scholar William Potter explain in a 2004 study:

> Consequences stemming from a terrorist-detonated nuclear weapon in an American city would emanate beyond the immediate tens or hundreds of thousands of fatalities and the massive property and financial damage. Americans who were not killed or injured by the explosion would live in fear that they could die from future nuclear terrorist attacks. Such fear would erode public confidence in the government and could spark the downfall of the administration in power. The tightly interconnected economies of the United States and the rest of the world could sink into a depression as a result of a crude nuclear weapon destroying the heart of a city.[6]

This threat stems not only from the 27,000 nuclear weapons held by eight or nine nations today but also from the possibility that new nations or even terrorist groups will join this deadly club. Many therefore conclude that we must find a non-nuclear alternative to global security. Upon receiving the 2005 Nobel Peace, Prize Mohamed ElBaradei, the director general of the International Atomic Energy Agency, said, "I have no doubt that, if we hope to escape self-destruction, then nuclear weapons should have no place in our collective conscience, and no role in our security."[7]

This book reviews the history, theory, and current trends in nuclear proliferation before coming to several conclusions about current policy and how it can be improved to significantly reduce the global nuclear threats.

Our story begins with an historical look back for a very good reason: we forget most of what we learn. This is true of individuals and of nations. The first three chapters serve both as a narrative for an elaboration of the science and technology of nuclear weapons and as a reminder that many of today's challenges are new in form, but not in substance, from those of the past. Policies to address these threats have been debated for over sixty years. We now have a solid historical record to use in judging which strategies worked and which did not. Just as the policy choices made in the early days of the nuclear age shaped the Cold War nuclear threats, the decisions we make in the next few years will determine whether we will roll back today's challenges or launch instead into a new wave of proliferation.

This brief look at the history of nuclear weapons should help readers better understand the various policy options described in the second half of the book. To help navigate these nuclear waters, we have also included a glossary, and extensive footnotes provide ideas for further readings. With these tools, readers can come to their own insights and conclusions about what the future of these weapons should be. For these should be policy decisions decided not by a small group of officials behind closed doors but by an informed public with the full benefit of considered debate. We hope this study contributes to that discussion.

ACKNOWLEDGMENTS

    This book was written while I was in my eighth year as director for nonproliferation at the Carnegie Endowment for International Peace. While at Carnegie I had the opportunity to directly engage some of the top scholars and senior officials in the field, both in the United States and around the world. Their insights inform the discussion of the history, theory, and future of nuclear weapons within this volume. I have tried to cite as many of them as possible and refer the reader to their works for more in-depth discussion. To all, named and unnamed, I owe a debt of gratitude.

    During the two years of writing for this book, I relied heavily on the dedication and assistance of Jane Vaynman and Joshua Williams, two of the finest researchers at Carnegie. Both worked for months to provide historical data, reviews of literature on the history and theory of proliferation, first drafts, informed comments, and painstaking corrections. Ben Bain and Caterina Dutto also pored over volumes of writings on nuclear issues and diligently delivered references, tables, charts, and insights. Georgetown University graduate student Courtney Radsch and Carnegie researcher Revati Prasad got this book off to a strong start with research that informed the proliferation theory chapter. My colleagues and my coauthors of *Deadly Arsenals*, Jon B. Wolfsthal and Miriam Rajkumar, educated and sustained me not only during the drafting of this study but throughout our years together at the Endowment. The book could not have been written without this outstanding Carnegie nonproliferation team.

As always, the Carnegie library staff of Kathleen Higgs and Chris Henley cheerfully and quickly provided vital research materials. Carnegie president Jessica Mathews and vice president George Perkovich, whose leadership has made the Endowment one of the premier global research institutions, graciously tolerated my obsession with this book and the time it took away from other vital projects.

I would also like to thank Mark Strauss, editor of the *Bulletin of the Atomic Scientists*, for allowing me to develop this historic analysis as an article, "Lessons Lost," in the November 2005 issue of his essential magazine, and Jon Lottman of Dot-Org Digital for producing a spectacular video presentation based on my lecture, "A Brief History of the Atomic Age," posting it on the web, and packaging it in a beautiful DVD. This presents a video overview of the first two chapters of this book. Thank you also to John Podesta, for bringing me on as senior vice president at the Center for American Progress, and to the team there that supported my lecture tour on this book. After two years at the center, I am grateful to the board of directors of the Ploughshares Fund for appointing me as its new president and to the foundation's executive director, Naila Bolus, for her unselfish partnership as I take on this new mission.

I am grateful for the generous past support of the John T. and Catherine D. MacArthur Foundation, the Carnegie Corporation of New York, the Nuclear Threat Initiative, the Prospect Hill Foundation, the Ford Foundation, the Ploughshares Fund, the Newland Foundation, and the George Family Foundation. Thanks also to the editors of Columbia University Press for inviting me to write this study, for patiently awaiting its delivery, for greatly improving what they received, and updating the book for the paperback edition.

My wife, Priscilla Labovitz, and my two wonderful, accomplished children, Amy and Peter Cirincione, have given me the most supportive and loving family a man could want. They are in great part responsible for the optimism the reader will find in the final chapters.

Joseph Cirincione
Washington, D.C.
March 2008

BOMB SCARE

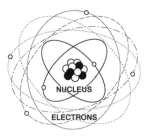

THE ATOM
Figure from the Department of Energy

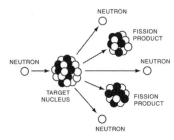

FISSION
Figure from Ohio State University, Department of Physics

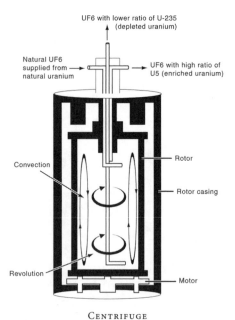

CENTRIFUGE
Figure from Cirincione, Wolfsthal, and Rajkumar, *Deadly Arsenals: Nuclear, Chemical, and Biological Threats*
(Carnegie Endowment for International Peace, 2005)

CHAPTER ONE

BUILDING THE BOMB

Albert Einstein signed the letter. Years later he would regret it, calling it the one mistake he had made in his life. But in August 1939, Adolf Hitler's armies already occupied Czechoslovakia and Austria and his fascist thugs were arresting Jews and political opponents throughout the Third Reich. Signing the letter seemed vital. His friends and fellow physicists, Leo Szilard and Eugene Wigner, had drafted the note he would now send to President Franklin D. Roosevelt.

The scientists had seen their excitement over the recent breakthrough discoveries of the deepest secrets of the atom turn to fear as they realized what unleashing atomic energies could mean. Now the danger could not be denied. The Nazis might be working on a super-weapon; they had to be stopped.

In his famous letter, Einstein warned Roosevelt that in the immediate future, based on new work by Szilard and the Italian physicist Enrico Fermi, "it may become possible to set up a nuclear chain reaction in a large mass of uranium, by which vast amounts of power and large quantities of new radium-like elements would be generated." This "new phenomenon," he said, could lead to the construction of "extremely powerful bombs of a new type." Just one of these bombs, "carried by boat and exploded in a port, might very well destroy the whole port together with some of the surrounding territory." The Nazis might already be working on such a bomb. "Germany has actually stopped the sale of uranium from Czechoslovakian mines, which she has taken over," Einstein reported.[1] He urged Roosevelt to speed up American experimental work by providing government funds and coordinating the work of physicists investigating chain reactions.

Roosevelt responded, but tentatively. He formed an Advisory Committee on Uranium to oversee preliminary research on nuclear fission. By the spring of 1940, the committee had allocated only $6,000 to purchase graphite bricks, a critical component of experiments Fermi and Szilard were running at Columbia University. In 1941, however, engineer Vannevar Bush, the president of the Carnegie Institution of Washington and the president's informal science advisor, convinced Roosevelt to move faster. British Prime Minister Winston Churchill also weighed in, sending the president new, critical studies by scientists in England.

The most important was a memorandum from two German refugee scientists living in England, Otto Frisch and Rudolph Peierls. From their early experiments and calculations, they detailed how vast the potential destructive power of atomic energy could be—and such power's military implications. Their memo to the British government estimated that the energy liberated from just 5 kilograms of uranium would yield an explosion equal to several thousand tons of dynamite.

> This energy is liberated in a small volume, in which it will, for an instant, produce a temperature comparable to that in the interior of the sun. The blast from such an explosion would destroy life in a wide area. The size of this area is difficult to estimate, but it will probably cover the center of a big city.
>
> In addition, some part of the energy set free by the bomb goes to produce radioactive substances, and these will emit very powerful and dangerous radiations. The effects of these radiations is greatest immediately after the explosion, but it decays only gradually and even for days after the explosion any person entering the affected area will be killed.
>
> Some of this radioactivity will be carried along with the wind and will spread the contamination; several miles downwind this may kill people.[2]

The scientists concluded:

If one works on the assumption that Germany is, or will be, in the possession of this weapon, it must be realized that no shelters are available that would be effective and that could be used on a large scale. The most effective reply would be a counter-threat with a similar bomb. Therefore it seems to us important to start production as soon and as rapidly as possible.[3]

They did not, at the time, consider actually using the bomb, as "the bomb could probably not be used without killing large numbers of civilians, and this may make it unsuitable as a weapon for use by this country."[4] Rather, they thought it necessary to have a bomb to deter German use. This was exactly the reasoning of Einstein, Szilard, and others.

Soon after the Frisch-Peierls memo circulated at the highest levels of the British government, a special committee on uranium, confusingly named the MAUD committee for a British nurse who had worked with the family of Danish physicist Niels Bohr, began assessing the two scientists' conclusions.[5] The MAUD report on "Use of Uranium for a Bomb" would have an immediate impact on the thinking of both Churchill and Franklin Roosevelt in the summer and fall of 1941. It concluded that a "uranium bomb" could be available in time to help the war effort: "the material for the first bomb could be ready by the end of 1943."[6] Upon meeting with Vannevar Bush and learning of the MAUD committee's dramatic conclusions on October 9, 1941, Roosevelt authorized the first atomic bomb project.

Bush, then head of the newly formed National Defense Research Committee, asked Harvard President James Conant to direct a special panel of the National Academy of Sciences to review all atomic energy studies and experiments. Though Bush's committee recommended the "urgent development" of the bomb, the December 1941 attack on Pearl Harbor gave other conventional military concerns greater precedence. It was not until a year later that work began in earnest.

The Manhattan Project, formally the "Manhattan Engineering District," was created in August 1942 within the Army Corps of Engineers. The laboratory research now became a military pursuit, in part to mask its massive budget.

Brigadier General Leslie Groves assumed leadership of the project in September 1942 and immediately accelerated work on all fronts. Historian Robert Norris says of Groves, "Of all the participants in the Manhattan Project, he and he alone was indispensable."[7]

Groves was the perfect man to direct the massive effort needed to create the raw materials of the bomb, having just finished supervising the construction of the largest office building in the world, the new Pentagon. He needed to find a partner who could mobilize the scientific talent already engaged in extensive nuclear research at laboratories in California, Illinois, and New York. At the University of California at Berkeley, Groves met physicist J. Robert Oppenheimer for the first time and heard his plea for a laboratory purely devoted to work on the bomb itself.[8] Groves thought Oppenheimer "a genius, a real genius," and soon convinced him to head the scientific effort.[9] Together they chose a remote southwestern mesa as the perfect site for the greatest concentration of applied nuclear brainpower the world had ever seen.

An Atomic Primer

When the young scientists recruited for the Manhattan Project moved into the stark buildings of Los Alamos, New Mexico, surrounded by barbed wire, they understood that they would be working on a top-secret project that could win the war. Most knew that they were there to build the world's first atomic bomb, but didn't know much more beyond that. To bring everyone up to speed, physicist Robert Serber gave five lectures in early April 1943 on the scientific and engineering challenges ahead. His lecture notes, mimeographed and given to all subsequent arrivals, became knows as *The Los Alamos Primer*. Today, it still serves as a valuable guide to the essentials of an atomic bomb.

Serber got right to the point: "The object of the Project is to produce a practical military weapon in the form of a bomb in which the energy is released by a fast neutron chain reaction in one or more of the materials known to show nuclear fission."[10]

The discovery of fission was new, but the idea of the atom goes back to the early Greek thinkers. In about 400 BCE, Democritus reasoned that if you continuously divided matter, you would eventually get down to the smallest, undividable particle, which he called an atom, meaning "uncuttable." By the beginning of the twentieth century, scientists realized the atom had an internal structure. In 1908 Ernest Rutherford discovered that atoms had a central core, or nucleus, composed of positively-charged protons, surrounded by the negatively charged electrons detected by J. J. Thompson eleven years earlier. In 1932 James Chadwick discovered that there were particles equal in weight to the proton in the nucleus, but without an electrical charge. He dubbed them neutrons. This led to the atomic model that we are familiar with today, of an atom as a miniature planetary system, with a nucleus of hard, round balls of protons and neutrons with smaller electron balls orbiting around. (See the first diagram on the page facing page 1.)

Familiar, but not quite right. Danish physicist Niels Bohr, among his many other contributions, found that a large nucleus behaved more like a water droplet. His insight led to a breakthrough discovery in 1939. German scientists Otto Hahn and Fritz Strassman, working with physicist Lise Meitner, had been bombarding uranium, the heaviest element found in nature, with neutrons and observing the new elements that seemed to form. Uranium has an atomic number of 92, meaning it has 92 protons in its nucleus. The scientists thought that the neutrons were being absorbed by the uranium atoms, producing new, man-made elements, but chemical analysis indicated that this was not the case. When Meitner and physicist Otto Frisch applied Bohr's water droplet model to these experimental results, they realized that under certain conditions the nucleus would stretch and could split in two, like a living cell. Frisch named the process after its biological equivalent: fission. (See the second diagram.)

Three events happen during fission. The least important, it turns out, is that the uranium atom splits into two smaller atoms (usually krypton and barium). Scientists had finally realized the dream of ancient alchemists—the ability to transform one element into another. But it is the other two events that made the discovery really interesting. The two newly created atoms weigh almost exactly what the uranium atom weighed. That "almost" is important. Some of the weight loss is attributable to neutrons flying out of the atom. These are now available for splitting other, nearby uranium nuclei. For every one neutron that splits a uranium nucleus, two more, on average, are generated. Splitting one nucleus can, under the right conditions, lead to the splitting of two additional nuclei, then four, then eight, on up. This is the chain reaction that can start from a single neutron.

The third event is the real payoff. Each fission converts a small amount of the mass of the atom into energy. The first scientists to discover fission applied Einstein's famous formula, $E = mc^2$, and quickly realized that even this small amount of matter m multiplied by the speed of light squared c^2 equals a very large amount of energy E.[11]

Energy at atomic levels is measured in electron volts. Normal chemical reactions involve the forming or breaking of bonds between the electrons of individual atoms, each releasing energies of a few electron volts. Explosives, such as dynamite, release this energy very quickly, but each atom yields only a small amount of energy. Splitting a single uranium nucleus, however, results in an energy release of almost 200 million electron volts. Splitting all 2,580,000,000,000,000,000,000,000 (2.58 trillion trillion) uranium atoms in just one kilogram of uranium would yield an explosive force equal to ten thousand tons of dynamite. This was the frightening calculation behind the Frisch-Peierls memo and Einstein's letter to Roosevelt. One small bomb could equal the destructive force of even the largest bomber raid.

THE RIGHT STUFF

Understanding these calculations was the easy part. There wasn't any great "secret" to atomic energy (and there isn't now). Physicists at the time in the United States, Great Britain, Russia, Germany, Italy, and Japan all quickly grasped the significance of nuclear fission. The hard part, and this is still true today, is producing the materials that can sustain this chain reaction. Some concluded that the material could not be made, or at least not made in time to affect the course of the war. Others disagreed—among them the influential authors of the MAUD committee report. The crucial difference in the United States was not superior scientific expertise but the industrial capability to make the right materials. Groves used this capability to build by the end of the war the manufacturing equivalent of the American automobile industry—an entirely new industry focused on creating just one product.[12]

To understand the challenge the United States faced then, and which other nations who want nuclear weapons face today, we have to delve a little deeper into atomic structures. Ordinary uranium cannot be used to make a bomb. Uranium, like many other elements, exists in several alternative forms, called isotopes. Each isotope has the same number of protons (and so maintains the same electric charge) but varies in the number of neutrons (and thus, in weight). Most of the atoms in natural uranium are the isotope U-238, meaning that they each have 92 protons and 146 neutrons for a total atomic weight of 238. When an atom of U-238 absorbs a neutron, it can undergo fission, but this happens only about one-quarter of the time. Thus, it cannot sustain the fast chain reaction needed to release enormous amounts of energy. But one of every 140 atoms in natural uranium (about 0.7 percent) is of another uranium isotope, U-235. Each U-235 nucleus has 92 protons but only 143 neutrons. This isotope will fission almost every time a neutron hits it. The challenge for scientists is to separate enough of this one part of fissile uranium from the 139 parts of non-fissile uranium to produce an amount that can sustain a chain reaction. This quantity is called a critical mass. The process of separating U-235 is called enrichment.

Almost all of the $2 billion spent on the Manhattan Project (about $23 billion in 2006 dollars) went toward building the vast industrial facilities needed to enrich uranium. The Army Corps of Engineers built huge buildings at Oak Ridge, Tennessee, to pursue two different enrichment methods. The first was gaseous diffusion. This process converts the uranium into gas, then uses the slightly different rates at which one isotope diffuses across a porous barrier to separate out the U-235. The diffusion is so slight that it requires thousands of repetitions—and hundreds of diffusion tanks. Each leg of the U-shaped diffusion plant at Oak Ridge was a half-mile long.

The other system was electromagnetic separation. Again, the uranium is converted into a gas. It is then moved through a magnetic field in a curved, vacuum tank. The heavier isotope tends to fly to the outside of the curve, allowing the lighter U-235 to be siphoned off from the inside curve. Again, this process must be repeated thousands of times to produce even small quantities of uranium rich in U-235. Most of the uranium for the bomb dropped on Hiroshima was produced in this way.

Both of these processes are forms of uranium enrichment and are still in use today. By far the most common and most economical method of enriching uranium, however, is to use large gas centrifuges. (See the third diagram on the page facing the opening of chapter 1.) This method (considered but rejected in the Manhattan Project) pipes uranium gas into large vacuum tanks; rotors then spin it at supersonic speeds. The heavier isotope tends to fly to the outside wall of the tank, allowing the lighter U-235 to be siphoned off from the inside. As with all other methods, thousands of cycles are needed to enrich the uranium. Uranium enriched to 3–5 percent U-235 is used to make fuel rods for modern nuclear power reactors. The same facilities can also enrich uranium to the 70–90 percent levels of U-235 needed for weapons. (This inherent "dual-use" capability is one of the key problems in controlling the spread of nuclear weapons and is explored further in chapters 2, 4, and 6.)

There is a second element that can sustain a fast chain reaction: plutonium. This element is not found in nature and was still brand-new at the time of the Manhattan Project. In 1940, scientists at Berkeley discovered that after absorbing an additional neutron, some of the U-238 atoms transformed into a new element with 93 protons and an atomic weight of 239. (The transformation process is called beta-decay, where a neutron in the nucleus changes to a proton and emits an electron.) Uranium was named after the planet Uranus. Since this new element was "beyond" uranium, they named it neptunium after the next planet in the solar system, Neptune. Neptunium is not a stable element. Some of it decays rapidly into a new element with 94 protons. Berkeley scientists

Glenn Seaborg and Emilio Segré succeeded in separating this element in 1941, calling it plutonium, after the next planet in line, Pluto.

Plutonium-239 is fissile. In fact, it takes less plutonium to sustain a chain reaction than uranium. The Manhattan Project thus undertook two paths to the bomb, both of which are still the only methods pursued today. Complementing the uranium enrichment plants at Oak Ridge, the Project built a small reactor at the site and used it to produce the first few grams of plutonium in 1944. The world's first three large-scale nuclear reactors were constructed that year in just five months in Hanford, Washington. There, rods of uranium were bombarded with slow neutrons, changing some of the uranium into plutonium. This process occurs in every nuclear reactor, but some reactors, such as the ones at Hanford, can be designed to maximize this conversion process.

The reactor rods must then be chemically processed to separate the newly produced plutonium from the remaining uranium and other highly radioactive elements generated in the fission process. This reprocessing typically involves a series of baths in nitric acid and other solvents and must be done behind lead shielding with heavy machinery. The first of the Hanford reactors went operational in September 1944 and produced the first irradiated slugs (reactor rods that had been bombarded with neutrons) on Christmas Day of that year. After cooling and reprocessing, the first Hanford plutonium arrived in Los Alamos on February 2, 1945. The lab had gotten its first 200 grams of U-235 from Oak Ridge a year earlier and it now seemed that enough fissile material could be manufactured for at least one bomb by August 1945.

The Manhattan Project engineers and scientists had conquered the hardest part of the process—producing the material. But that does not mean that making the rest of the bomb is easy.

BOMB DESIGN

The two basic designs for atomic bombs developed at Los Alamos are still used today, though with refinements that increase their explosive yield and shrink their size.

In his introduction lectures, Robert Serber explained the basic problem that all bomb designers have to solve. Once the chain reaction begins, it takes about 80 generations of neutrons to fission a whole kilogram of material. This takes place in about 0.8 microseconds, or less than one millionth of one second. "While this is going on," Serber said, "the energy release is making the material very hot, developing great pressure and hence tending to cause an explosion."[13]

This is a bit of an understatement. The quickly generated heat rises to about 10 billion degrees Celsius. At this temperature the uranium is no longer a metal but has been converted into a gas under tremendous pressure. The gas expands at great velocity, pushing the atoms further apart, increasing the time necessary for neutron collisions, and allowing more neutrons to escape without hitting any atoms. The material would thus blow apart before the weapon could achieve full explosive yield. When this happens in a poorly designed weapon it is called a "fizzle." There is still an explosion, just smaller than designed and predicted.

Led by Robert Oppenheimer, the scientific teams developed two methods for achieving the desired mass and explosive yield. The first is the gun assembly technique, which rapidly brings together two subcritical masses to form the critical mass necessary to sustain a full chain reaction. The second is the implosion technique, which rapidly compresses a single subcritical mass into the critical density.

The gun design is the least complex. It basically involves placing a subcritical amount of U-235 at or around one end of a gun barrel and shooting a plug of U-235 into the assembly. To avoid a fizzle, the plug has to travel at a speed faster than that of the nuclear chain reaction, which works out to about 1,000 feet per second.[14] The material is also surrounded by a "tamper" of uranium that helps reflect escaping neutrons back into the bomb core, thus reducing the amount of material needed to achieve a critical mass.

The nuclear weapon that the United States dropped on Hiroshima, Japan, on August 6, 1945, was a gun-type weapon. Called "Little Boy," the gun barrel inside weighed about 1,000 pounds and was six feet long. The science was so well understood, even at that time, that it was used without being explosively tested beforehand. Today, this is almost certainly the design that a terrorist group would try to duplicate if they could acquire enough highly enriched uranium. The Hiroshima bomb used 64 kilograms of U-235.[15] Today, a similar bomb could be constructed with approximately 25 kilograms, in an assembled sphere about the size of a small melon.

Gun-design weapons can use only uranium as a fissile material. The chain reaction in plutonium proceeds more rapidly than the plug can be accelerated, thus causing the device to explode prematurely. But plutonium can be used in another design that uniformly compresses the material to achieve critical mass (as can uranium). This is a more complex design but allows for a smaller device, such as those used in today's modern missile warheads. The implosion design was used in the first nuclear explosion, the Trinity test at Alamogordo, New Mexico, on July 16, 1945, and in the "Fat Man" nuclear bomb dropped on Nagasaki, Japan, on August 9, 1945.

The implosion method of assembly involves a sphere of bomb material surrounded by a tamper layer and then a layer of carefully shaped plastic explosive charges. With exquisite microsecond timing, the explosives detonate, forming a uniform shock wave that compresses the material down to critical mass. A neutron emitter at the center of the device (usually a thin wafer of polonium that is squeezed together with a sheet of beryllium) starts the chain reaction. The Trinity test used about 6 kilograms of plutonium,[16] but modern implosion devices use approximately 5 kilograms of plutonium or less—a sphere about the size of a plum.[17]

By Spring 1945 the Los Alamos scientists were franticly rushing to assemble what they called the "gadget" for the world's first atomic test. Although they had spent years in calculation, the staggering 20-kiloton magnitude of the Trinity explosion surpassed expectations. Secretary of War Henry Stimson received word of the successful test while accompanying President Truman at the Potsdam Conference. At the close of the conference, Truman made a deliberately veiled comment to Stalin, alluding to a new U.S. weapon. The Soviet premier responded with an equally cryptic nod and "Thank you."[18]

Back in the U.S. the wheels were in motion, and the first atomic bomb, "Little Boy," was on a ship headed to Tinian, an island off the coast of Japan. In the months leading up to Trinity, top government officials had selected targets and formed a policy of use. The eight-member Interim Committee, responsible for A-bomb policy and chaired by Stimson, concluded that "we could not give the Japanese any warning; that we could not concentrate on a civilian area; but that we should seek to make a profound psychological impression on as many of the inhabitants as possible ... [and] that the most desirable target would be a vital war plant employing a large number of workers and closely surrounded by workers' houses."[19] On August 6, 1945, Little Boy exploded with a force of 15 kilotons over the first city on the target list, Hiroshima.

DROPPING THE BOMB

To this day, the decision to drop the bomb on Japan remains controversial and historians continue to dispute the bomb's role in ending the Pacific war. The traditional view argues that Truman faced a hellish choice: use the bomb or subject U.S. soldiers to a costly land invasion. Officials at the time did not believe that Japan was on the verge of unconditional surrender, and the planned land invasion of the home islands would have resulted in extremely high casualties on both sides. The months preceding the atomic bombings had witnessed some of the most horrific battles of the war in the Pacific, with thousands of U.S. troops dying in island assaults. Historians Thomas B. Allen and Norman Polmar write:

> Had the invasions occurred, they would have been the most savage battles of the war. Thousands of young U.S. military men and perhaps millions of Japanese soldiers and civilians would have died. Terror weapons could have scarred the land and made the end of the war an Armageddon even worse than the devastation caused by two atomic bombs.[20]

Immediately after the bombing of Hiroshima and Nagasaki, there was significant moral backlash, expressed most poignantly in the writings of John Hersey, whose gripping story of six Hiroshima residents on the day of the bombing shocked readers of the *New Yorker* in 1946. But the debate was not over whether the bombing was truly necessary to end the war. It was not until the mid-1960s that an alternate interpretation sparked a historiographical dispute.[21] In 1965, Gar Alperovitz argued in his book *Atomic Diplomacy* that the bomb was dropped primarily for political rather than military reasons. In the summer of 1945, he says, Japan was on the verge of surrender. Truman and his senior advisors knew this but used the atomic bomb to intimidate the Soviet Union and thus gain advantage in the postwar situation.[22] Some proponents of this perspective have disagreed with Alperovitz on the primacy of the Soviet factor in A-bomb decision making, but have supported his conclusion that the bomb was seen by policy makers as a weapon with diplomatic leverage.[23]

A middle-ground historical interpretation, convincingly argued by Barton Bernstein, suggests that ending the Pacific war was indeed Truman's primary reason for dropping the bomb, but that policy makers saw the potential to impress the Soviets, and to end the war before Moscow could join an allied invasion, as a "bonus."[24] This view is buttressed by compelling evidence that most senior officials did not see a big difference between killing civilians with fire bombs and killing them with atomic bombs. The war had brutalized everyone. The strategy of intentionally attacking civilian targets, considered beyond the pale at the beginning of the war, had become commonplace in both the European and Asian theaters. Hiroshima and Nagasaki, in this context, were the continuation of decisions reached years earlier. It was only after the bombings that the public and the political leaders began to comprehend the great danger the Manhattan Project had unleashed and began to draw a distinction between conventional weapons and nuclear weapons.

CHAPTER TWO

CONTROLLING THE BOMB

Soon after using the bomb, President Harry Truman began wrestling with how to control it. "The hope of civilization," he said in his message to Congress in October 1945, "lies in international arrangements looking, if possible, to the renunciation of the use and development of the atomic bomb." In November 1945, Truman advanced the first government nonproliferation plan when he joined with British Prime Minister Clement Attlee and Canadian Prime Minister Mackenzie King to propose to the new United Nations that all atomic weapons be eliminated and that nuclear technology for peaceful purposes be shared under strict international controls, implemented by a UN Atomic Energy Commission. By 1946, he had a detailed plan that included many of the nuclear nonproliferation proposals still debated today, including a ban on the production of any new weapons or the fissile material for weapons, international control of nuclear fuel, a strict inspection regime, and complete nuclear disarmament. Truman was not alone in considering new policies that might be able to stop the spread of this terrible new weapon. In fact, the origins of this first U.S. plan can be found in the troubled conversations some atomic scientists held in the closing days of the war.

FRANCK WARNING

A-bomb research was conducted primarily in Los Alamos, while scientists at the Manhattan Project's Metallurgical

Laboratory in Chicago focused on the production of fissile materials that would form the core of the explosive device. In December 1942, the first test nuclear reactor went critical in the squash courts under the stadium at the University of Chicago. While Los Alamos raced to finish the bomb, by the spring of 1945 work at Chicago had slowed and scientists were drawn to thoughts of the future. That June, when the defeat of Nazi Germany eliminated the major reason why many of the scientists had rallied to the atomic project, Chicago physicist and Nobel laureate James Franck formed a committee to consider the implications of the bomb. It included Eugene Rabinowitch, the ultimate drafter of the report (and later that year a founder of the *Bulletin of the Atomic Scientists*) and Leo Szilard, who agonized about its use on Japan after Hitler's defeat. They were increasingly concerned about the uncontrolled spread of atomic energy and the moral implications of using the atomic bomb.

The scientists warned that the United States could not rely on its current advantage in atomic weaponry. Nuclear research would not be an American monopoly for long, and secrecy would not mean protection. Staying ahead in production was also a false source of security, since a "quantitative advantage in reserves of bottled destructive power will not make us safe from sudden attack." If no international agreement were developed after the first detonation of the bomb, they concluded, then there would be a "flying start of an unlimited armaments race."[1]

The report identified nuclear materials as the critical choke point. The scientists believed that the rationing of uranium ores could be the simplest way to control nuclear technology. Under an international agreement, uranium could be accounted for, and there would be a check on the conversion of natural uranium into fissile material. Any international agreement must, they said, be backed by controls: "No paper agreement can be sufficient since neither this or any other nation can stake its whole existence on trust in other nations' signatures."

The Franck report also argued that the use of the bomb on Japan without warning would have both moral and political repercussions:

It will be very difficult to persuade the world that a nation which was capable of secretly preparing and suddenly releasing a weapon, as indiscriminate as the rocket bomb and a thousand times more destructive, is to be trusted in its proclaimed desire of having such weapons abolished by international agreement.

Rather than immediately drop the bomb, they contended, there should be a technical demonstration of its enormous explosive power to warn the Japanese of what would happen if they failed to surrender.

After a discussion of the Franck report in mid-June, the interim committee decided that the technical demonstration pushed by the scientists would not convince Japan to surrender. It did not seriously consider the recommendations on international control of atomic energy.

But the Chicago scientists had hit upon a core truth: preventing proliferation had to be a universally accepted political solution; the science of nuclear technology could not be otherwise contained. They could not have been more clear:

We urge that the use of nuclear bombs in this war be considered as a problem of long-range national policy rather than military expediency, and that this policy be directed primarily to the achievement of an agreement permitting an effective international control of the means of nuclear warfare.

ENTER BARUCH

This impulse found new life after the war. The Truman-Attlee-King proposal to form a commission was adopted by the United Nations in December 1945. On June 14, 1946, the United States representative to the commission, conservative financier Bernard Baruch, presented the nation's detailed recommendations. At the United Nations, Baruch was nothing if not dramatic. "We are here to make a choice between the quick and the dead," he said. "That is our business. . . . If we fail, then we have damned every man to be the slave of fear."

Baruch based his plan on the Acheson-Lilienthal report, which had been submitted to President Truman by Undersecretary of State Dean Acheson and U.S. Atomic Energy Commission Chairman David Lilienthal in March 1946. The plan sought to establish an International Atomic Development Authority that would own and control all "dangerous" elements of the nuclear fuel cycle, including all uranium mining, processing, conversion, and enrichment facilities. Only "non-dangerous" activities would be allowed on a national level, and even then only with a license granted by the proposed International Authority. Baruch reasoned that this structure would make verification relatively simple since the mere possession of a uranium conversion or enrichment plant by a national authority would be a clear violation. Baruch's version of the plan also included automatic punishment for violations, which went a step further than the recommendations of Acheson and Lilienthal.[2]

Since the objective of the Baruch Plan was not only to restrain the spread of nuclear weapons, but also to prevent an arms race and eliminate the bomb altogether, it proposed that once the International Authority could ensure that no other state was able to construct the bomb, the United States would guarantee the elimination of its entire nuclear stockpile.

Approved by the UN Atomic Energy Commission on December 31, 1946, the plan was opposed by the Soviet Union in the UN Security Council. Stalin saw the bomb as more than a weapon. It was also a symbol of industrial might, scientific accomplishment, and national prestige. Stalin told his scientists, "Hiroshima has shaken the whole world. The balance has been broken. Build the Bomb—it will remove the great danger from us."[3]

Stalin was not about to accept any plan that limited Soviet national sovereignty and that might have locked in, even if only for a short time, America's nuclear advantage. Knowing that the Americans would refuse, the Soviets proposed that any agreement require Washington to disarm prior to the establishment of some form of international authority.

Stalin was right. Truman and Baruch would not compromise. There was a growing sense among prominent American officials that the United States should retain a nuclear monopoly. Leslie Groves argued that the Soviets would not be able to build the bomb for one to two more decades. Secretary of State James Byrnes saw the bomb as a trump card in meetings with Stalin and Soviet Foreign Minister V. M. Molotov. Even Baruch came to believe that the plan could only be accepted on its own terms since "America can get what it wants if she insists on it. After all, we've got it and they haven't."[4]

The combination of Soviet opposition and growing faith in the sustainability of American superiority proved too much for the Baruch Plan. For a brief time in 1946, this revolutionary vision to abolish the ultimate weapon seemed within reach. In a matter of months, it was defunct.

A Bomb for Russia

Historian David Holloway and others argue persuasively that even if Truman had followed physicist and Nobel laureate Niels Bohr's advice to tell the Soviets about the bomb before it was built, Stalin would still have pursued a Russian bomb. "As the most powerful symbol of American economic and technological might, the atomic bomb was ipso facto something the Soviet Union had to have too," Holloway writes. [5] In fact, by the time of the Baruch Plan, Russia was seriously committed to her atomic bomb project.

The Soviet effort commenced with little fanfare in 1943. Stalin did not expect the bomb to be ready in time to influence the war with Germany, and the nuclear program was instead started as "a rather small hedge against future uncertainties."[6] The head of the Soviet project, physicist Igor Kurchatov, struggled to attain both the fissile materials and the political support necessary to speed up development of the bomb. Even in the spring and summer of 1945, Stalin remained skeptical. When Truman cryptically mentioned a "new weapon of unusual destructive force" at the Potsdam Conference in July 1945, Stalin most likely understood the atomic bomb reference.[7] But the reality of the weapon as a tool of both destruction and diplomacy was not apparent to Stalin until the bombing of Hiroshima and Nagasaki.[8]

Moscow's effort was greatly accelerated following the end of World War II. Stalin was determined, and he spared no expense, telling his nuclear scientists, "Ask for whatever you like. You won't be refused."[9] Thrown full force into a greatly expanded nuclear program, Soviet scientists knew they were several years behind the Americans. But they also had a significant advantage: the U.S. had shown it could be done. The American design, while not the most efficient, was successful, and the Soviet Union did not have time to take chances. Soviet intelligence provided scientists with the key elements of the American bomb design.[10] But as the source of the bomb design was kept secret, experimental results had to be reconstructed and steps retraced. Apart from Kurchatov and a few other select members of the project, Soviet physicists did not know they were working on copied designs.

It took the U.S.S.R. four years to catch up, achieving the bomb in almost the exact same time it took the U.S.[11] The first Soviet nuclear test took place on August 29, 1949. The test was set up in remote Kazakhstan, at a site known as Semipalatinsk-21. The area around the settlement, later renamed after Kurchatov, was to be the site of over 450 nuclear tests through the course of the Cold War.

AN ATOMIC EDGE?

The American monopoly was over. For Stalin, the bomb wasn't a threat to all of humanity, but rather a source of security and power. Truman saw it more than ever as a tool to contain Stalin and preserve American security. He ordered a rapid increase in the then small U.S. atomic arsenal.

Atomic weapons were becoming the currency of power. Policy was increasingly influenced by the strong belief in the diplomatic utility of these new weapons. As we will see later, this view retains a powerful hold on policy makers in many countries today. It began early on, as some within the U.S. government argued that dropping the bomb on Japan would also have a deterrent effect on the Soviet Union. The Soviets understood this, but did not respond as predicted. Molotov said years later that the Soviets rejected the Baruch Plan because they believed that the bombs dropped on Japan "were, of course, not against Japan but against the Soviet Union: 'See, remember what we have. You don't have the atomic bomb, but we do—and these are what the consequences will be if you stir.' Well, we had to adopt our tone, to give some kind of answer, so that our people would feel more or less confident."[12]

The idea that political power comes from the barrel of a gun-assembly fission bomb took hold in both American and Soviet policy. Even James Conant, the president of Harvard who had overseen the Manhattan Project and was a voice for nuclear restraint, wrote Henry L. Stimson in 1947, "I am firmly convinced that the Russians will eventually agree to the American proposals for the establishment of an atomic energy authority of world-wide scope, *provided* they are convinced that we would have the bomb in quantity and would use it without hesitation in another war" (emphasis in original).[13] But Conant was wrong. The American shift to more and bigger bombs did not convince the Soviets to forgo their own arsenal. Instead, it encouraged Moscow to respond in kind.

CHAPTER THREE

RACING WITH THE BOMB

After the 1948 coup in Czechoslovakia and the Berlin crisis that same year, President Truman ordered an increase in weapons production. By late 1949, the United States had more than 200 atomic bombs. When the Soviets tested their first fission bomb that November, Truman raised the stakes, accelerating a program to build the "Super," or hydrogen bomb.[1] David Lilienthal, chairman of the U.S. Atomic Energy Commission (AEC), wrote in his diary, "More and better bombs. Where will this lead . . . is difficult to see. We keep saying, 'We have no other course'; what we should say is 'We are not bright enough to see any other course.'"[2]

Many of the scientists responsible for the first nuclear weapon, including Robert Oppenheimer and James Conant, strongly opposed the "Super." The AEC had asked for the advice of its General Advisory Committee on the entire nuclear weapons program. Oppenheimer and Conant joined in the unanimous opinion of the eight-member group against the hydrogen bomb. They believed it to be a weapon of genocide: "The use of this weapon would bring about the destruction of innumerable human lives; it is not a weapon which can be used exclusively for the destruction of material installations of military or semi-military purposes. Its use therefore carries much further than the atomic bomb itself the policy of extermination of civilian populations."[3] Even if the Soviets developed the H-bomb, they argued, the United States could deter its use with atomic weapons.

The scientists' views did not prevail. Albert Einstein wrote in March 1950, "The idea of achieving security through national armaments is, at the present state of military technique, a disastrous illusion. . . . The armament race between the USA and the USSR, originally supposed to be a preventive measure, assumes hysterical character."[4]

The Super project inaugurated the design and testing of the advanced weapon that now composes the large majority of modern arsenals. Fission bombs create temperatures equal to those of the surface of the sun, but fusion bombs truly are the equivalent of bringing a small piece of the sun down to earth. The energy of all stars (including our own sun) comes not from the splitting of atoms, but from their fusion. The enormous gravity and high temperatures within stars fuses atoms together by overcoming the electromagnetic resistance that keeps them apart. Each fusion releases enormous energies, including the sunlight that makes possible life on earth.

The smaller the electrical charge of the atom, the lower the temperature needed to fuse the atoms. Thus, the process in the sun and other stars begins with the fusing of the lightest atoms, hydrogen, into helium, then continues crushing heavier atoms together until they can no longer overcome the resistance of the created atoms. For the sun, this process has been continuing for about 4.5 billion years and will end some 5–6 billion years hence when most of the its atoms have been fused up the chain into carbon, oxygen, silicon, magnesium, and sulfur. Massive stars, many times the size of our sun, can synthesize atoms all the way to iron before collapsing in a supernova explosion whose shockwave forges trace amounts of the heavier elements up to and including uranium and scatters all these elements into the universe. Every one of these atoms found on earth was created by this nuclear synthesis. The iron in our blood came from a supernova.

This science was now applied to weapons. Fusion weapons have two or more separate nuclear components in the same device that are ignited in stages—the energy released in the exploding fission "primary" is used to compress and ignite nuclear reactions in the separate fusion "secondary," vastly increasing the explosive yield. The energy released in these weapons is generated primarily by the fusion of isotopes of hydrogen, hence the name, hydrogen bomb. A hydrogen atom normally has one proton and one electron. The hydrogen isotopes best suited for fusion are known as deuterium (one proton, one neutron, and one electron) and tritium (one proton, two neutrons, and one electron). Fusion devices are also called thermonuclear weapons, because of the high temperature required to fuse these light isotopes together.[5]

The United States tested the first hydrogen device in the southern Pacific Ocean on November 1, 1952. Whereas the first fission nuclear explosion—the Trinity device—had a force of 20,000 metric tons of TNT (that is, 20 kilotons), the first hydrogen explosion had a force of 10,400,000 metric tons of TNT (10.4 megatons).

The Soviet Union tested its first fusion device a year later on August 12, 1953. The American *Bravo* test of March 1, 1954, exploded the first deliverable H-bomb (with a yield of 15 megatons) and the Soviets dropped their first true H-bomb on November 23, 1955.

Atoms for Peace

America's leaders were enthusiastic about both nuclear power and nuclear weapons in the 1950s. Expert witnesses told Congress that nuclear energy was the miracle power of the immediate future. They predicted atomic-powered cars, airplanes, and homes. They said that nuclear reactors would make electricity so cheap that we would no longer meter it. Winston Churchill, once again prime minister, envisioned atomic energy as "a perennial fountain of world prosperity."[6] President Dwight Eisenhower also believed in the promise of nuclear energy, but was more worried than many of his subordinates were about the dangers of nuclear weapons. He sought a way to promote peaceful use of the atom while also restricting military use. On December 8, 1953, Eisenhower stepped to the podium of the United Nations to unveil his Atoms for Peace program. The former general wrote in his diary two days after the speech that he was inspired by "the clear conviction that the world was racing toward catastrophe," and that he had to act.[7]

At the time of his speech the United States had detonated 42 nuclear test explosions and military leaders were beginning to integrate the much more powerful H-bombs into their operational forces. Eisenhower explained to the General Assembly, "A single air group, whether afloat or land-based, can now deliver to any reachable target a destructive cargo exceeding in power all the bombs that fell on Britain in all of World War II."

But the Soviet Union was now also testing and deploying nuclear weapons, as was the United Kingdom. Eisenhower warned, "the knowledge now possessed by several nations will eventually be shared by others—possibly all others."[8] While countries were already beginning to build warning and defensive systems against nuclear air attack, he cautioned, "Let no one think that the expenditure of vast sums for weapons and systems of defense can guarantee absolute safety for the cities and citizens of any nation. The awful arithmetic of the atomic bomb does not permit any such easy solution."[9]

Eisenhower proposed the creation of the International Atomic Energy Agency (IAEA) to promote the peaceful uses of atomic energy while the nuclear powers "began to diminish the potential destructive power of the world's atomic stockpiles." By the time the IAEA opened for membership in 1956, the disarmament components of the original vision were gone, as was the idea of the IAEA as a uranium bank that would equitably receive and redistribute fissile material. This hope disappeared with Soviet reluctance to contribute to the uranium bank, with American and Soviet nuclear arms policy, and with the strong views in Congress that the United States should be the one to decide who would receive its fissile material and nuclear technology.

But the promotion of atomic energy remained, now through bilateral agreements between each nuclear power (the United States, the United Kingdom, the Soviet Union), and whomever they chose to provide with nuclear assistance (most typically with research reactors, but also with power reactors, fissile material, heavy water, collaborative research efforts, and more). Eisenhower's initiative has divided historians into two opposing schools of thought.

The first group—the proponents of the program—argue that nuclear technology was already beginning to spread, and that Atoms for Peace was the only way for responsible nations like the United States to regulate that spread in an attempt to ensure that it would remain peaceful. Former chairman of the IAEA Board of Governors Bertrand Goldschmidt believes "the Atoms for Peace policy has contributed to the slowing down of horizontal proliferation . . . The acceptance of a system of safeguards as a normal condition of international nuclear commerce is without any doubt the major achievement of the Atoms for Peace program."[10]

The second group's view is just the opposite. From their perspective, Atoms for Peace was driven by a budding nuclear industry concerned that it might lose market share to the British, French, and Soviets, and by Cold War strategists who believed that, as a 1955 National Security Council directive put it, sharing nuclear technology would "strengthen American world leadership and disprove the Communists' propaganda charges that the United States is solely concerned with the destructive uses of the atom." Atoms for Peace spread nuclear technology too quickly and too recklessly, they contend. Not only was nuclear technology aggressively promoted, but an acceptable safeguards regime was not even put into place until the late 1960s. They point to the countries—such as India, Israel, Argentina, and Brazil—that benefited from the program and used it as a springboard to build, or attempt to build, nuclear weapons. As Leonard Weiss, a former Senate staff expert on the program, put it, "It is legitimate to ask whether Atoms for Peace has accelerated proliferation by helping some nations achieve more advanced arsenals earlier than would have otherwise been the case. The jury has been in for some time on this question, and the answer is yes."[11]

LEARNING TO LOVE THE BOMB

While Atoms for Peace was promoting nuclear technology for peaceful purposes, the U.S. military was equipping their troops with thousands of nuclear weapons, adapting them for use in nuclear depth charges, nuclear torpedoes, nuclear mines, nuclear artillery, and even a nuclear bazooka. (This infantry weapon, called the Davy Crockett, would fire a nuclear warhead about half a mile.) Both the United States and the Soviet Union developed strategies to fight and win a nuclear war, created vast nuclear weapon complexes, and began deploying intercontinental ballistic missiles and fleets of ballistic missile submarines.

The effective abandonment of international control efforts and the race to build a numerical and then a qualitative nuclear advantage resulted in the American nuclear arsenal mushrooming from just under 400 weapons in 1950 to over 20,000 by 1960. The Soviet arsenal likewise jumped from 5 warheads in 1950 to roughly 1,600 in 1960. The United States was ahead but afraid. As the atomic scientists had warned in the Franck report, numerical superiority did not bring security. Tensions were high, and confrontations in Berlin (1961) and Cuba (1961 and 1962) put the world on edge.

Baby boomers remember this era vividly. Most towns tested their air raid sirens and civil defense emergency broadcast radio stations at noon every Saturday. Schools conducted regular "duck and cover" drills and brought students down to basements stocked with barrels of water and cartons of crackers. The new shopping plazas opening up in the growing suburbs regularly showed in their parking lots models of prefabricated fallout shelters that could be buried in the backyard. Nuclear fears found artistic expression in books such as *On the Beach* and movies including *Fail-Safe* and most famously,

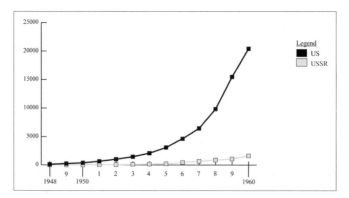

FIGURE 3.1. U.S. AND U.S.S.R. NUCLEAR WEAPON STOCKPILES, 1948–1960
Global Nuclear Stockpiles, 1945–2002, *NRDC: Nuclear Notebook, Bulletin of the Atomic Scientists* (Nov./Dec. 2002).

Dr. Strangelove, or How I Learned to Stop Worrying and Love the Bomb. Russia's launch of *Sputnik*, the world's first satellite, in 1957 brought home a chilling new reality: atomic bombs could now be carried by long-range missiles that could destroy cities within thirty minutes of launching. Anyone who was a child of that era can remember at least one moment when they were safely riding a bike or tucked in bed and the sound of a plane or a siren made them suddenly think, "This might be it. The Russians are bombing us."

Moreover, the threat no longer came from just two states. The United Kingdom had joined the nuclear club in 1952, France in 1960, and China was not far off (they would test their first atomic weapon in 1964). In 1958, the U.S. intelligence community concluded that, if things proceeded as they had over the previous ten years, then as many as sixteen states could have nuclear weapons by 1968.[12]

NUCLEAR RESTRAINT

American leaders were thus faced with the crucial question of how to protect the United States in the face of such a severe threat. Build more weapons or try to climb down? For John F. Kennedy, the answer was clear. In September 1961 the new president said that "the risks inherent in disarmament pale in comparison to the risks inherent in an unlimited arms race."[13]

TABLE 3.1. 1958 NATIONAL INTELLIGENCE ESTIMATE

16 POTENTIAL NUCLEAR WEAPON STATES	
France	Canada
Sweden	East Germany
West Germany	Czechoslovakia
Italy	Poland
Belgium	Japan
Netherlands	China
Switzerland	India
Norway	Israel

During the presidential campaign, Kennedy had gone after his opponent, Vice President Richard Nixon, from the right. He criticized the Eisenhower-Nixon administration for failing to protect American national security from the rising nuclear threats. In their third presidential debate in October 1960, Kennedy said the administration had not done enough to end nuclear testing and stop the spread of nuclear weapons. "There are indications, because of new inventions," he said, "that ten, fifteen or twenty nations will have a nuclear capacity—including Red China—by the end of the presidential office in 1964."[14] While offering his support for an increase in conventional forces and production of the new Minuteman and Polaris nuclear missiles, he went on:

> One of my disagreements with the present administration has been that I don't feel a real effort has been made on this very sensitive subject, not only of nuclear controls, but also of general disarmament. Less than a hundred people have been working throughout the entire federal government on this subject.... If I have anything to do with it, the next administration will make one last great effort to provide for control of nuclear testing, control of nuclear weapons. If possible, control of outer space free from weapons and also to begin again the subject of general disarmament levels.[15]

Kennedy was realistic. He balanced his disarmament proposals with programs that modernized the U.S. nuclear forces (and in the campaign accused his opponent—falsely—of allowing a "missile gap" to develop with the Soviet Union). The combined approach worked. As president, Kennedy kept his promises and worked forcefully for ways to reduce the nuclear threats. He created the Arms Control and Disarmament Agency to pursue his vision and to provide some balance in national policy discussions.

If he had any doubts about the urgency of reducing nuclear dangers, these were dispelled by the 1962 Cuban Missile Crisis. The discovery that the Soviet Union had placed missiles in Cuba capable of hitting the United States set off a diplomatic and military confrontation that terrified the world. Former Kennedy speech writer Arthur Schlesinger Jr. recalled the crisis in 2006:

> The Cuban missile crisis was not only the most danger-ous moment of the Cold War. It was the most dangerous moment in all human history. Never before had two con-tending powers possessed between them the technical ca-pacity to destroy the planet. Had there been exponents of preventive war in the White House, there probably would have been nuclear war.[16]

Only decades later, with the collapse of the Soviet Union and the opportunity for the participants in the crisis to sit down and discuss these events, did previously secret and terrifying information come to light. We now know what Kennedy and the Joint Chiefs did not know then: the Soviet Union had already placed over 100 nuclear warheads in Cuba and that the submarines escorting the cargo ships toward the American blockade of Cuba were armed with nuclear-tipped torpedoes.[17] Any attack on either the ships or Cuba would have almost certainly unleashed an atomic reaction.

After the crisis, relieved that the United States and Russia had avoided nuclear war (however narrowly), Kennedy was determined never to come so close to the precipice again. He renewed the stalled Eisenhower administration negotiations for a Comprehensive Nuclear Test-Ban Treaty and began pursuit of a global nonproliferation pact. He signed the Lim-ited Test Ban Treaty with the Soviet Union in 1963, banning nuclear tests in the atmosphere, in space, and underwater, calling it a "first step" in a series of threat reduction mea-sures he hoped would follow.[18] "The weapons of war must be abolished," he had told the United Nations in his first year in office, "before they abolish us."[19] He was now backing up his words with actions.

Kennedy did not live to finish the job, but Lyndon Johnson picked up where Kennedy left off. On July 1, 1968, LBJ signed the diplomatic crown jewel of his presidency: the Treaty on the Non-Proliferation of Nuclear Weapons, popularly known as the Non-Proliferation Treaty or NPT.

THE REGIME EMERGES

Richard Nixon had some criticisms of the NPT while campaigning against Hubert Humphrey in 1968, but as president secured its ratification by the Congress and signed it into force in a Rose Garden ceremony in March 1970. "Let us trust that we will look back," he said, "and say that this was one of the first and major steps in that process in which the nations of the world moved from a period of confrontation to a period of negotiation and a period of lasting peace."[20] The treaty went into effect in 1970 with almost one hundred nations as original signatories.

The treaty has become a mainstay of the international security system, enjoying near universal acceptance, with almost every nation in the world today a member of the treaty regime (India, Pakistan, and Israel remain outside the treaty and North Korea left the agreement). The basic pact is simple: 183 nations have pledged never to acquire nuclear weapons; in addition, the five nuclear powers recognized by the treaty (the United States, Russia, the United Kingdom, France, and China) are all members and have committed to reduce and eventually eliminate their arsenals. Those states that have nuclear technology also promise to sell it to those states that do not as long as the receiving countries pledge to use it for peaceful purposes only. This system regulates international commerce in nuclear power reactors, nuclear fuel, and nuclear technology for agricultural or medicinal purposes under a system of safeguards and inspections run by the IAEA.

Initially proposed by the Irish delegation to the United Nations General Assembly in 1958 as a way to stem the arms race, the treaty emerged from bilateral negotiations between the United States and the Soviet Union on preventing the transfer of nuclear weapons to states that did not already possess them. It was not until the rest of the world got involved with the negotiations that its most contentious provisions—those calling for sharing nuclear technology for peaceful purposes and for the gradual elimination of the nuclear weapon states' arsenals—were debated and finally accepted.

As former Atomic Energy Commission chairman (and discoverer of plutonium) Glenn Seaborg has written, "The nonnuclear countries were not about to accept without resistance a pact that they believed to be highly discriminatory against them . . . the United States and the Soviet Union found themselves in an unaccustomed alliance as they sought to fend off the demands of the nonnuclear-weapon countries."[21]

The treaty reflected the international realities of the times. Alliance security arrangements, including the promise that the United States would extend a "nuclear umbrella" over Europe and Japan, undoubtedly made it easier for several industrial nations to abandon their nuclear weapons programs and embrace the treaty. The Soviet Union simply enforced nonproliferation on its alliance system. The United States was not averse to using strong-arm tactics to convince, for example, Taiwan and South Korea to abandon nuclear weapons research and join the treaty regime. In many developing nations, nuclear ambitions ran into the formidable financial and technological obstacles to both nuclear power and nuclear weapon development. (These issues are discussed further in chapter 4.)

These financial, technical, and alliance factors were not in themselves sufficient barriers to proliferation. These same factors were present in the 1960s as well as in the 1970s. But before the signing of the NPT, proliferation was on the rise; afterward it was on the decline. The critical importance of the NPT is that it provided the international legal mechanism and established the global diplomatic norm that gave nations a clear path to a non-nuclear future. It captured rather than created the consensus view developing within many nations that their security was better assured without nuclear weapons than with them. Sweden, for example, officially announced its decision to forgo a nuclear weapons program in 1968, not because of the treaty but after an extensive domestic debate about the security impact of an independent Swedish arsenal.

Over time, however, the treaty established an international standard—seeking or selling nuclear weapons has become something done only by pariah states on the periphery of the international system. "The basic purpose of the NPT was to provide another choice," explains George Bunn, a principal member of the U.S. NPT negotiating team, "to establish a common nonproliferation norm that would assure cooperating nuclear weapon 'have-not' countries that if they did not acquire nuclear weapons, their neighbors and rivals would not do so either."[22]

David Fischer, a historian of the regime, wrote:

> A broadly shared perception that one's national interest is better served by not possessing nuclear weapons is thus the foundation of the international non-proliferation regime. . . . [T]he former Axis nations had no choice in the matter but since then their enforced renunciation has become firmly embedded in national policy. In some cases renunciation presupposed that the USA would shield them with her nuclear umbrella but even that link has now lost most of its relevance. In many small developing countries nuclear abstention may simply reflect technical inability. But in several countries the decision to forego nuclear weapons came after prolonged internal debate as in Sweden, Switzerland, Belgium, Yugoslavia, Turkey, Egypt, and Spain. Even in Australia there were once powerful voices in favor of nuclear weapons.[23]

Within the United States, the NPT was a bipartisan effort that produced a measurable increase in national and international security. The NPT and the test ban proved the substantive link between controlling existing nuclear arsenals and controlling the spread of nuclear weapons to other nations. Though hotly debated today, it was clearly recognized at the time. In 1958, when only three countries had nuclear weapons, a now declassified National Intelligence Estimate noted:

> A US-USSR agreement provisionally banning or limiting nuclear tests would have a restraining effect on independent production of nuclear weapons by fourth countries. However, the inhibiting effects of a test moratorium would be transitory unless further progress in disarmament—aimed at effective controls and reduction of stockpiles—were evident.[24]

Subsequent NIEs reaffirmed this linkage. The first assessment done during Kennedy's presidency, in September 1961, looked at fifteen countries that might develop nuclear weapons programs during that decade. It judged seven as unlikely to do so in the next few years, but warned, "These attitudes and views could change in the coming years with changing circumstances, e.g., if it became increasingly clear that progress on international disarmament was unlikely. . . ."[25]

Four years later, President Johnson's Gilpatric Committee report,[26] primarily authored by National Security Council staffer Spurgeon Keeny, concurred with the sentiment of the earlier NIEs: "It is unlikely that others can be induced to abstain indefinitely from acquiring nuclear weapons if the Soviet Union and the United States continue in a nuclear arms race."[27]

The collective successes of the test ban, the NPT, and other disarmament efforts had an impact on the likelihood of new nations pursuing nuclear weapons. NIEs in 1963, 1964, and 1966 confirmed a steady decrease in the number of "likely" or "possible" new nuclear states. The danger then (as now) was that increased national arsenals and decisions by new states to "go nuclear" would lead to a cascade of proliferation. For example, the 1958 assessment judged five states as likely to develop weapons, four as possible, and seven as possible but unlikely. But if disarmament efforts faltered and if several states did go nuclear, then the estimate changed. Many more states might take the leap. These were not "outlaw states," but developed nations including Belgium, Italy, the Netherlands, Switzerland, West Germany, and Japan.

By the signing of the NPT, even though France and China did test nuclear weapons, only two other states were of real concern, India and Israel. The arms control efforts of the previous ten years had made a tangible difference. Proliferation no longer seemed inevitable. The diplomatic dam held.

Ambassador George Bunn said,

The first and greatest success of the NPT is that only these nine countries are believed to have nuclear weapons: the NPT-permitted P-5 plus India, Pakistan, Israel and North Korea. Without the NPT, I believe that 30–40 countries would now have nuclear weapons. That would have included at least these nine plus Argentina, Australia, Belarus, Brazil, Canada, Egypt, Germany, Indonesia, Italy, Japan, Kazakhstan, the Netherlands, Norway, Romania, South Africa, South Korea, Spain, Sweden, Switzerland, Taiwan (China), Ukraine, the former Yugoslavia—all of which have had nuclear research programs or other nuclear activities. If, without the NPT, these countries had continued their research to the point of making nuclear weapons, some of their neighbors and rivals would no doubt have sought nuclear weapons as well.[28]

These nonproliferation victories were not so obvious or desirable to some. While popular with the public, they were fiercely opposed by Cold War hawks. The limited test ban was a particularly tough fight, and rhetoric was at fever pitch. Phyllis Schlafly, a strong voice for conservative Republicans, told the Senate Committee on Foreign Relations in 1963, "If the Senate approves the Moscow treaty, then America—the last, best hope of mankind—may be at the mercy of the dictators who already control a third of the world."[29] Senator William Fulbright (D-AR) chaired the Senate Foreign Relations Committee that recommended the treaty's approval. But Senator John Stennis (D-MS) held his own hearings and his subcommittee report opposed the ban on atmospheric and underwater tests, citing the need for nuclear dominance. "Soviet secrecy and duplicity require that this nation possess a substantial margin of superiority in both the quality and quantity of its implements of defense," the report said. It claimed that the test ban posed "serious—perhaps even formidable—military and technological disadvantages to the U.S." and further, that it would block the ability to produce "the highest quality of weapons of which our science and technology are capable."[30]

A few years later, opponents of the NPT were equally adamant. Senator Strom Thurmond (R-SC) opposed the treaty because it would "prevent the modernization of armaments in the Western European countries, thereby removing a counterforce to Soviet designs."[31] Stennis called it "unilateral disarmament."[32]

The Regime Evolves

Despite the conservative criticisms, the success of the NPT and improving relations with the Soviet Union encouraged other nonproliferation efforts in the 1970s. In addition to the NPT, President Nixon negotiated or initiated many of the other cornerstones of today's international control regimes. To implement controls over the export of nuclear fuel, materials, and equipment, Nixon established the NPT Exporters Committee (known as the Zangger Committee after its first chair, the Swiss expert Claude Zangger). This group of nuclear supplier nations worked out standards and procedures to regulate their nuclear exports to non-nuclear weapon states. Nixon negotiated and implemented the U.S.-Soviet Strategic Arms Limitation Treaty (SALT) limiting offensive arms and the companion Anti-Ballistic Missile Treaty limiting defensive armaments, both signed in May 1972.

Nixon also announced in 1969 that the United States would unilaterally and unconditionally renounce biological weapons. He ordered the destruction of the considerable U.S. biological weapons stockpile and the conversion of all production facilities for peaceful purposes. He reversed fifty years of U.S. reluctance, and sought ratification of the 1925 Geneva Protocol prohibiting the use in war of biological and chemical weapons (the protocol was subsequently ratified under President Gerald Ford). The president successfully negotiated the Biological Weapons Convention (BWC), signed in 1972 and ratified by the Senate in 1974, prohibiting the development, production, stockpiling, acquisition, and transfer of biological weapons.

The nuclear weapons treaties were only partially effective, however, and existing arsenals grew over the course of the decade. Though the SALT treaties set limits on the number of "delivery vehicles" the United States and the Soviet Union could have (bombers, missiles, and submarines), they did not limit how many warheads each country could deploy. Each nation developed the technology to allow individual warheads to be independently targeted. A large missile, therefore, could release in space three, five or even ten warheads, known as multiple independently targeted reentry vehicles (MIRVs).

"We have gone on piling weapon upon weapon, missile upon missile, new levels of destructiveness upon old ones," said George Kennan, a principal architect of U.S. Cold War policy, in 1981. "We have done this helplessly, almost involuntarily, like the victims of some sort of hypnotism, like men in a dream, like lemmings headed for the seas."[33]

With the newly MIRV'ed missiles, global nuclear arsenals continued to grow. In 1960, four states had a total of 22,000 nuclear weapons, with 93 percent of these held by the United States. During the mid and late 1960s, the U.S. arsenal leveled off and even began to decline. But by 1970, there were five nuclear powers and global stockpiles had grown to 38,100 nuclear weapons, with U.S. weapons accounting for 68 percent of the total. By 1980 global stockpiles grew by an additional 44 percent to 54,700 total weapons. Although the US stockpile again decreased slightly, the number of Soviet nuclear weapons rose dramatically from 11,600 to 30,000[34]

During the 1970s, the number of nuclear states also increased. India decided not to sign the 1968 NPT and went against the newly established international norm. In May 1974, India carried out a "peaceful test" of a nuclear device, becom-

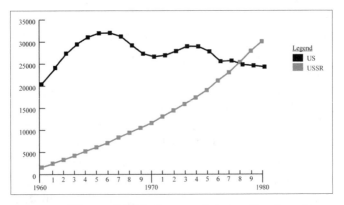

FIGURE 3.2. U.S. AND U.S.S.R. NUCLEAR STOCKPILES, 1960–1980
Global Nuclear Stockpiles, 1945–2002, *NRDC: Nuclear Notebook, Bulletin of the Atomic Scientists* (Nov./Dec. 2002).

ing the sixth nation in the world to test. Most Indians were overjoyed. The *Washington Post* noted a day after the test that "it was almost impossible today to find an Indian who did not take enormous pride in the government's achievement."[35] The Soviet Union and China, by not criticizing the test, seemed to give their general approval. Even the United States, as experts noted at the time, "seemed to give . . . official U.S. blessing to India's new status by calling on India to act responsibly in considering the export of nuclear technology."[36] For others, George Perkovich says in his definitive history of India's program, "India's blast amplified the alarms and prompted demand for corrective nonproliferation action by the United States and other nations."[37] These concerns soon prompted a more dramatic U.S. response. Perkovich describes the innovation implemented bySecretary of State Henry Kissinger:

> According to then-ACDA Director Fred Ikle, Kissinger hit upon the idea of a multilateral control arrangement instead of the unilateral approach. In April 1975, Kissinger convened a secret meeting in London of what became the Nuclear Suppliers Group. The United States sought additional agreements by nuclear technology suppliers to strengthen the safeguards they would require in importing states. A major aim was to plug loopholes such as those that had allowed India to produce its "peaceful" nuclear explosive. An extensive list of equipment necessary to produce fissile materials and other requisites of nuclear weapons became subject to controls. The Nuclear Suppliers Group became a relatively effective nonproliferation cartel.[38]

The Nuclear Suppliers Group continues today to set export control guidelines on all items that are unique to the production of nuclear weapons or materials, as well as sixty-five "dual-use" items that have legitimate non-nuclear uses. The forty-four member nations of the group agree not to ship these items to non-nuclear weapon states for use in any unsafeguarded facilities, that is, nuclear installations that are not subject to inspections by the International Atomic Energy Agency. President George Bush's 2006 nuclear deal with India would break the barriers Richard Nixon constructed by, for the first time, selling nuclear reactors, fuel, and technology to a state that has not opened all its facilities to inspection. India agreed to put two-thirds of its 22 current and planned reactors under IAEA safeguards, but has kept 8 outside inspections and dedicated to weapons production.

India's 1974 test also reinvigorated the probability of further proliferation by pushing Pakistan to pursue its own nuclear weapons. Prime Minister Zulfiqar Ali Bhutto famously remarked, "If India builds the bomb, we will eat grass or leaves, even go hungry, but we will get one of our own."[39] Pakistan had already started a secret program in 1972, aided by designs and technical information Abdul Qadeer Khan had brought back from his years working in the Netherlands at uranium enrichment facilities operated by the European consortium URENCO (Uranium Enrichment Company). Khan enabled Pakistan to begin production of centrifuges and then of highly enriched uranium. The secret smuggling operations he started to acquire machinery for this effort later formed the basis of his global nuclear black market that provided equipment to Iran, Libya, North Korea and perhaps other nations beginning in the 1980s. (More information on AQ Khan can be found in Chapter 4.)

THE TWO RONALD REAGANS

After almost two decades of arms limitation agreements and an overall increase in global nuclear arsenals the pendulum swung back with the inauguration of Ronald Reagan as president in 1981. Treaties were out, and talk of preparing to fight and win a global thermonuclear war was in. Richard Perle, then assistant secretary of defense for international security policy, told *Newsweek* in 1983, "Democracies will not sacrifice to protect their security in the absence of a sense of danger, and every time we create the impression that we and the Soviets are cooperating and moderating the competition, we diminish the sense of apprehension."[40]

President Reagan began programs to increase U.S. nuclear and conventional military power, including production of the

MX missile (a new ten-warhead intercontinental ballistics missile), the B-1 intercontinental strategic bomber, additional Trident ballistic missile submarines, and, most famously, the elaborate anti-missile program knows as the Strategic Defense Initiative, or "Star Wars." The private conservative Committee for the Present Danger, which counted Perle, Paul Wolfowitz, Paul Nitze, and Eugene Rostow among its leading members, had organized support for these and other military programs to provide what they saw as a needed corrective to the drift and "appeasement" policies of the 1970s. They saw the nuclear trends not as Soviet efforts to catch up to the U.S., but as part of a plan for global domination. "Since the final bitter phases of the Vietnam War," said Rostow, "our governments have been reacting with the same fear, passivity, and inadequacy which characterized British and American policy so fatally in the thirties and British policy before 1914."[41]

As president, Reagan implemented the promises he had made as a candidate. Frances FitzGerald summarizes the core of Reagan's campaign speeches in her study of Reagan and the Star Wars program, *Way Out There in the Blue:*

> "We now enter one of the most dangerous decades of Western civilization," Reagan warned in January 1980. The Soviets, he claimed in subsequent speeches, were menacing Iran and the whole Middle East; Hanoi had "annexed" Indochina; Castro, as an agent of the Kremlin, was trying to turn the Caribbean into a "red sea" that would engulf Mexico. As for the United States, the country, he said, had been through an era of "vacillation, appeasement and aimlessness." . . . Carter, he said, had made a "shambles" of defense. . . . As a result, the Soviets had pulled way ahead. . . . Reagan estimated that the Soviets had spent $240 billion more than the U.S. on defense over the past decade and were now outspending America by fifty billion dollars a year. . . . We were, he said repeatedly, in an arms race, "but only one side is racing."[42]

It did not look that way to Reagan's critics. "The White House carefully cultivated an image of American military weakness and Soviet duplicity," says University of St. Andrews history professor Gerard DeGroot. "With smoke and mirrors, the administration convinced Congress and the American people of the urgent need for massive increases in military spending."[43]

Whether by change of heart, by design, or by the increased influence of the pragmatic Secretary of State George Shultz over the more hawkish Secretary of Defense Caspar Weinberger, President Reagan followed a first term characterized by defense budget increases and new nuclear weapon programs with a second term marked by a flurry of arms control agreements. He had campaigned against President Jimmy Carter's unratified SALT II treaty, but in office he largely observed the limits it would have imposed. He went further by negotiating and signing the landmark Intermediate-Range Nuclear Forces Treaty (INF) in 1987, ending the U.S.-Soviet competitive deployment of missiles in Europe by requiring the destruction of all 2,700 U.S. and Soviet missiles and their launchers with ranges between 500 and 5,500 kilometers (a treaty some argue should be globalized to prohibit all missiles of this range anywhere in the world). That same year, Reagan initiated the Missile Technology Control Regime (MTCR)— the first effort to control the spread of ballistic missile technology. He also negotiated the first strategic treaty that actually reduced (rather than limited) deployed strategic nuclear forces. The Strategic Arms Reduction Treaty (START) cut both U.S. and Soviet-deployed strategic nuclear forces down to an agreed limit of 6,000 warheads each.

Today, defenders of both Reagan's first- and second-term policies insist the buildup was necessary to encourage Soviet reform and to reach real arms reduction agreements. "It was Ronald Reagan, by his arms buildup and his inability to contemplate anything but an American victory," says Irving Kristol, "that persuaded the Soviet leaders they were fighting a losing war. And so they folded their tents and stole away."[44]

Not so, says Anatoly Dobrynin, longtime Soviet ambassador to the United States. "The impact of Reagan's hard-line policy on the internal debates in the Kremlin and on the evolution of the Soviet leadership was exactly the opposite from the one intended by Washington," he says. "It strengthened those in the Politburo, the Central Committee, and the security apparatus who had been pressing for a mirror-image of

Reagan's own policy."[45] George Kennan agreed; "The general effect of Cold war extremism was to delay rather than hasten the great change that overtook the Soviet Union at the end of the 1980's."[46]

That "great change" was the economic and political collapse of a Soviet empire rotting from within. Popular protests in Eastern Europe, most notably the *Solidarnösc* (Solidarity) union movement in Poland and the "Velvet Revolution" in Czechoslovakia, exposed the weakness of the Soviet regimes and propelled a breakdown in 1989 few had predicted. The end of the Warsaw Pact and then the Soviet Union in 1991 gave new impetus to arms control efforts.

President George H. W. Bush signed Reagan's START treaty in 1991 and kept the momentum going by negotiating and signing in January 1993 the START II treaty, the most sweeping arms reduction pact in history. The treaty required that deployed U.S. and Russian forces be no higher than 3,500 warheads each. President Bush also negotiated and signed the Chemical Weapons Convention (CWC) prohibiting the development, production, acquisition, stockpiling, transfer, or use of chemical weapons. In 1991 President Bush announced that the United States would unilaterally withdraw all of its land- and sea-launched tactical nuclear weapons and would dismantle all of its land- and many of its sea-based systems (thereby denuclearizing the Army and the Navy surface fleet). The president also unilaterally ended the twenty-four-hour alert status of the U.S. bomber force and took a substantial portion of the land-based missile force off of hair-trigger alert (readiness to launch within fifteen minutes). Two weeks later, Russian President Mikhail Gorbachev reciprocated with similar tactical weapon withdrawals and the de-alerting of 503 Soviet intercontinental ballistic missiles.

While the process was begun by Eisenhower, inspired by Kennedy, and pushed by Johnson, most of the major diplomatic lifting was actually done by Presidents Nixon, Reagan, and Bush, who either negotiated or brought into force almost all the instruments that make up the interlocking network of treaties and arrangements we refer to as the nonproliferation regime. In the 1990s, President Clinton added the Agreed Framework with North Korea that froze that nation's nascent nuclear program; won Senate ratification of George Bush's START II treaty and chemical weapons ban; helped denuclearize Belarus, Kazakhstan, and Ukraine after the dissolution of the Soviet Union; won the permanent extension of the NPT in 1995; negotiated and signed the long-sought Comprehensive Nuclear Test-Ban Treaty (CTBT), which is still awaiting entry into force; and implemented the Nunn-Lugar Cooperative Threat Reduction programs to secure and eliminate Russian nuclear weapons and materials.

President George W. Bush signed what he hoped would be the last arms reduction treaty negotiated with Russia on May 24, 2002. Ratified by the US Senate on March 6, 2003 and by the Russian Duma on May 14, 2003, the Strategic Offensive Reductions Treaty commits the two nations to reduce their "operationally deployed" strategic warheads to 1,700–2,200 by December 2012. The treaty has been subject to both praise and criticism; while it establishes the lowest nuclear arsenal levels to date, it does not include provisions for destruction of warheads and delivery systems or for detailed verification of treaty compliance. Both nations will still keep thousands of warheads for tactical use and as reserves.

By 2006, the U.S arsenal had been cut to approximately 9,900 total warheads; the Russians to about 16,000; with the two accounting for all but about one thousand of the estimated 26,900 warheads held by eight or nine nations. This is the lowest the global arsenals have been since 1962 and they are expected to continue shrinking over the rest of the decade. President George W. Bush has also maintained threat reduction programs that assist Russia in dismantling delivery systems, securing nuclear materials and warheads, and redirecting former weapons scientists.

Over time, the nonproliferation regime emerged as an adaptable organism capable of evolving to meet new challenges. The result is a network of agreements to reduce the demand for nuclear weapons, help guarantee the security of those nations that give up the nuclear option, and prevent the unregulated and widespread diffusion of dangerous nuclear technology and know-how. But it is also a regime with serious, built-in flaws, and one heavily dependent on the will of its members to sustain and enforce its rules.

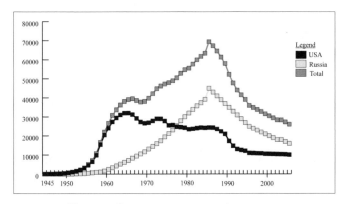

FIGURE 3.3. NUCLEAR STOCKPILES, 1945–2006
For the U.S. (through 1988) and Russia (through 1985), the number of
stockpiled warheads is used; from those years to the present, the total intact
warheads number is used.
Data used in graph taken from NRDC, Archive of Nuclear Data, available at
http://www.nrdc.org/nuclear/nudb/datainx.asp.

AN UNCERTAIN FUTURE

The good news is that the nonproliferation regime has
worked. The nuclear threat is less severe today than it was in
1970 when the Non-Proliferation Treaty entered into force.
The number of nuclear weapons in the world has declined
from a peak of 65,000 in 1986 to roughly 27,000 today.[47]
Since the signing of the NPT, many more countries have
given up nuclear weapon programs than have begun them.
In the 1960s, 23 states had nuclear weapons, were conducting weapons-related research, or were actively discussing
the pursuit of nuclear weapons. Today, only 10 states have
nuclear weapons or are believed to be seeking them.[48] Before the NPT entered into force, only six nations abandoned
indigenous nuclear weapon programs that were under way
or under consideration: Egypt, Italy, Japan, Norway, Sweden,
and West Germany. Since then, Argentina, Australia, Belarus, Brazil, Canada, Iraq, Kazakhstan, Libya, Romania, South
Africa, South Korea, Spain, Switzerland, Taiwan, Ukraine,
and Yugoslavia have all abandoned nuclear weapon programs or nuclear weapons (or both). Now North Korea, Iran,
and Pakistan are the only three states in the world that began

TABLE 3.2. COUNTRIES WITH NUCLEAR WEAPONS OR PROGRAMS, PAST AND PRESENT[a]

STATES WITH NUCLEAR WEAPONS	PROGRAMS TERMINATED OR CONSIDERATION ENDED AFTER 1970	
China	Argentina**	Romania
France	Australia***	South Africa
Russia	Belarus*	South Korea
United Kingdom	Brazil	Spain**
United States	Canada****	Switzerland***
India	Iraq	Taiwan
Pakistan	Kazakhstan*	Ukraine*
Israel	Libya	Yugoslavia
SUSPECTED PROGRAMS OR WEAPONS	PROGRAMS TERMINATED OR CONSIDERATION ENDED BEFORE 1970	
North Korea	Egypt	Norway***
Iran	Italy***	Sweden
	Japan***	West Germany***

[a] Table adapted from George Perkovich et al., *Universal Compliance: A Strategy for Nuclear Security* (Carnegie Endowment, 2005).
* Gave up weapons inherited after collapse of USSR in 1991.
** Country had an active program, but intent to produce weapons is unconfirmed.
*** A program for nuclear weapons was debated, but active nuclear programs were civilian in nature.
**** Canada had between 250 and 450 U.S.-supplied nuclear weapons deployed on Canadian delivery systems until the early 1980's. In 1978, Prime Minister Pierre Trudeau declared that Canada was "the first nuclear-armed country to have chosen to divest itself of nuclear weapons." See Duane Bratt, "Canada's Nuclear Schizophrenia," *Bulletin of the Atomic Scientists*, March/April 2002, 58, no. 2, pp. 44-50.

acquiring nuclear capabilities after the NPT entered into force and they have not ceased their efforts. Interestingly, no new nation has begun a nuclear weapon program since the end of the Cold War. The programs in North Korea and Iran both began in the 1980s.

There is more good news. Today, programs are in place that, if implemented effectively and urgently, would virtually eliminate the looming threat of nuclear terrorism.

TABLE 3.3. THE 15 COUNTRIES THAT HAVE OR ARE SUSPECTED
OF HAVING NUCLEAR, BIOLOGICAL OR CHEMICAL WEAPONS OR
PROGRAMS

COUNTRY	NUCLEAR	BIOLOGICAL	CHEMICAL
Albania			W*
China	W	W?	W?
Egypt		R?	W
France	W		
India	W		X
Iran	R	R?	W?
Israel	W	W?	W
Libya			W*
North Korea	W	W?	W
Pakistan	W		
Russia	W	W?	W*
South Korea			W*
Syria		R?	W
United Kingdom	W		
United States	W		W*

Key: W = has known weapon or agents; R = has known research program;
? = is suspected of having weapons or programs; and W* = has chemical
weapons but has declared them under the Chemical Weapons Convention
and is in the process of destroying them.

Moreover, not only is the nuclear threat declining, but so
are the threats posed by biological and chemical weapons
and the ballistic missiles used to deliver them. Since the
entry into force of the Biological Weapons Convention and
the Chemical Weapons Convention, state arsenals of these
two weapons have been almost eliminated. They are widely
seen as unusable in conflict, and very few states continue
to attempt to produce and stockpile them. Over all, there
are only fifteen states in the world that have or are suspected of having any nuclear, biological, or chemical weapons
or programs.

Lastly, the number of countries with ballistic missiles keeps
on declining. In 2002, 36 nations possessed ballistic missiles.
In 2005, only 30 had them. And of these 30, only 11 have ballistic missiles that can travel more than 1,000 kilometers in

distance.[49] The embarrassing failure of North Korea's July 4, 2006, test of its Taepodong medium-range missile and the "fizzle" of its October 9, 2006, nuclear test (which exploded with a much smaller yield than expected) underscored how daunting the technological obstacles to a successful military capability are.

Overall, the twenty-first century has begun with the number of nuclear, biological, and chemical weapons and ballistic missiles shrinking steadily. The number of states with programs for these weapons is also contracting. The bad news is that we, and the nonproliferation regime, face formidable challenges. If the right steps are not taken to meet these challenges, we could face a new, dangerous wave of proliferation. North Korea has pulled out of the NPT and declared it has nuclear weapons. Iran is pursing advanced nuclear technologies which it claims are for peaceful development but which can be used for decidedly non-peaceful purposes. Determining correctly what these steps should be requires an understanding of what motivates states to build—or not build—nuclear weapons.

CHAPTER FOUR

WHY STATES WANT NUCLEAR WEAPONS—AND WHY THEY DON'T

Nuclear weapons are the most terrifying weapons ever created by humankind. They are unique in their destructive power and in their lack of direct military utility. Most national leaders repeatedly express their hope that these weapons will never be used.

Why, then, do states devote enormous human and financial resources to develop these weapons? What are the principal desires and fears that drive these expensive, demanding programs? And why don't more states have these weapons? What are the main barriers that prevent proliferation, and have these motivations, strategies and obstacles changed over time?

THE FIVE DRIVERS AND THE FIVE BARRIERS

Simply stated, the five main reasons that states acquire nuclear weapons are security, prestige, domestic politics, technology, and economics. Each has been developed by international relations theorists into distinct, but often complementary, models that help answer our questions. The "national security" model argues that states seek nuclear weapons in order to enhance their own security. The "prestige" model emphasizes the symbolic value of nuclear weapons: states see the weapons as a prerequisite for great power status. The "domestic political" model views states as units made up of competing internal factions within which influential bureaucratic and military actors can lead a state to nuclear weapons. The "technology" model, or technological determinism, contends that if a state is technologically capable of developing nuclear weapons, then the allure of such a scientific accomplishment will be too much for most leaders to resist. Finally, economic factors, though not enough to stand on their own as a causal model, interact with the other four drivers of nuclear proliferation, sometimes encouraging nuclear proliferation and sometimes restraint. Each of these theories can illuminate decisions to develop nuclear weapons, but few experts claim that any one motive is robust enough to explain all cases.

If there are so many incentives for states to pursue nuclear weapons—greater security, an enhanced international position, satisfying parochial interests, and a sense of technological triumph—then why are there only nine or ten states with nuclear weapons or programs to acquire them?[1] What has kept the other 180-plus states in the world from reaching for these arms of unequaled power and destruction? So many states have shown nuclear restraint over such a long period of time that there must be equally enticing reasons why states do *not* want nuclear weapons.

It turns out that the reasons why states do not develop nuclear weapons can be grouped into the same set of reasons why they do: security, prestige, domestic politics, technology, and economics. Just as every atomic particle has a matching antiparticle of the same mass but an opposite charge, each motivation for acquiring nuclear weapons has a matching one that pulls in the opposite direction. That is, states decide not to build nuclear weapons—or, in some cases, to give up weapons they have acquired or programs that they have started—because they decide that the security benefits are greater without nuclear weapons, that prestige is enhanced by non-nuclear-weapon status, because domestic politics convinces leaders not to pursue these programs, or because the technological and economic barriers are too significant to overcome.

These are not abstract issues, interesting only for classroom discussion. National leaders at the highest level must understand the drivers for and against building nuclear weapons in order to plan their own nation's security. This requires studying not just their enemies, but their friends as

TABLE 4.1. PROLIFERATION DRIVERS AND BARRIERS

DRIVERS OF PROLIFERATION	BARRIERS TO PROLIFERATION
Security: States acquire nuclear weapons to protect their own sovereignty.	*Security:* States forgo nuclear weapons when it is in their security interest to do so and/or when they can gain protection from a nuclear ally.
Prestige: States acquire nuclear weapons to fulfill perceptions of national destiny or to be viewed as a "great power" in international affairs.	*Prestige:* States forgo nuclear weapons because of the international norm against the weapons. They seek acceptance or leadership in the international community.
Domestic Politics: States acquire nuclear weapons when a set of well-placed bureaucratic actors convince political leaders of the need for them.	*Domestic Politics:* States forgo nuclear weapons when there is significant public opposition to nuclear programs, when there is a change in regime or in government priorities, and/or when well-placed bureaucratic actors convince political leaders that nuclear weapons are unnecessary.
Technology: States acquire nuclear weapons because they have the technical ability to do so.	*Technology:* States forgo nuclear weapons when they cannot develop or acquire the technology or technical know-how necessary to make fissile material and build a bomb.
Economics: Economics generally do not drive a state to pursue nuclear weapons, though advocates of nuclear weapons do argue that a nuclear defense is cheaper than a conventional defense.	*Economics:* States may forgo nuclear weapons because they are too costly, because of the economic sanctions that result from a nuclear weapons program, or because of the economic benefits that follow the abandonment of such a program.

well. When John Kennedy became president in 1961, his director of central intelligence prepared a National Intelligence Estimate that examined the likelihood of additional countries pursuing nuclear weapon programs.

Titled "Nuclear Weapons and Delivery Capabilities of Free World Countries Other Than the US and UK," the document began with an overview of capabilities, then pulled back to describe the drivers and barriers to nuclear acquisition and how they interact. It is just as useful a primer today, as we consider whether some of the 40-plus countries that have the technical ability to make nuclear weapons might actually do so.

> Decisions to go ahead on a [nuclear weapon] program, or to carry out such a program once launched, will depend upon a complex of considerations both domestic and international. These include in the case of any specific country the nature of its political relations with other states, its estimated military requirements, and general psychological and emotional factors such as the intensity of the desire to increase national prestige, the domestic opposition to the acquisition of nuclear weapons, etc. The economic burden of such a program would in all cases be a major factor to be considered since even a program for a few crude weapons and an unsophisticated delivery system would cost several hundred million dollars. A more ambitious program, involving modern aircraft or missiles with compatible warheads, would require expenditures of up to several billions of dollars.
>
> The weight of the factors mentioned above is not fixed and may change as costs and difficulties change and the political-strategic factors alter. The prospect of an agreement among the major powers for a nuclear test ban, for example, especially if it were viewed as a forerunner to broader disarmament steps, would undoubtedly strengthen forces opposed to the spread of nuclear capabilities. Growing pessimism as to the likelihood of any realistic disarmament agreement could in some cases (e.g., Sweden, India) tend to undermine opposition to the acquisition of a national nuclear capability.[2]

We will look at each of these drivers more closely, weighing it against the barriers to weapons acquisition and illustrating it with case studies of particular nations. We will come to some general conclusions about how to use these tools to assess proliferation trends.

THE SECURITY IMPERATIVE

The national security model remains the leading explanation for nuclear proliferation and is based in the long-standing international relations theory of realism. Realism, at its essence, relies on two major assumptions. First, it views the international system as anarchic. While individuals can be controlled by a central government, individual states are not regulated by any equivalent authority. Second, states will do whatever is necessary to guarantee their security and sovereignty in this Hobbesian jungle. As Thomas Hobbes summarized his own philosophy in his seminal work, *Leviathan*, humankind's natural state is "of every man against every man," a state characterized by "continual fear, and danger of violent death; and the life of man, solitary, poor, nasty, brutish, and short."[3]

Nuclear weapons, from this perspective, are the ultimate security guarantor. A nuclear arsenal can deter any state rival. When a state faces an acute threat to its security, such as a potential adversary developing nuclear weapons, then that state will almost certainly have to match that capability or risk its very existence. In this view, once the United States developed nuclear weapons in 1945, the Soviet Union had to respond. China also cited U.S. nuclear threats for its decision to build the bomb: "So long as U.S. imperialism possesses nuclear bombs, China must have them, too."[4] (China later added the threat from the Soviet Union as the former allies split in the late 1960s.) India's leaders say China's test forced them to consider its nuclear options. "The nuclear age entered India's neighborhood when China became a nuclear power in October 1964," claims former Indian foreign minister Jaswant Singh. "From then on, no responsible Indian leader could rule out the option of following suit."[5] Once India detonated its "peaceful nuclear explosive" in 1974, Pakistan had no choice but to begin a nuclear weapons program of its own. When India tested weapons in 1998, Pakistan followed within days. From this perspective, nuclear proliferation is inevitable. As one state goes nuclear another state is forced to do so, and then another and another. In short, "proliferation begets proliferation."[6]

NUCLEAR DETERRENCE OF A CONVENTIONAL THREAT: SOUTH AFRICA AND ISRAEL   Though nuclear proliferation is most often a strategic decision taken to balance the power of a nuclear rival, some states have felt so threatened by conventional rivals that they have chosen to pursue nuclear weapons. According to Columbia University professor Richard Betts, these states may be so isolated or conventionally inferior that they feel they cannot meet their own security needs without nuclear weapons.[7]

South Africa is a prime example. Ostracized because of its apartheid policies, South Africa in the mid-1970s saw an increasing threat from the buildup of Cuban forces in Angola. Cuban forces had been dispatched to Angola as Soviet proxies to support the cause of the leftist forces in the ongoing civil war. In 1977, South Africa's white leaders determined that their secret research on a "peaceful nuclear explosive" for the country's mining operations should be accelerated to produce a nuclear arsenal.[8]

They clandestinely built six nuclear weapons. Officials have since said that they were intended as part of a "three-phase nuclear strategy to deter potential adversaries . . . and to compel Western involvement should deterrence fail."[9] These three phases consisted of first, a policy of opacity, neither confirming nor denying South Africa's nuclear capability; second, revealing their capability to Western leaders to force those countries' intervention should South Africa be seriously threatened; and third, if the previous two steps had failed, to conduct an overt nuclear test to demonstrate their capability to the world.[10]

Some other states have high levels of security anxiety, even though their conventional forces are superior to any potential rival. For largely historical reasons, they feel acute existential threats from neighbors.[11] Israel, whose right to exist is still not recognized by a number of its neighbors, is one example.

Israel now has a conventional military force that can overcome any Arab or Muslim state or combination of states, but that was not always so. As Avner Cohen writes, "Israel's nuclear project was conceived in the shadow of the Holocaust, and the lessons of the Holocaust provided the justification and motivation for the project."[12] Nuclear weapons were seen as essential even after resounding conventional victories in the wars of 1949, 1967, and 1973. Israel's nuclear weapons program, says Cohen, was driven by Prime Minister David Ben Gurion's "vision of an Israel secured against existential threats. . . . The Jews of Israel will never be like the Jews in the Holocaust. Israel will be able to visit a terrible retribution on those who would attempt its destruction."[13] Israel developed its first nuclear weapons in 1966–1967, and currently may have 100–170 nuclear weapons deployed on missiles, aircraft, and submarines.[14]

Betts cites South Korea and Pakistan as other examples of this security imperative. Similar security considerations take place today in countries outside what scholars James Goldgeier and Michael McFaul call the "core" of the international system—states with shared democratic values and interdependent economies.[15] Together these "core" states make up a "pluralistic security community" whose members have little security-based need to consider nuclear weapons.[16] Countries such as North Korea, Iran, and formerly Libya and Iraq, however, are on the "periphery" of the international system. These states are not economically integrated with the core states and feel far more acute threats to their national security. Glenn Chafetz concludes that these peripheral states "possess strong incentives to acquire or develop nuclear weapons."[17] Unlike the core states, they have much to gain and little to lose.

In this realist approach to nuclear proliferation, domestic politics, technology and economics play minor roles. Domestic politics are subordinate to supreme national security interests, technology can be acquired one way or the other, and the expense of a program is irrelevant for a state that must ensure its own security.

THE SECURITY BARRIER   There is a flip side to the security model. As Zachary Davis puts it, "Nations accumulate power to reduce insecurity, but they face a dilemma that too much power may cause other states to feel insecure and inspire them to increase their own power."[18] For example, if Brazil, the fast growing and emerging power in Latin America, developed a nuclear weapon, Argentina might feel it could not afford to abstain from doing likewise. The short-term effects of a nuclear arsenal would benefit Brazil greatly, making it an unrivaled military power in the region. In the long run, however, it would actually be less secure once it faced an equal nuclear power on its southwestern border.[19] This is the essence of the security dilemma. Unilateral possession of nuclear weapons may provide security; a region of many nuclear weapon states increases insecurity. For this reason, most states have concluded that they are more secure without nuclear weapons.

Because the security model is the dominant explanation of why countries do or do not get nuclear weapons, we will take a closer look at the variations on this theory before discussing, in turn, the other explanations.

A CLOSER LOOK AT THE SECURITY MODEL: THE CASE OF WEST GERMANY   States have a variety of options when faced with a nuclear rival. One certainly is to develop an independent arsenal, but another is to ally with a nuclear partner, benefiting from its guarantee of protection, or "nuclear umbrella." These protections are a form of extended deterrence and are referred to as positive security assurances. *Credible* assurances can prevent states from developing their own nuclear arsenal. But credibility can be hard to maintain, as national leaders will continue to ask themselves, "Would the president of the United States risk Washington to protect my capital city?"

For example, just a decade after its defeat in World War II, West Germany considered developing its own nuclear arsenal. It was one of the countries examined in the 1961 intelligence review, discussed above. The U.S. analysts weighed the proliferation drivers, such as the desires of West Germany's military to acquire modern weapons and of its political leaders to restore the country as a major power, against the barriers, such as the political dissension within both the nation and the North Atlantic Treaty Organization (NATO) alliance that such a decision would provoke. Although analysts estimated that West Germany was then in a technical and economic position to develop a nuclear weapon within five years of a decision to do so, they judged that the nation's leaders would choose to seek the benefits of a nuclear capability through cooperation with its allies, rather than strike out on its own.

That is in fact what happened. The Germans did not develop their own bombs. German Chancellor Helmut Kohl reflected both current and past German thinking when he said in 1992, "Why should we have them? I am very happy that my French friends have them. I live 40 kilometers from the French border. It does not disturb my peace of mind to know that seven hours flying time from me the U.S. president has the decision-making power over nuclear weapons to protect us Germans and that 40 minutes from my home there is a French president who has the same powers. We must state the facts. We do not need them at all."[20]

As was the case for other members of the NATO alliance, West Germany's decision was made easier by the knowledge that they would enjoy the perceived benefits of nuclear deterrence, including participation in the Nuclear Planning Group of NATO and having nuclear weapons deployed on their soil at NATO bases. Similarly, though considerably less democratically, the nations of the former Warsaw Pact became part of the Soviet Union's extended deterrence system and did not acquire nuclear weapons of their own. Only now, more than fifteen years after the Cold War ended, is Germany seriously considering the final removal of the remaining U.S. nuclear weapons from Europe and basing German security firmly on a non-nuclear deterrent.

A CLOSER LOOK AT THE SECURITY MODEL: THE
CASE OF SOUTH KOREA   South Korea provides an illuminating example of what can happen when security
assurances such as those provided by the United States are
called into question. It shows how a security barrier can
transform into a security driver.

Since the Korean War, South Korea (formally, the Republic of Korea or ROK) has felt threatened by the actions and
rhetoric of its bellicose neighbor to the north. This insecurity was addressed in large part by the superior South Korean conventional forces and by American assurances that
Washington would aid the south in the face of any northern
aggression. The United States, as part of its defensive posture, stationed troops and hundreds of nuclear weapons in
and near South Korea. Yet this did not prevent South Korean
leaders from beginning their own nuclear weapon program
in the early 1970s.

The decision was above all a reaction to what many saw
as the "changing role of the United States" in East Asia.[21]
The first jolt to South Korea came from the Nixon Doctrine,
announced by President Richard Nixon in July 1969. At a
time when anti–Vietnam War protests were reaching new
heights in the United States, the doctrine was part of Nixon's effort to fulfill his campaign promise to "bring an hon-
orable end to the war in Vietnam."[22] The new policy held
that America's Asian allies would have to become more self-
reliant, implying that the United States would not always be
willing or able to come to their aid by projecting force into
the region.

The Nixon Doctrine was followed by two other rattling
events. First, in 1971, the Nixon administration withdrew an
entire military division from South Korea. U.S. troops had
been stationed just south of the 38th parallel dividing the two
Koreas since the end of the Korean War. They were there to
serve as a "trip wire," forcing the United States to intervene in
the instance of a North Korean invasion. The removal of even
just a portion of these forces made Seoul uneasy.

Then, shortly after the troop withdrawal, Nixon made
his historic visit to China in February 1972, confirming and

accelerating the Sino-American rapprochement. This move certainly had far greater implications for Taiwan than for South Korea, but the shifting American approach was highly unnerving to leaders in South Korea's "Blue House."

In early 1974, South Korea began negotiating with Canada to buy a heavy-water CANDU (for "Canadian deuterium-uranium") reactor—better suited for the production of weapons-grade plutonium as compared to light-water reactors—and with France to purchase a facility for reprocessing the spent fuel rods from the reactor, separating out the plutonium. Light-water reactors use enriched uranium fuel, which is difficult to manufacture domestically, and allow for easy international monitoring because a shutdown of the reactor core is required for refueling. In contrast, the CANDU heavy-water reactors are fueled with more easily attainable natural uranium, the fuel can be replaced while the reactor is operating, and the spent fuel can contain a higher concentration of plutonium-239 used in weapons. Together, the CANDU reactor and reprocessing facility would have allowed South Korea to produce the material for nuclear bombs.

Washington wheeled into action, not only pressuring Seoul to cancel this program, but also strong-arming the allies that were supplying the crucial nuclear technology. In their study of this issue, College of William and Mary scholar Mitchell Reiss and Naval War College professor Jonathan Pollack say, "Washington brought both indirect and direct pressure to bear upon Seoul to forsake its nuclear weapons ambitions."[23] U.S. officials intervened directly with Paris, Ottawa, and others to cut off sales, "pressed Seoul to ratify the Non-Proliferation Treaty, and threatened to terminate all civilian nuclear energy cooperation."[24] Washington forced Seoul to choose. As U.S. Ambassador Richard Sneider ominously warned South Korean President Park Chung Hee in late 1975, "If the ROK [government] proceeds as it has indicated to date, [the] whole range of security and political relationships between the U.S. and ROK will be affected."[25]

South Korea chose to terminate its reprocessing program and join the NPT, winning reaffirmed security assurances from the United States. But the story did not end there.

President Jimmy Carter in 1977 planned to withdraw almost all U.S. forces and nuclear weapons from Korea, and the South Koreans once again rattled their nuclear weapons program. Their primary goal, according to Reiss, was not actually to develop their own weapons, which would have led to a cutoff of the nuclear technology trade necessary for its burgeoning civilian nuclear power program, but "to use the *threat* of an ROK nuclear arsenal in order to persuade Washington to maintain it conventional and nuclear forces in the South."[26] When President Ronald Reagan won election in 1980, he assured the South Korean president that the United States would not withdraw any forces. Whether the U.S. assurances helped stop the South Korean program or the South Korean program helped keep the U.S. assurances is a bit unclear, but the outcome satisfied both nations.

There is one final footnote to this story. New inspection authority granted to the IAEA helped uncover secret experiments South Korean scientists had conducted in the 1970s and 1980s and as recently as 2000. These involved uranium enrichment tests and the separation of small amounts of plutonium. These may have been unauthorized experiments, as the government claims, or evidence that South Korean leaders were hedging their bets by preserving some nuclear weapon expertise.[27] It is also unclear whether nuclear security assurances are as important to South Korea today as they once were. The United States withdrew all its nuclear weapons from South Korea beginning in 1991, with little Korean resistance. On the other hand, Japan still seems to want American assurances in lieu of an independent nuclear weapons program.

NUCLEAR PRESTIGE

It should be clear that national security considerations offer a compelling explanation of why states do or do not want nuclear weapons. But there are many cases that cannot be explained by security imperatives alone.

The second major factor to consider is prestige. Countries have perceptions of what makes any given state modern, legitimate, and strong. These perceptions are based in part on a country's observation of other states' actions. They are also influenced by the way in which each state views itself, its national identity, and its role in the world. Some states, consequently, believe that nuclear weapons are necessary to meet their national destinies. Possession of nuclear weapons, proponents of the prestige model would argue, makes these states feel more powerful, relevant, and respected. Stanford University professor Scott Sagan says that nuclear weapons may serve "important symbolic functions—both shaping and reflecting a state's identity."[28]

France is an illustrative case. In the 1950s, the Soviet Union was a grave national security concern for Paris. The French, given their long history of continental scuffles, also viewed both East and West Germany with suspicion, concerned that one of these new states might be inclined to obtain nuclear weapons. French President Charles de Gaulle wondered whether his American counterpart would be willing to risk Soviet retaliation to defend France.

Yet in the 1950s, other European states had the same security concerns. West Germany was at the front line of the American-Soviet confrontation in Central Europe. Belgium, Italy, the Netherlands, Norway, Sweden, Switzerland, and many others also faced serious threats from Moscow. "If the critical cause of proliferation in France was the lack of credibility in the U.S. nuclear guarantees" Sagan writes, "why then did other nuclear-capable states in Europe, faced with similar security threats at the time, not also develop nuclear weapons?"[29]

France, more than most European states, considered itself to be a great power in the world, the bearer of Enlightenment values and democracy. After World War II, though, it was a fading colonial power, forced out of Vietnam and facing a growing insurgency in Algeria. It was starting to lose its influence in the global community as the two superpowers came to dominate virtually every facet of foreign affairs. Sagan says, "the governments of both the Fourth and Fifth Republics vigorously explored alternative means to return France to its historical great power status."[30] The most symbolically powerful of these means were nuclear weapons.

For many in France in the middle of the twentieth century, this evolving national character was nothing less than an existential crisis. As de Gaulle himself put it to a French nuclear strategist, the issue at the heart of Paris's nuclear weapons program was, "Will France remain France?"[31] For McGeorge Bundy, national security adviser to U.S. Presidents John F. Kennedy and Lyndon B. Johnson, there is little doubt that this is the explanation for the French nuclear decision. "The bomb," he wrote, "was [de Gaulle's] passport to international grandeur. It would place France back where she belonged, among the Great Powers."[32] Bundy believed that the prestige driver accounts for both the British and French decisions to acquire nuclear weapons:

> I am persuaded that the basic objective, historically, for both the British and French governments has been to have a kind of power without which these two ancient sovereign powers could not truly be themselves. . . . It is not a matter of deterrent strategy as such. It is rather a matter of what Britain and France must have, as long as others have it, in order to meet their own standards of their own rank among nations.[33]

In the British case, the matter of prestige was clearly a strong factor for keeping a nuclear arsenal. Historian Lawrence Wittner captures these motives in an illuminating description of a December 1962 meeting of President Kennedy and British Prime Minister Harold Macmillan. Wittner says that McMillan argued

> that Britain needed independent control of nuclear weapons "in order to remain something in the world." He conceded that "the whole thing is ridiculous," for the modest British nuclear force did not add much "to the existing nuclear strength, which is enough to blow up the world." Still, "countries which have played a great role in history must retain their dignity." Britain had to "increase or at least maintain the strength of its foreign policy, so that it could not be threatened with impunity."[34]

At the end of the century, India's Jaswant Singh displayed the same motivation defending India's 1998 tests. "Nuclear weapons remain a key indicator of state power," he wrote, "Since this currency is operational in large parts of the globe, India was left with no choice" if it wanted to be recognized as a great power.[35]

THE MAJORITY VIEW: THE REAL PRESTIGE IS GET-TING RID OF NUCLEAR WEAPONS   Most countries, however, do not share the views of the eight nuclear-weapon states. That is, they do not believe that nuclear weapons are essential to their national identity or place in the world. It took some time for this non-nuclear position to prevail. In the middle of the last century, when the United Kingdom, France, and China were developing nuclear arsenals, there was a pervasive view among political elites in many nations that nuclear weapons were acceptable, desirable, even necessary. The increasing size of nuclear arsenals and alarm over the spread of deadly radioactive fallout from nuclear tests, however, stoked fears of nuclear dangers. Distinguished philosopher Bertrand Russell and Albert Einstein (in one of his last acts before his death) issued the Russell-Einstein Manifesto in July 1955. "We have to learn to think in a new way," they wrote. "We have to learn to ask ourselves, not what steps can be taken to give military victory to whatever group we prefer, for there no longer are such steps; the question we have to ask ourselves is: what steps can be taken to prevent a military contest of which the issue must be disastrous to all parties?"[36] After several global showdowns brought the world close to nuclear war, including the 1962 Cuban Missile Crisis, officials and publics in many nations moved to being decidedly anti-nuclear. Over time, and particularly with the signing of the Nuclear Non-Proliferation Treaty in 1968, the majority of governments came to view nuclear weapons as dangerous and unnecessary.

Today, most of the 183 nations that have signed the Non-Proliferation Treaty and that do not have nuclear weapons believe what the treaty says: nuclear weapons should be eliminated. Several of these states find that they gain prestige by their leadership in the nonproliferation movement. Ireland was perhaps the first to demonstrate the important role smaller nations can play in great power politics by introducing the first resolution at the United Nations in 1958 calling for a treaty on the nonproliferation of nuclear weapons.

South Africa is a more recent example. In 1993, on the eve of the transition to majority rule, the apartheid government disclosed its secret nuclear program and announced that all its weapons had been dismantled. Nelson Mandela, the first president of the new majority government, could have reversed this decision. But he decided that South African security was better served in a continent where there were no nuclear weapons than in one where there was a nuclear arms competition. South African representatives made their new government's first major foray into international affairs at the 1995 Non-Proliferation Treaty review conference. South Africa stepped in at a critical moment to forge a compromise agreement between the nuclear and non-nuclear weapon states that allowed for the strengthening and indefinite extension of the treaty, to the applause of all the attending nations. Similarly, in June 1998 the governments of Brazil, Egypt, Ireland, Mexico, New Zealand, Slovenia, South Africa, and Sweden launched a "New Agenda" initiative to resuscitate the disarmament process. Their efforts shaped international discussions in the following years and helped bring about a successful joint program agreed to at the 2000 NPT conference for thirteen practical steps for nonproliferation and reductions of nuclear weapons.

Libya has clearly gained prestige by its 2003 decision to abandon its nuclear weapons program. President George Bush calls Libyan President Muammar Qaddafi "a model" that other leaders should emulate. In his official announcement of Libya's intention to dismantle its program, President Bush said that "leaders who abandon the pursuit of chemical, biological, and nuclear weapons, and the means to deliver them, will find an open path to better relations with the United States and other free nations. . . . Libya can regain a secure and respected place among the nations, and over time, achieve far better relations with the United States."[37] British Prime Minister Tony Blair visited Libya in

March 2004, signifying Libya's reintegration into the international community.

The decision of the Nobel Prize Committee to grant the Nobel Peace Prize to IAEA Director Mohamed ElBaradei in 2005 can be seen as a conscious effort to add to the prestige of nonproliferation champions. ElBaradei himself recognized the importance of perception. "Unless we have created the environment in which nuclear weapons are seen as an historical accident from which we are trying to extricate ourselves as soon as we can," he told an international conference in November 2005, "we will continue to have this cynical environment that all the guys in the minor leagues will try to join the major leagues. That is a reality. It has nothing to do with ideology.... They will say, 'I would like to emulate the big boys if I have a security problem. If the big boys continue to rely on nuclear weapons, why shouldn't I?'"[38]

DOMESTIC NUCLEAR POLITICS

Both the national security and the prestige models of why states want nuclear weapons make the same assumption: states are monolithic actors. These theories portray policy decisions as being made by the state itself, in the interest of the entire nation. In reality, however, policy-making is a much more complicated process. Foreign policy, like domestic policy, is the product of competing internal arguments championed by a variety of individuals with unique parochial and bureaucratic interests. There is a flaw in drawing a "strict dichotomy ... between domestic and international politics," says Glenn Chafetz.[39] Just as international developments influence domestic policy (such as military budgets, civil liberties, and political campaigns), domestic concerns can impact foreign policy.

Proponents of the domestic political model contend that bureaucratic actors, with certain vested interests that may or may not be consistent with the broader national interest, ultimately make the case for or against a nuclear weapons program. These individuals are not passive actors in the policy-making process, simply accepting decisions from above and implementing them. Rather, they are active participants, lobbying and persuading, doing their best to achieve a policy outcome conforming to their views. It is often these actors who convince political leaders, not the other way around. Nuclear decisions are decided by whoever wins these internal debates.[40]

This brief introduction to the theory leads us to ask two essential questions. First, who are these well-placed individuals and how do they win or lose from certain nuclear choices? Second, how are they able to convince leaders that they must develop nuclear weapons?

THE THREE NUCLEAR MUSKETEERS   Three sets of actors play the dominant roles in nuclear decisions: the scientists, the soldiers, and the state leaders. Scott Sagan calls the first group the nuclear energy establishment, including public employees who work in national nuclear laboratories and civilian reactor facilities doing research and development for a wide range of nuclear applications. Nuclear physicists and engineers have a great interest in a nuclear weapons program because, he says, "it is technically exciting and keeps money and prestige flowing to their laboratories."[41]

The case of Pakistan's A. Q. Khan, now known as the infamous leader of a black market proliferation ring that sold nuclear technology to Iran, Libya, and other nations, illustrates this point. Khan is also known as the father of the Pakistani nuclear weapons program. When Khan returned home to Pakistan in 1975 after three years working at the European nuclear energy consortium URENCO, he brought with him stolen sensitive nuclear knowledge, including blueprints for centrifuges. Khan used this information to accelerate the newly begun, clandestine Pakistani nuclear weapons program. By the mid-1980s, Pakistan had the capability to make nuclear weapons.[42] After their first and only set of nuclear tests in 1998, Pakistani Prime Minister Nawaz Sharif congratulated the "accomplishments of the Pakistan Atomic Energy Commission, Dr. AQ Khan Research Laboratories, and all affiliated organizations."[43] Shortly thereafter, twenty-three nuclear scientists and engineers received "different civil awards in recognition of their meritorious contribution."[44] Khan is a revered national hero and has grown rich from his nuclear science and trade. Most nations elevate their nuclear scientists in a similar, if not so grand, manner.

The second group consists of certain members of the professional military, often the leaders of the air force and the navy, who benefit most from a nuclear arsenal. Both of these services stand to gain from nuclear weaponry because the development of such arms leads to requirements for more and better weapon systems and a larger role for the respective services. The air force will press for nuclear weapons because it will guarantee the need for ballistic missiles and nuclear-capable bombers. The navy will be spurred on by the prospect of nuclear-propelled submarines and nuclear ballistic missile submarines.

A fascinating illustration of this is a little-known incident in 1961, when, after the Cuban Missile crisis, President Kennedy visited the headquarters of the Strategic Air Command (SAC) in Omaha, Nebraska. In the words of historian Robert S. Norris, Kennedy's "host that day was Thomas Power, the commander-in-chief of SAC. . . . Power reportedly spoke of a requirement of 10,000 Minuteman ICBM's, and is known to have personally suggested that figure to President Kennedy. . . . [Air Force Chief of Staff Curtis] LeMay and Power and others throughout this period wanted a nuclear weapon for every conceivable mission."[45]

This is one example of how the nuclear laboratories and the pronuclear elements of the military must convince the third, and most indispensable, set of actors in the domestic political model: political leaders. It is this final group that makes the ultimate decision whether or not to proceed with a nuclear weapons program. In many instances, top political leaders do not have built-in parochial interests in favor of nuclear weapons. Consequently, unless there is widespread popular support for a nuclear program, the first two sets of bureaucratic actors must become what Peter Lavoy calls "nuclear mythmakers" and convince the political leadership of the necessity of nuclear weapons.[46]

The nuclear energy establishment and the pronuclear elements of the military, Lavoy notes,cannot just convince their state's leaders to start a nuclear weapons program out of thin air. There must be a clear rationale behind their arguments.

"Nuclear weapons programs are not obvious or inevitable solutions to international security problems," notes Sagan; "instead, nuclear weapons programs are solutions looking for a problem to which to attach themselves so as to justify their existence."[47] From the domestic politics perspective, these assertive bureaucratic actors emphasize, and perhaps even exaggerate, external security threats from rivals while also focusing on the great security and prestige benefits to be gained from nuclear weapons possession. In the case cited above, LeMay and Power were clearly overstating the threat and requirement. Secretary of Defense Robert McNamara beat back the Air Force request, and they ultimately settled on 1,000 Minuteman ICBMs.

In short, proponents of this model view security and prestige as necessary but insufficient drivers of nuclear weapons programs. What is needed to push a state over the top is a strong coalition of influential pronuclear actors. Lavoy argues that "a state is likely to go nuclear when national elites, who want the state to develop nuclear weapons, emphasize the country's insecurity or its poor international standing to popularize the myth that nuclear weapons provide military security and political power."[48]

NUCLEAR MYTHMAKERS: THE CASE OF INDIA   One example of the domestic political model is India.[49] Conventional wisdom holds that the Indian nuclear weapons program was a security-driven response to China's first nuclear test in 1964 and a prestige-driven decision resulting from India's own "ambition to be regarded as a major power in a world where the recognized great powers rely on nuclear weapons."[50] Security and prestige concerns were not alone, however, in producing an Indian nuclear weapons capability by 1974 and an overt Indian bomb by 1998. Domestic actors, such as the first head of the Atomic Energy Commission (AEC), Homi Bhabha, played decisive roles. According to Carnegie Endowment expert George Perkovich, the "leaders of the strategic weapons establishment, an enclave of scientists and engineers in India's defense research and atomic energy institutions ... for five decades had been pushing India to join the exclusive club of nuclear weapon states."[51] Lavoy focuses on Bhabha's singular importance, writing, "India's efforts to launch a military nuclear program cannot be understood apart from Homi Bhabha's pivotal role as a nuclear mythmaker."[52]

Following the Chinese nuclear test, and despite former foreign minister Singh's claim noted above that "from then on, no responsible Indian leader could rule out the option of following suit,"[53] there was no immediate Indian consensus on whether nuclear weapons were essential for national security. The most important actor in this battle, Prime Minister Lal Bahadur Shastri, quickly positioned himself against a nuclear weapons program. In 1964 Shastri said, "We cannot at present think in terms of making atomic bombs in India. We must try to eliminate the atomic bombs in the world rather than enter into a nuclear arms competition."[54] Clearly, "Shastri believed in this singular Indian mission, as Mahatma Gandhi and Jawaharlal Nehru had."[55] Bhabha, however, "loudly lobbied for development of nuclear weapons," and took great pains to minimize the anticipated cost of such an effort, making an official estimate that excluded the expense of the nuclear reactors and plutonium separation plants.[56] By the end of 1964, Shastri had compromised with Bhabha, agreeing to a "Peaceful Nuclear Explosives" program. Only two years after this initial agreement, however, Shastri and Bhabha both passed away unexpectedly, throwing the Indian program into a state of uncertainty.

Indira Gandhi, wholly inexperienced with Indian nuclear policy, became prime minister. Bhabha's position was filled by Vikram Sarabhai, a physicist more cautious about the supposed benefits of nuclear weapons. "Unlike in the Bhabha days," Perkovich tells us, "now India's nuclear establishment was headed by a bomb agnostic if not a skeptic."[57] The pro-bomb scientists at the AEC were thus restrained, at least until Sarabhai's own death in 1971. They then persuaded Prime Minister Gandhi to allow the "peaceful" test of May 1974.

Political leaders subsequently resisted the lobbying of the nuclear establishment until the elections of March 1998, when the conservative Bharatiya Janata Party (BJP) formed a stable government coalition for the first time. BJP had made the nuclear program a campaign issue. In January 1998, their foreign policy spokesman said, "Given the security environment, we have no option but to go nuclear."[58] The hesitant political leadership that had previously restrained the nuclear lobbyists was no longer an obstacle. In May 1998, India conducted five underground nuclear tests. Perkovich says, "A handful of politicians instigated by a handful of scientists with little experience in international affairs [pushed] India across a portentous strategic threshold whose implications they did not fully appreciate."[59]

DOMESTIC BARRIERS   There are also powerful domestic interests opposed to nuclear weapons programs. Most obvious are the large citizens' campaigns against nuclear weapons that rise and fall over the decades, sometimes restraining programs such as in the United States and Europe, and sometimes becoming a permanent part of the national identity, as in Japan.[60] Scientists also often play a leading role in opposing the initiation or expansion of programs, as noted above and in chapter 1.

Less appreciated, perhaps, is the role played by military leaders who doubt the utility of these weapons. Colin Powell recalls that as a young officer in 1958 he was assigned to guard a unit in West Germany equipped with 280 mm atomic cannons. These weapons fired atomic artillery shells with a yield of 15 kilotons, roughly equal to the size of each of the bombs dropped on Japan. Powell learned that his mission in time of war was to lay down a barrage on advancing Soviet troops:

> We were not talking simply about dropping a few artillery shells at a crossroad. No matter how small these nuclear payloads were, we would be crossing a threshold. Using nukes at this point would mark one of the most significant political and military decisions since Hiroshima. The Russians would certainly retaliate, maybe escalate. At that moment, the world's heart was going to skip a beat. From that day on, I began rethinking the practicality of these small nuclear weapons. And a few years later, when I became Chairman of the Joint Chiefs

of Staff, I would have some ideas about what to do with tactical nukes.[61]

His idea as chairman of the Joint Chiefs in 1990 was to get rid of these weapons. He thought they were "trouble-prone, expensive to modernize, and irrelevant in the present world of highly accurate conventional weapons."[62] His friend and chief of staff of the Army, General Carl Vuono, opposed him. "The nukes were a matter of prestige to the artillery," Powell explains. "I was asking his branch to give up a part of itself. Carl, the senior artilleryman in the U.S. Army, was not about to preside over the dismantling of his nukes." Vuono lined up the other service chiefs to oppose Powell. The senior civilians in the defense department weighed in. Powell calls them "a refuge of Reagan-era hard-liners, who stomped all over it, from Paul Wolfowitz on down." Secretary of Defense Richard Cheney rejected Powell's proposal.

But Powell was not done. In 1991, in the wake of the Gulf War and the dissolution of the Soviet Union, President George H. W. Bush wanted new ideas on nuclear disarmament. Within days, Powell's staff developed plans to get rid not just of nuclear artillery but all short-range nuclear weapons, such as the Army's Lance missiles and the Navy's nuclear torpedoes and depth charges. "The chiefs, now responding to a radically changed world, signed on, as did Paul Wolfowitz and his hard-liners," says Powell, with some delight, "Cheney was ready to move with the winds of change."[63] On September 27, 1991, President George H. W. Bush announced these unilateral nuclear disarmament measures and other steps to national and international acclaim. Today, with few or no nuclear missions to defend, many Army, Marine, and Navy leaders see nuclear weapons and their delivery systems as draining limited resources that could be used for other critical conventional needs.

JAPAN'S NUCLEAR ALLERGY   Kurt Campbell and Tsuyoshi Sunohara convincingly demonstrate the power of domestic political pressure in creating and reinforcing Japan's non-nuclear choice. "Having experienced the horrors of Hiroshima and Nagasaki," they write, "Japan's political structures and national psyche have engendered a deeply enshrined cultural taboo ... against even public discussion of the nuclear option."[64]

When Japanese leaders "indicated in unguarded moments their support for Japan's acquiring an independent nuclear weapons capacity ... pressure both from domestic constituencies and from Japan's most important security ally, the United States, kept them from acting on their desires," they say.[65] In fact, strong public opposition to nuclear weapons acquisition contributed to the resignations of multiple leaders in the wake of ill-advised comments on the nuclear issue, including by Prime Minister Nobusuke Kishi in 1957, Agriculture and Forestry Minister Tadao Kuraishi in 1968, and Vice Defense Minister Shingo Nishimura in 1999.[66]

Public opinion compelled Eisaku Sato, prime minister from 1964 to 1972 and perhaps the most pronuclear of any Japanese leader, to announce the three non-nuclear principles—not to manufacture, possess, or permit the deployment of nuclear weapons in Japan. When the United States ceded control of Okinawa in 1972, Washington had to assure Tokyo that all nuclear weapons based there would be gone before the transfer of control was completed.

In the past few years, public and political opposition to nuclear weapons has gradually softened, as Japan has adopted a more assertive military policy. Still, public opposition to a nuclear-armed Japan coupled with U.S. security assurances make it unlikely that Tokyo will amend its non-nuclear policy. Campbell and Sunohara conclude, "The depth of antinuclear sentiment is such that only major changes in the international or domestic environment, and probably only a combination of such changes could engender a domestic political environment more permissive toward Japan's acquiring nuclear weapons."[67]

TECHNOLOGICAL DETERMINISM

Some experts contend that if a state has the technological ability to develop nuclear weapons, then it will do so; the awesome power of nuclear technology and arms is too much for most leaders to resist. This argument often appeared as nuclear scientists debated among themselves the morality of building atomic, then hydrogen bombs. If we know these bombs can be built, then they will be built, some said, since every weapon that could be made, has been made. Edward Teller said in arguing for the H-bomb, "There is among my scientific colleagues some hesitancy as to the advisability of this development on the grounds that it might make the international problems even more difficult than they are now. My opinion is that this is a fallacy. If the development is possible, it is out of our powers to prevent it."[68]

The United Kingdom is a clear example of technology as a dominant factor in a country's decision to acquire nuclear weapons. As discussed previously, the country had serious security concerns and there was also a healthy prestige factor as Britain sought to retain the global role it had played for centuries. But its close alliance with the United States (which opposed a British bomb) and domestic and economic factors might have stayed its hand were it not for one overriding fact: British scientists knew how to build a bomb and build one quickly.

British scientists, in fact, had begun nuclear research before the Americans, and were close partners in the Manhattan Project. After World War II, a secret committee was formed to address the question of atomic energy and to establish a nuclear material production complex in the United Kingdom. In 1947, after American interest in a collaborative relationship with Britain cooled considerably and the 1946 Atomic Energy Act declared the U.S. intent to not share nuclear technology with any country, British leaders decided to do it on their own. "There was a kind of scientific imperative at work to regain the momentum that was under way in 1941 and 1942 and bring it to completion," concluded nuclear expert Robert Norris and his colleagues, "British scientists had begun to pursue the bomb as early as 1940 only to be interrupted. With the war over, it was now time to resume the quest."[69] It did not take long. The United Kingdom conducted its first nuclear test in October 1952.

Technology, however, seems to be a more important factor in determining the pace and extent of a nation's nuclear program *after* the initial weapons are built. Once the technology is in hand, or seems fairly easy to acquire, it becomes much more difficult for national leaders to resist the entreaties of the military, industrial, or scientific proponents of new and better weapons.

The decision of the United States to build the hydrogen bomb is probably the most compelling example of technological determinism at work. Four months after the Soviet atomic test ended the U.S. monopoly, President Truman announced that the United States would build new, more powerful weapons. Washington would develop the hydrogen bomb with 1,000 times more explosive force than the fission bombs used on Japan.

There was no urgent security rationale for pursuing such a weapon. The nuclear scientific panel advising the government on nuclear policy unanimously opposed the plan, arguing that the atomic fission bombs that the United States already possessed were devastating enough to deter the Soviet Union's emerging nuclear arsenal (see chapter 1). The panel, called the General Advisory Committee, wrote that "the extreme dangers to mankind inherent in the [H-bomb] proposal wholly outweigh any military advantage that could come from this development."[70]

The former leaders of the Manhattan Project, including Ernest Lawrence, Arthur Compton, J. Robert Oppenheimer, and Enrico Fermi, had argued that a change in political and international relations could blunt the technological drive for more and more powerful weapons. They understood the technological pull and tried to resist it. "The development, in the years to come, of more effective atomic weapons would appear to be a most natural element in any national policy of maintaining our military forces at great strength," they wrote earlier, in 1945. "Nevertheless we have grave doubts that this further development can contribute essentially or permanently to the prevention of war."[71] Their pleas were rejected both after the war and in the quest for the H-bomb.

Understanding the technological imperative does not

make one immune to it. The allure of the science and technology, not security or prestige concerns, eventually changed
even Oppenheimer's mind. He wrote in 1954:

> My feeling about development [of the H-bomb] became
> quite different when the practicabilities became clear.
> When I saw how to do it, it was clear to me that one had to
> at least make the thing. Then the only problem was what
> one would do about them when one had them.[72]

Oppenheimer's perspective may have accurately reflected
that of some nuclear scientists at Los Alamos. It seems to have
been Edward Teller's primary motivation from the first time
he realized such a weapon was possible and had urged Oppenheimer to forget about the atomic bomb and go straight to the
hydrogen bomb.

Still, the American choice can be understood independent of the theory of technological determinism. Washington policy makers seem to have had more basic motives.
Even though there was no *objective* security rationale for
developing these immensely powerful weapons, there was
a widely held *perception* among the foreign policy elite that
it would be a political and security disaster to allow the Soviets to gain such technology first. As Senator Brien Mc-
Mahon (D-CT) put it, "if we let Russia get [the H-bomb]
first, catastrophe becomes all but certain."[73] President Truman likewise viewed the issue as an unquestionable security imperative. Immediately prior to making his decision, Truman asked his advisors, "Can the Russians do it?"
When told they could, he concluded, "In that case, we have
no choice."[74]

Today, with technology spreading at a faster rate than at
any other time in human history, some argue that proliferation is inevitable. As an overall explanation of national motives, however, technological determinism does not hold up
to the historical record. There are forty-four "nuclear-capable"
states—that is, states with the industrial and technological
infrastructure to develop nuclear weapons if they so chose.
Less than one-fourth of these nations have nuclear weapons
or are attempting to develop them. Why haven't states like

Argentina, Australia, Belgium, Brazil, Germany, Italy, Japan, the Netherlands, Sweden, Switzerland, South Korea, and Taiwan built and deployed nuclear weapons? In the words of international relations theorist Benjamin Frankel, "although [nuclear weapons proliferation] requires technological capabilities to be sustained ... the spread of nuclear weapons is determined by international politics."[75] Our previous examination of several of these national decisions confirms this judgment: politics trumps technology.

TECHNOLOGICAL BARRIERS   Nuclear weapon technology has been around for more than sixty years. Just because it is possible, however, does not mean it is easy. Building a bomb still poses significant scientific and engineering challenges.

Two major obstacles stand in the way of nuclear weapons development. The more challenging of the two is producing the highly enriched uranium (HEU) or plutonium that gives an atomic bomb its unmatched explosive power. Luckily for champions of nonproliferation, this material can only be produced through a series of complex steps—uranium mining, milling, conversion, enrichment (and reprocessing in the case of plutonium), and fabrication into a metal core—all of which require advanced equipment, such as high-speed centrifuges, and years of intensive labor.

The second technological barrier to getting the bomb is putting all the necessary pieces together once the requisite HEU or plutonium has been made. Peter Zimmerman writes, "The technical barriers to weaponization of fissile material come down to designing and proving the explosive sets needed to assemble the supercritical mass; producing a reliable initiator; coping with the physical and chemical properties of the fissile materials; and performing the necessary proof testing of the designs."[76] Most experts agree, however, that this challenge pales in comparison to that of making the fissile material. Michael May, former director of Lawrence Livermore National Laboratory, argues, "Once fissile material is in hand, sophisticated technology is not needed to enter the nuclear weapons club."[77]

Technological barriers do not affect the most advanced countries of the world. Japan, for example, has long since known how to reprocess plutonium. These barriers do, however, affect developing countries that desire nuclear weapons. Reinforced by IAEA safeguards and export control regimes such as the Nuclear Suppliers Group, technological barriers can, in some instances, foil a nuclear bomb program altogether. May says that for many of the "poorest countries in the world . . . the export controls that have been imposed on most necessary materials, parts and technologies since 1992, probably erect an insuperable barrier to the acquisition of nuclear weapons, unless a country can steal them or the material to make them."[78]

Even developing countries with some advanced capabilities and access to nuclear black markets such as the A. Q. Khan network can be slowed or stopped by a technology-denial strategy. Sanctions against Iraq for its failure to cooperate with UN inspectors were so severe that it triggered humanitarian concerns about their effects on the Iraqi population. When inspectors were allowed to return in November 2002, they found that the combination of sanctions and UN inspections had crippled a nuclear program that senior U.S. officials erroneously claimed had been reconstituted. Less than two weeks before the U.S.-led invasion, IAEA Director General Mohamed ElBaradei told the UN Security Council, "During the past four years, at the majority of Iraqi sites, industrial capacity has deteriorated substantially."[79] In late 2003, David Kay, who was leading the postwar search for nuclear, biological, and chemical weapons, commented, "We have been struck in probably 300 interviews with Iraqi scientists, engineers and senior officials how often they refer to the impact of sanctions and the perceived impact of sanctions in terms of regime behavior."[80]

Intense scrutiny from the IAEA and the leading nations of the UN Security Council is retarding Iran's nuclear efforts today. Iran voluntarily agreed to the suspension of all uranium enrichment-related activities for over two years starting in November 2003, and by mid-2006 had still not built a centrifuge cascade large enough to enrich enough uranium for even one bomb, though it did produce a minuscule quality of low-enriched uranium with great fanfare in April 2006. Moreover, Iran has run into problems with uranium conversion, a necessary precursor to uranium enrichment. The gas is reportedly contaminated with heavy metals. Until Iran can reliably convert uranium yellowcake into the gaseous uranium hexafluoride that goes into centrifuges, they will not be able to enrich in any significant quantity. With the technology and assistance Iran purchased from the Khan network now cut off and leading nations refusing to supply technology beyond that required for the construction of reactors, it is not clear where Iran could obtain the necessary additional technical aid. Indigenous efforts could succeed in time, but without external help, Iran's program will progress much more slowly. It is unlikely that Iran could produce either fuel for reactors or material for bombs before the beginning of the next decade. [81]

Iraq and Iran are not the only cases in which technological barriers have slowed or stopped nuclear programs. In his detailed study of the Brazilian and Argentine programs, for example, Mitchell Reiss concluded, "Despite heavy investments in uranium enrichment and spent-fuel reprocessing capabilities, neither Buenos Aires nor Brasilia ever had the technical wherewithal to produce material for nuclear bombs."[82] Indeed, Argentina never completed its Ezeiza plutonium reprocessing plant and never enriched uranium-235 past 20 percent. (Uranium-235 is normally enriched to 90 percent to form the core of a nuclear weapon.) Brazil never enriched past 7 percent uranium-235. Reiss points out that restrictions on nuclear commerce "increased the amount of time needed to complete projects and raised their costs. . . . The examples of Argentina and Brazil strongly suggest that export controls can make a significant difference in preventing countries from increasing their nuclear competence."[83]

Clearly, the higher that countries can make the technological barriers, the more difficult it is for other nations to pursue nuclear weapons quickly or successfully. International efforts to raise technological barriers have a second effect, as the experiences of Brazil and Argentina indicate. They increase the daunting economic costs of a nuclear weapons program.

ECONOMIC DRIVERS

Nuclear weapons are big-ticket items. They and their delivery systems are expensive to make. Economic considerations alone cannot explain a state's pursuit of nuclear weapons. A country does not launch a nuclear program just because it can afford one. Nor will economic costs have much impact if a state decides nuclear weapons are vital to its national security.

Pakistan is the most often-cited example of a state that neglected the well-being of its people for nuclear weapons capability. Evidence indicates that North Korea operates on this same principle today. Despite being one of the world's poorest countries, with a Gross Domestic Product (GDP) per capita of $1,700, Pyongyang continues to pursue nuclear weapons and spends 25 percent of its GDP on defense each year.[84]

Nuclear proponents do use economic arguments to help drive their case, however. To convince political leaders that nuclear weapons are beneficial, bureaucratic actors must de-emphasize the budget strains incurred by such a program. Homi Bhabha's misleading estimate that a small Indian nuclear arsenal would cost less than $21 million is just one example of many.

Proponents also often argue that developing nuclear weapons is more affordable than building up conventional defenses to enhance national security. In the 1950s, for instance, U.S. nuclear policy was driven in part by the belief that nuclear weapons were a cost-effective deterrent, that they provided a "bigger bang for a buck." As William Weida wrote in the comprehensive *Atomic Audit*, "Basing the nation's defenses on nuclear weapons appeared to be less expensive because it was considered easier to implement than alternative strategies for deterring the Soviet threat, principally the perceived imbalance of conventional forces in Europe."[85] A proposed Senate resolution introduced by Senator McMahon in 1951 illustrates Weida's point: "The cost of military fire power based upon atomic bombs is hundreds of times cheaper, dollar for dollar, than conventional explosives."[86]

These arguments are misleading. Nuclear weapons are very expensive, and are always deployed in addition to conventional forces, not as substitutes for those forces. The United States spent approximately $7.5 trillion developing, producing, deploying, and maintaining tens of thousands of nuclear weapons from 1940 to 2005.[87] No country should take on these programs with the illusion that they are some-how going to save defense dollars.

ECONOMIC BARRIERS   Economic factors more often help tip the balance against the pursuit of nuclear weapons. Libya, Ukraine, Argentina, and Sweden provide good case studies of how economic considerations combine with security, prestige, domestic, and technology barriers to stop nuclear programs.

Libya's desire to get out from sanctions and become re-integrated in the international community was the primary driver of President Muammar Qaddafi's decision to end his clandestine nuclear pursuits. On December 19, 2003, Libya announced that it would abandon its thirty-three-year old nuclear weapons quest in exchange for improved diplomatic and economic relations with the West. After nearly two de-cades of U.S. and international sanctions against his country, Qaddafi wanted to revive the sputtering Libyan economy. Brookings Institution scholar and former State Department and National Security Council official Flynt Leverett explains: "An explicit quid pro quo was offered: American officials in-dicated that a verifiable dismantling of Libya's weapons proj-ects would lead to the removal of our own sanctions. . . ."[88]

Dismantlement of Libya's nuclear program (in addition to its chemical weapons and ballistic missile programs) pro-ceeded in three phases from January to September 2004. In January, with the first phase nearly complete, a bipartisan congressional delegation traveled to Libya for the first time in thirty years.[89] In March, during British Prime Minister Tony Blair's meeting in Libya with Qaddafi, it was announced that the Anglo-Dutch Shell oil company had signed a deal worth up to $1 billion with the Libyan National Oil Corporation to do exploration off the Libyan coast.[90] By June 2004, Libya and the United States had normalized relations and some U.S. sanctions had been lifted. By September, President Bush had lifted most remaining sanctions and direct flights be-tween the two countries were allowed. The following month, the European Union formally lifted its sanctions, which dated back to 1992. Finally, in January 2005, just thirteen months after it formally gave up the nuclear program, Libya consummated oil and gas exploration deals with American oil companies.[91]

In a January 2005 interview, Qaddafi confirmed the importance of economic integration in his decision-making. He emphasized that providing greater economic assistance would make Libya a model for others that are pursuing nuclear weapons: "There must be at least a declaration of a program like the Marshall Plan, to show the world that those who wish to abandon the nuclear weapon program will be helped."[92]

Ukraine's experience after the collapse of the Soviet Union shows that a state does not have to be suffering under sanctions to realize the linked economic and prestige benefits of forgoing or abandoning nuclear weapons. When it proclaimed independence from the Soviet Union in December 1991, Ukraine was the world's third-largest nuclear power. Kiev had retained between 4,500 and 6,300 nuclear weapons deployed on its territory during the Cold War.[93] It was by no means a foregone conclusion that Ukraine would surrender its nuclear inheritance, as it ultimately did. Just months after striking a December 1991 agreement with Russia to return all tactical nuclear weapons, for example, Ukrainian President Leonid Kravchuk announced the suspension of any further withdrawals. By mid-1992, even though Ukraine had committed to join the NPT as a non-nuclear weapon state and to give up all its nuclear weapons, it was still unclear whether the Rada (the Ukraine parliament) would sign off on the agreements, and when, if ever, these events would occur.[94]

In his detailed history of the nuclear debate in Ukraine, Mitchell Reiss pinpoints national security, international prestige, and financial concerns that needed to be satisfied before the Rada would consent to permanent non-nuclear status. Beyond the historical animosity between Ukraine and Russia, which included a territorial dispute over the Crimean peninsula, Reiss writes, "The gravest internal threat to Ukrainian security derived from its inability to create an economically viable state. . . . Economic conditions were appalling, with the inflation rate running at 90 percent per month."[95] Like many other former Soviet republics and satellites, Ukraine looked to the West for hope—and help. Kiev was seeking not only economic carrots for abandoning its nuclear weapons, however, but also an improved long-term relationship with the United States, the European Union, and NATO. In 1992 and 1993, "there was the growing perception that the West and especially the United States . . . was interested in Ukraine only so long as it retained nuclear weapons."[96] Persuading Ukraine to give up its weapons would mean convincing Kiev that non-nuclear status would bring more attention from the United States, not less. Concern of Western abandonment did not begin to wane until Secretary of State Warren Christopher visited Ukraine in October 1993 and assured President Kravchuk that the U.S.-Ukrainian relationship would not be limited to the issue of denuclearization.

Ukraine finally acceded to the NPT as a non-nuclear weapon state in December 1994, but not before it had won security assurances from Russia, the United States, and the United Kingdom, as well as promises of compensation from Russia for the warheads it returned, and a commitment from President Clinton to double U.S. aid to Ukraine. Most important, according to Reiss, was that Ukraine's ratification of the NPT "would facilitate greater Ukrainian integration with the U.S. and Western financial, political, and military institutions that could far better bolster the country's fortunes."[97]

The transition from military rule to civilian democracy in Argentina offers a window into how economic barriers can combine with shifting domestic political priorities to restrain a nation's nuclear weapons policy. In his study of Argentina's nuclear program, Leonard Spector notes that the state's nuclear bureaucracy had been largely protected from austerity measures even after Raul Alfonsín was elected president in October 1983, following seven years of military rule, "because the nuclear program was an important symbol of national prestige."[98] However, as Argentina's economic crisis worsened, the democratic government was forced to make budget cuts that delayed completion of Argentina's third nuclear power reactor and other facilities crucial to the production of fissile material. By the late 1980s, technical and financial problems plagued the country's nuclear installations, forcing shutdowns of the nuclear power plants and a halt in nuclear construction projects. Argentina's financial crisis did not directly end the nuclear weapons program, but it did slow its progress and significantly raise the social and political costs to the new government of continuing nuclear weapons investment.

Clearly, nuclear weapons are costly. Billions of dollars are required to produce and maintain a nuclear arsenal. Political and economic isolation is now the likely result of clandestinely pursuing nuclear weapons and materials. Still, there are even more costs to a nuclear weapons program. One of these is the opportunity cost—what the state could otherwise be doing with the resources poured into the nuclear program. Sweden is an interesting case in this regard. Scholars still debate why Sweden ultimately decided not to pursue a nuclear weapons program—offering sound analyses that emphasize national defense strategy, international prestige concerns, or domestic political sensitivities. No one can deny, however, that economic limitations also played a role in keeping Sweden non-nuclear. Scholar Jan Prawitz explains that Sweden viewed spending for nuclear weapons and conventional weapons as zero-sum: "Realistic defense planning dictated that a nuclear strike force in addition to the necessary conventional defense would not be possible within any conceivable peacetime level of Swedish defense expenditures."[99] In other words, Sweden had to choose between a conventional defense and a nuclear one. They chose to build SAAB jet fighters, not nuclear missiles.

Another often-neglected cost of nuclear weapons is environmental. In the 1996 study *Atomic Audit*, Stephen Schwartz concluded that the United States had spent between $216 billion and $410 billion in environmental cleanup costs related to its nuclear weapons program.[100] That is roughly $270 billion to $515 billion in 2006 dollars. Equivalent costs in the Soviet Union could be at least three times as great.[101] These expenses serve as a reminder of the true costs of a nuclear weapons program. Development and deployment of nuclear weapons is expensive, but so is the legacy that they leave.

Finally, there are often heavy political costs to be paid for the nuclear deployments. For example, while some in Europe felt reassured by the U.S. nuclear umbrella, others felt threatened. When the United States began deploying large numbers of nuclear cruise and ballistic missile in Europe in the

1980s to counter similar Soviet deployments, massive public protests roiled Europe's capitals for years. Decades later, that sentiment lingers in desires for a Europe more independent of U.S. policy.

Conclusion

The decision to pursue or not to pursue nuclear weapons is not as simple and clean cut as it might first appear. No single model can explain all of the different decisions made by distinct leaders in disparate states, each of which faces its own unique security threats, possesses its own national identity, and must contend with its own domestic political pressures. The only way to gain a complete understanding of nuclear proliferation is to take a holistic approach—examining each case, such as Iran, by testing it against all of the different models presented above. Is it an irrational hatred of the West that drives Iran's quest for nuclear technology or is it fear of a belligerent United States? Or are such efforts best understood through the prestige model as Iran strives to re-establish itself as the premier power in the Middle East? What are Iran's technical capabilities and limitations? What roles do domestic politics and internal government factions play in this choice? Can Iran afford to build these weapons and is it willing to suffer the economic penalties of sanctions and blocked trade agreements?

The most accurate conclusion that can be drawn from this analysis, then, is that states want nuclear weapons for a variety of distinct, yet closely related, reasons. Scott Sagan calls this "multicausality." In short, none of the explanatory models are perfect, but all are helpful. "Nuclear weapons proliferation," he says, "occurred in the past, and can occur in the future, for more than one reason: different historical cases are best explained by different causal models."[102]

Theoretical assumptions and conclusions both have enormous implications for nonproliferation policy. Each of the proliferation models leads us to draw different conclusions about how to best fight the spread of nuclear weapons. The result? Great difficulty in developing and sustaining a consistent and effective nonproliferation policy. Or as Yogi Berra said, "In theory there is no difference between theory and practice. In practice there is." One way to resolve some of the differences in the theoretical models is to get the analysts to all start from the same page. That is, to forge a consensus around an objective assessment of the nuclear threats. This can help put the discussion on a more practical level, filter out preconceived assumptions, and build support for an approach that tries to account for all the proliferation drivers. The next chapter develops such an assessment.

CHAPTER FIVE

TODAY'S NUCLEAR WORLD

Some say that the world is more dangerous now than it was during the Cold War. Most often these statements are made by political figures seeking to promote a new policy or by journalists eager to grab attention before anyone can flip the page or channel. But it is not true. Most military and political leaders of the past half century would likely have traded the threats of global war they faced for the challenges we face today. A moment's reflection is enough to help us realize that as serious as the current dangers are, they pale in comparison to the dangers we have just escaped.

There was arguably a much greater chance of an American city being destroyed by a nuclear explosion during the Cold War than there is today. During most of that earlier period, long-range bombers and long-range ballistic missiles threatened to bring instant, total destruction to the United States, the Soviet Union, many other nations, and, perhaps, the entire planet. Nevil Shute vividly portrayed these fears in his 1957 book, *On the Beach* (later made into a movie by Stanley Kramer, starring Gregory Peck and Ava Gardner). His story accurately captured the destruction of the Northern Hemisphere that would have resulted from a global thermonuclear war. He described the last few months of life of several survivors on the shores of Australia as they awaited the clouds of deadly radioactivity that would inevitably circle the globe to even their remote location. At the time the movie premiered in 1959, the Soviets deployed approximately 360 nuclear bombs on long-range planes and missiles; the United States fielded over 7,000.

By the 1980s, the nuclear danger had grown even worse. President Reagan's anti-missile system was supposed to defeat a first-wave attack of some 5,000 Soviet SS-18 and SS-19 missile warheads streaking over the North Pole. When Jonathan Schell's chilling book, *The Fate of the Earth,* was published in 1982, there were then 50,000 nuclear weapons in the world with a destructive force equal to roughly 20 billion tons of TNT, or 1,000,600 times the power of the Hiroshima bomb. "These bombs," Schell wrote, "were built as 'weapons' for 'war,' but their significance greatly transcends war and all its causes and outcomes. They grew out of history, yet they threaten to end history. They were made by men, yet they threaten to annihilate man."[1]

The threat of a global thermonuclear war is now near zero. The treaties negotiated in the 1980s, particularly the START agreements that began the reductions in U.S. and Soviet strategic arsenals and the Intermediate Nuclear Forces agreement of 1987 that eliminated an entire class of nuclear weapons (intermediate-range missiles that can travel between 3,000 and 5,500 kilometers), began a process that accelerated with the end of the Cold War. Between 1986 and 2006 the nuclear weapons carried by long-range U.S. and Russian missiles and bombers decreased by 61 percent.[2] These reductions are likely to continue through the current decade.

The dangers we face today are very serious, but they are orders of magnitude less severe than those we confronted just two decades ago from the overkill potential of U.S. and Russian arsenals. We no longer worry about the fate of the earth, but we still worry about the fate of our cities.

At the Carnegie International Non-Proliferation Conference in November 2005, National Public Radio's *Talk of the Nation* host Neal Conan asked a panel of top experts how they thought the nuclear risks today compared to those of the past decades. He wanted to know whether the famous *Bulletin of the Atomic Scientists* clock that depicts the world as just a few minutes from the "midnight" of a nuclear catastrophe should be moved forward or back. National Nuclear Security Administration director Linton Brooks said,

I think you have to distinguish very sharply between the threat we faced of the annihilation of societies and the threat we face that somebody may steal enough for a crude device. I don't mean to minimize the importance of nuclear security—I'm spending my life trying to improve it—but the nuclear threat that we faced in the Cold War dwarfs anything we face today.

Senator Richard Lugar (R-IN) said, "I have to agree with Linton that we are not talking about annihilation of the world. We are talking about a serious event in which a lot of people could be killed, and that would be an enormous tragedy." Former Senator Sam Nunn added,

I believe that the clock is further from midnight than it was during the Cold War. I would agree with Linton certainly in terms of any kind of all-out confrontation that would involve nuclear weapons between the United States and the Soviet Union. . . . The chances of a nuclear explosion by terrorists is greatly increased with the proliferation of weapon-grade material all over the globe . . . but the chance of an all-out nuclear attack has gone down very considerably.[3]

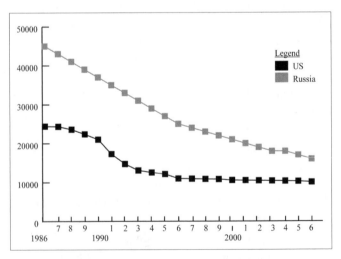

FIGURE 5.1. U.S. AND RUSSIAN STOCKPILES, 1986–2006
Data used in graph taken from NRDC, Archive of Nuclear Data, available at http://www.nrdc.org/nuclear/nudb/datainx.asp.

As these experts indicated, there are still very serious nuclear dangers. Despite its long record of success, the nonproliferation regime today is unstable. Early in the twenty-first century we face four nuclear threats:

- The danger of nuclear terrorism, though not new, is the most serious threat. Some Islamist terrorists are known to be actively seeking intact nuclear warheads or the fissile material necessary to construct a crude nuclear device.
- Existing nuclear arsenals pose a second serious challenge. Even as the stockpiles continue to decline, Russia and the United States still maintain thousands of warheads on hair-trigger alert, ready to launch within fifteen minutes, and they and some of the other nuclear weapon powers are actively researching options for new nuclear weapons. After nuclear terrorism, this is the most likely threat to American cities.
- There is also the danger of new nuclear weapon states emerging. If renewed nuclear efforts in Iran and North Korea are not stopped, they could trigger regional arms races that could end with five or six new nuclear states in the Middle East and Northeast Asia.
- Finally, there is the real risk that the entire nonproliferation regime could collapse, leading many states to reconsider their nuclear options. Indeed, some seem to be doing so already as they begin to construct plants to enrich uranium for fuel rods, a process that could easily be used to enrich uranium for nuclear bombs.

None of these dangers is unstoppable, however. Each can be diminished, if not eliminated entirely. Harvard's Graham Allison calls nuclear terrorism "the ultimate preventable catastrophe."[4] Just as the policy choices made in the early days of the nuclear age shaped the Cold War nuclear threats, the decisions we make in the next few years will determine whether we continue to roll back these four threats or launch instead into a new wave of proliferation.

To confront today's nuclear challenges effectively, it is important to recognize that developments in one of the threats will influence the others. For example, the emergence of

TABLE 5.1. THE FOUR NUCLEAR THREATS

NUCLEAR TERRORISM	EXISTING NUCLEAR ARSENALS
Some terrorists seeking to acquire nuclear weapons	27,000 nuclear weapons in eight or nine states.
Substantial risk of theft or illegal purchase	96 percent in U.S and Russia.
Russia and Pakistan are of greatest concern	Thousands of missiles on hair-trigger alert increase risk of mistaken launch
Civilian nuclear material stockpiles also at risk	Unstable double standard created by states retaining nuclear weapons for security, prestige, and diplomatic leverage
Programs are in place to reduce risk	
Progress is too slow	

NEW NUCLEAR STATES	NONPROLIFERATION REGIME COLLAPSE
New nuclear states could trigger regional chain reaction	Confidence eroding in treaties
A nuclear Iran could lead to nuclear programs in Saudi Arabia, Egypt, and Turkey	Nuclear states not living up to disarmament obligations
North Korea could push Japan, South Korea, and Taiwan to develop nuclear weapons	States cheating on treaties
Additional arsenals increase risk of terrorist access and use. More states acquiring facilities for fuel that could be used for bombs	Acceptance of states outside the NPT as legitimate nuclear powers

new nuclear states will present terrorists with more sources from which they could acquire weapons or materials and is likely to halt decreases in existing nuclear arsenals. Likewise, if the nuclear weapon states continue to be seen as dragging their feet on disarmament commitments or if new states acquire and test nuclear weapons without significant consequences, the Non-Proliferation Treaty would be seriously weakened and could collapse. The end of the regime and the subsequent spread of nuclear weapons and their related technology could quickly usher us into the frightening world of 15, 20, or 25 nuclear states that John F. Kennedy warned of in 1960. As Brent Scowcroft, national security advisor to both Gerald Ford and George H. W. Bush, wrote in 2004,

> The world may be on the verge of a major breakdown of the non-proliferation regime. . . . We are at a critical moment. Are we serious in our efforts to prevent nuclear proliferation, or will we watch the world descend into a maelstrom where weapons-grade nuclear material is plentiful and unimaginable destructive capability is available to any country or group with a grudge against society?[5]

Nuclear Terrorism: The Most Serious Threat

While *states* can be deterred from using nuclear weapons by fear of retaliation, *terrorists* have no fixed assets to protect and are more difficult to deter. Fortunately, the vast majority of terrorist groups around the world are not trying to acquire nuclear weapons. Harvard's Matthew Bunn writes:

> Most terrorist groups have no interest in threatening or committing large-scale nuclear destruction. Focused on local issues, seeking to become the governments of the areas now controlled by their enemies (and thus not wanting to destroy those areas), and needing to build political support that might be undermined by the horror and wanton destruction of innocent life resulting from a nuclear attack, all but a few terrorist groups probably would not want to get and use a nuclear bomb even if they could readily do so.[6]

The danger comes from apocalyptic or messianic groups that believe that mass destruction can bring about the global conflict they seek, helping them achieve their day of reckoning either in this world or the next. "Rather than inspire terror for the sake of achieving limited political objectives," scholars Charles Ferguson and William Potter note in their 2004 study *The Four Faces of Nuclear Terrorism*, "today's terrorism is often fueled by extremist religious ideologies that rationalize destruction, vengeance, and punishment as both necessary ends in themselves and as tools to achieve a better world."[7] The two prime examples are al Qaeda and the Japanese cult Aum Shinrikyo (which experimented with biological weapons and tried to buy components of nuclear weapons before settling for an attack with sarin nerve gas on the Japanese subway system that killed twelve people and injured hundreds).

A terrorist group with nuclear aspirations would prefer to acquire an intact nuclear warhead rather than try to construct it themselves. Russian officials "confirmed four incidents in 2001–2002 of terrorist teams carrying out reconnaissance on Russian nuclear warheads—two on nuclear warhead storage facilities and two on nuclear weapon transport trains."[8] Stealing (and later detonating) an intact warhead, however, would be extremely difficult. Nuclear expert and former National Security Council staffer Jessica Stern has written, "Stealing a warhead would require overcoming security at a site where weapons are stored or deployed, taking possession of the bomb, and bypassing any locks intended to prevent unauthorized detonation of the weapon."[9]

Nor can terrorist groups build a bomb from scratch. They cannot manufacture the highly enriched uranium (HEU) or plutonium necessary for the bomb's core. This requires substantial industrial facilities beyond the capabilities of any such group. But they can steal the uranium or plutonium, or buy it from corrupt officials. If terrorists could buy or steal 25 kilograms of highly enriched uranium, a well-organized group could probably also obtain the necessary technical expertise to fashion a gun-assembly type bomb, similar to the Hiroshima bomb.

In 1987, a group of U.S. nuclear weapons designers was commissioned to determine if this assumption was true. They concluded that such a task was achievable for "terrorists having sufficient resources to recruit a team of three or four technically qualified specialists."[10] Graham Allison finds:

Given the number of actors with serious intent, the accessibility of weapons or nuclear materials from which elementary weapons could be constructed, and the almost limitless ways in which terrorists could smuggle a weapon through American borders. . . . In my own considered judgment, on the current path, a nuclear terrorist attack on America in the decade ahead is more likely than not.

The danger of terrorist theft or purchase of weapons or material is often linked to so-called outlaw states. President George W. Bush most prominently did this in his 2002 State of the Union address: "States like [Iran, Iraq, and North Korea], and their terrorist allies, constitute an axis of evil, arming to threaten the peace of the world. By seeking weapons of mass destruction, these regimes pose a grave and growing danger. They could provide these arms to terrorists, giving them the means to match their hatred."[11]

In fact, these countries are not the most likely sources for terrorists since their stockpiles, if any, are small and exceedingly precious, and hence well guarded. Iran does not and Iraq did not have nuclear weapons or significant quantities of fissile materials. Nor is North Korea, a state that probably does have weapons-grade material, likely to give away what its leadership almost certainly sees as the most precious jewel in its security crown.

How can we determine where terrorists are likely to steal nuclear materials? When they asked the famous 1930s thief Willie Sutton why he robbed banks, he replied, "That's where the money is." If today's terrorists think like Willie Sutton they will not care about a state's geopolitical orientation; they will go where the material is. The largest, most accessible supply is in Russia and other former Soviet states. Other states, particularly Pakistan, have a volatile mixture of weapons, instability, and radical fundamentalism that make them attractive targets for terrorists hunting the bomb. And there are over forty states with civilian research reactors fueled by highly enriched uranium–perfect for a bomb, but still guarded as if they were library books.

Are terrorists really trying to get these materials? According to the IAEA Illicit Trafficking Database, there have been eighteen confirmed incidents involving HEU or plutonium through the end of 2004.[12] Osama bin Laden's best-documented attempt to acquire the material necessary for a nuclear device came in late 1993, when al Qaeda operatives reportedly tried to purchase $1.5 million of uranium in Sudan. Other reported incidents include efforts by bin Laden's aide Mamdouh Mahmud Salim to obtain HEU in the mid-1990s and al Qaeda contacts with a man in Kazakhstan who promised bin Laden a suitcase bomb in two years or less. This Kazakhstan deal evidently never went through.[13] It is not clear to what extent al Qaeda has dealt with actors well placed to follow through on their promises as opposed to scam artists looking to cash in on bin Laden's desire for a nuclear capability. Either way, two things are clear: some terrorists want this material, and there are too many avenues through which they could get it.

Russia today has thousands of nuclear weapons at approximately 150–210 sites and hundreds of tons of nuclear material at approximately 49 sites.[14] The actual amount of weapon-usable nuclear material in Russia may not even be known by the Russian government. Reliable estimates indicate that Moscow holds 180–185 tons of separated plutonium and about 1,100 tons of highly enriched uranium.[15] Roughly half is thought to be in existing weapons with the remainder in storage. The only thing between this material and a nuclear terrorist capability is the quality of security at storage sites across Russia. This means both physical security and human security: the quality of physical protection and the commitment of the insiders and guards who work at and protect each site.

If Russia is the state of primary concern when it comes to nuclear terrorism, then Pakistan is a close second. Terrorist organizations and radical fundamentalist groups operate within Pakistan's borders. National instability or a radical change in government could lead to the collapse of state control over nuclear weapons and materials and to the migration of nuclear scientists to the service of other nations or groups.

In November 2001, *USA Today* reported that the Taliban and al Qaeda had contacted at least ten Pakistani nuclear scientists since 1999.[16] The magnitude of this problem is uncer-

TABLE 5.2. PROGRESS IN SECURING AND DESTROYING FORMER SOVIET WEAPONS

The Nunn-Lugar Program provides U.S. funding and expertise to help the former Soviet Union safeguard and dismantle its large stockpiles of nuclear, chemical, and biological weapons, related materials, and delivery systems.

AS OF 2008, THE NUNN-LUGAR PROGRAM HAS ELIMINATED:[a]

SYSTEM	# DESTROYED/ ELIMINATED	% OF FINAL GOAL
Warheads	7,260	80%
ICBMs	671	58%
ICBM Silos	496	81%
ICBM Mobile Launchers	119	35%
Bombers	155	100%
Air-surface missiles	906	100%
Submarine launchers	456	80%
Submarine-launched missiles	622	89%
Strategic submarines	30	77%
Nuclear Test Tunnels/ Holes	194	100%

SECURING NUCLEAR WARHEADS AND MATERIALS: HOW MUCH WORK HAVE U.S.-FUNDED PROGRAMS COMPLETED?[b]

Comprehensive Upgrades on Weapons-Usable Nuclear Material Buildings in the Former Soviet Union	55%
At Least Rapid Upgrades on Weapons-Usable Nuclear Material Buildings in the Former Soviet Union	70%
Security Upgrades Completed on Russian Nuclear Warhead Sites	50%
Global HEU-Fueled Research Reactors Upgraded to Meet IAEA Security Recommendations	80%
Global HEU-Fueled Research Reactors Upgraded to Defeat Demonstrated Threats	20%
Global HEU-Fueled Research Reactors With All HEU Removed	25%

[a]Senator Richard G. Lugar, "Nunn-Lugar Report," January 22, 2008, available at http://lugar.senate.gov/nunnlugal/scorecard.html.
[b]Matthew Bunn and Anthony Weir, "Securing the Bomb 2007," Harvard University, Nuclear Threat Initiative, September 2007, p. vii. All percentages listed are as of the end of FY 2006.

tain, but a few Pakistani experts might be all that al Qaeda or other Islamist groups need to take stolen fissile material and make an effective nuclear device. Pakistani nuclear experts may have already helped al Qaeda. In August 2001, just weeks before the September 11 attacks on the United States, two senior Pakistani nuclear physicists held a series of top-secret meetings over two or three days with Osama bin Laden and his deputy, Ayman al-Zawahiri, at a compound in Kabul, Afghanistan. At these meetings, the Pakistani scientists, Sultan Bashir-ud-Din Mahmood and Chaudiri Abdul Majeed, answered detailed questions about nuclear, biological, and chemical weapons. According to a 2001 White House fact sheet, "In one meeting, a bin Laden associate indicated he had nuclear material and wanted to know how to use it to make a weapon. Mahmood provided information about the infrastructure needed for a nuclear weapon program and the effects of nuclear weapons."[17] According to the *Washington Post*, Mahmood gave bin Laden detailed information on the construction of nuclear weapons.[18] Neither Mahmood nor Majeed have been incarcerated. As is nuclear black marketer and fellow countryman A.Q. Khan, they are under house arrest in Pakistan.

The other point of concern in Pakistan is the possibility that extremist groups within the country could gain control of Pakistani nuclear facilities, including fissile material. Not once, but twice in 2003, President General Pervez Musharraf escaped death by a matter of inches. Assassination attempts against the Pakistani leader raised the scary specter of a government in shambles and a country in chaos. What would become of Pakistan's reserves of highly enriched uranium—enough to make 50 to 110 bombs? Who would take control of the facilities where this material is stored? How would the Pakistani military react? A destabilized Pakistan with Kashmiri militants to the northeast and al Qaeda and Taliban insurgents to the northwest would be a global security nightmare.

While Russia and Pakistan are the states of primary concern when it comes to nuclear terrorism, groups determined to wreak havoc on an atomic scale will not limit their efforts to only two states. They will look for the weakest link. There is a substantial risk of terrorist theft from the civilian nuclear stockpiles in more than forty countries around the world. It only takes about 25 kilograms of HEU or 8 kilograms of plutonium to make a nuclear weapon.[19] There is enough fissile material in the world for 300,000 bombs. There are 1,850 metric tons of HEU and plutonium in civil stockpiles. Nine countries have at least 1 metric ton of HEU and 32 countries have at least 1 metric ton of plutonium.[20] Many do not have adequate protection measures in place. These civilian facilities designed for academic research or production of medical isotopes could become the source for a bomb that vaporizes a city.

THE RISK FROM EXISTING ARSENALS

There are grave dangers inherent in countries such as the United States and Russia maintaining thousands of nuclear weapons and others like China, France, the United Kingdom,

TABLE 5.3. GLOBAL STOCKS OF PLUTONIUM AND HEU

GLOBAL STOCKS[a]				
CATEGORY	PLUTONIUM	HEU	TOTAL	BOMB EQUIVALENT
Civil Stocks	1,675	175	1850	216,800
Military Stocks	155	1725	1880	88,400
Total	1830	1900	3730	304,800
Bomb Equivalent	228,800	76,000	304,800	

Note: Military stocks include all material in weapons, in reactors and in storage. All bomb equivalents are calculated using the official IAEA estimates of 25kg of HEU or 8kg of Plutonium for each nuclear weapon and then rounded to the nearest 100. Many experts believe these estimates are conservative and that sophisticated nuclear devices can use as little as 15kg of HEU or 4kg of Plutonium. Calculations based on these smaller fissile material amounts lead to much higher estimates of bomb equivalency, up to 584,200 total possible weapons.

[a]All fissile material totals (in metric tons) are as of the end of 2003, according to the report "Global Stocks of Nuclear Explosive Materials," by David Albright and Kimberly Kramer, Institute for Science and International Security, August 2005.

TABLE 5.4. THE FIFTY COUNTRIES WITH WEAPONS-USABLE URANIUM[a]

Argentina	Germany	Mexico	South Korea
Australia	Ghana	Netherlands	Sweden
Austria	Greece	Nigeria	Switzerland
Belarus	Hungary	North Korea	Syria
Belgium	India	Norway	Taiwan
Brazil	Iran	Pakistan	Turkey
Bulgaria	Israel	Poland	Ukraine
Canada	Italy	Portugal	United Kingdom
Chile	Jamaica	Romania	United States
China	Japan	Russia	Uzbekistan
Czech Republic	Kazakhstan	Serbia	Vietnam
France	Latvia	Slovenia	
Georgia	Libya	South Africa	

[a]All numbers are as of the end of 2003. David Albright and Kimberly Kramer, "Global Stocks of Nuclear Explosive Materials," Institute for Science and International Security (August 2005).

Israel, India, and Pakistan holding hundreds of weapons. While these states regard their personal nuclear weapons as safe, secure, and essential to security, each views others' arsenals with suspicion.

Though the Cold War has been over for more than a dozen years, Washington and Moscow maintain thousands of warheads on hair-trigger alert, ready to launch within fifteen minutes. This greatly increases the risk of an unauthorized launch. Because there is no time buffer built into each state's decision-making process, this extreme level of readiness also enhances the possibility that either side's president could prematurely order a nuclear strike based on flawed intelligence.

Sam Nunn argues, "We are running the irrational risk of an Armageddon of our own making. . . . The more time the United States and Russia build into our process for ordering a nuclear strike the more time is available to gather data, to exchange information, to gain perspective, to discover an error, to avoid an accidental or unauthorized launch."[21] We came close to such a disaster in January 1995, when Russian

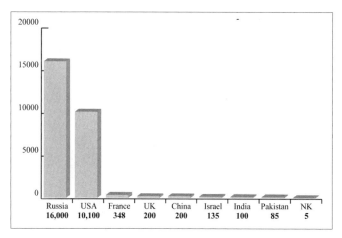

FIGURE 5.2. WORLDWIDE NUCLEAR STOCKPILES
The weapon totals for many of these countries are uncertain. The median of
the range of the best weapon estimates were used for India, Pakistan, Israel,
and North Korea (100, 85, 135, 2 respectively).
     Carnegie Endowment for International Peace, Nuclear Numbers. Available
at http://www.carnegieendowment.org/npp/numbers/default.cfm.

forces mistook a Norwegian weather rocket for a U.S. submarine-launched ballistic missile. Russian President Boris
Yeltsin had the "nuclear suitcase" open in front of him for
the first time in the nuclear age. He had just a few minutes
to decide if he should push the button that would launch a
barrage of nuclear missiles, but concluded the alert had to
be a mistake. As Russian capabilities continue to deteriorate,
the chances of accidents only increase. Limited spending on
the conventional Russian military has led to greater reliance
on an aging nuclear arsenal, whose survivability would make
any deterrence theorist nervous. Moreover, Russia's early
warning systems are "in a serious state of erosion and disre-
pair,"[22] making it all the more likely that a Russian president
could panic and reach a different conclusion than Yeltsin did
in 1995.
     Existing regional nuclear tensions already pose serious
risks. The decades-long conflict between India and Pakistan
has made South Asia the region most likely to witness the first
use of nuclear weapons since World War II. An active missile
race is under way between the two nations, even as India and

TABLE 5.5. NUCLEAR WEAPON STATES' CAPABILITIES[a]

UNITED STATES	RUSSIA	UNITED KINGDOM	FRANCE
10,000 warheads	16,000 warheads	200 warheads	348 warheads
• 5,735 active/operational	• 7,200 active/operational		
5,235 strategic	3,800 strategic		
500 nonstrategic	3,400 nonstrategic		
• 4,225 reserve/inactive	• 8,800 reserve/inactive		
DELIVERY VEHICLES	DELIVERY VEHICLES	DELIVERY VEHICLES	DELIVERY VEHICLES
ICBMs 500 (1,050 warheads)	ICBMs 585 (2,270 warheads)	SLBMs 58	Aircraft 70 (60 warheads)
SLBMs 336 (2,016 warheads)	SLBMs 192 (672 warheads)		SLBMs 48 (288 warheads)
Bombers 115 (1,955 warheads)	Bombers 78 (872 warheads)		
Nonstrategic 325 (500 warheads)			

CHINA	INDIA	PAKISTAN	ISRAEL
130–200 warheads	40–50 assembled warheads	Enough fissile material for 50-110[b]	Enough fissile material for 100-170[d]
	Enough fissile material for 75-110[c]		

TABLE 5.5. Nuclear Weapon States' Capabilities[a] (continued)

DELIVERY VEHICLES	DELIVERY VEHICLES	DELIVERY VEHICLES	DELIVERY VEHICLES
Land-based missiles 80 (80 warheads)	Land-based missiles	Land-based missiles	Land-based missiles
SLBMs 12 (12 warheads)	Aircraft		Sea-based cruise missiles
Aircraft 20 (40 warheads)			Aircraft
Stored 70			

[a] All data, unless otherwise specified, is derived from the NRDC Nuclear Notebook, available at http://www.thebulletin.org/nuclear_weapons_data/. For more detailed information, including nuclear deployment policy, delivery capabilities, etc., see Joseph Cirincione, Jon B. Wolfsthal, Miriam Rajkumar, *Deadly Arsenals*, Carnegie Endowment for International Peace, 2005.

[b] Joseph Cirincione, Jon B. Wolfsthal, Miriam Rajkumar, *Deadly Arsenals*, Carnegie Endowment for International Peace, 2005, p. 221. Weapon estimates are based on 4 to 5 kilograms of plutonium per weapon.

[c] Joseph Cirincione, Jon B. Wolfsthal, Miriam Rajkumar, *Deadly Arsenals*, Carnegie Endowment for International Peace, 2005, p. 239. Weapon estimates are based on 13 to 18 kilograms of HEU per weapon.

[d] Joseph Cirincione, Jon B. Wolfsthal, Miriam Rajkumar, *Deadly Arsenals*, Carnegie Endowment for International Peace, 2005, p. 262. Weapon estimates are based on 4 to 5 kilograms of plutonium per weapon.

Note: North Korea exploded a nuclear device on October 9, 2006, with an estimated yield of 0.5 kilotons. North Korea may have enough plutonium for as many as 12 nuclear weapons. Without further tests, it is unlikely that North Korea could build weapons small enough and sturdy enough to be delivered by missiles or perhaps even by airplanes.

China continue their rivalry. And though some progress toward détente has been made, with each side agreeing to notify the other before ballistic missile tests, for example, quick escalation in a crisis could put the entire subcontinent right back on the edge of destruction.

For some, nuclear weapons can act as a stabilizing force, even in these regions. There is some evidence to support this view. Relations between India and Pakistan, for example, have improved overall since the 1998 nuclear tests. Even the conflict in the Kargil region between the two nations that came to a boil in 1999, and again in 2002 (with over one million troops mobilized on both sides of the border) ended in negotiations, not war. Kenneth Waltz argues, "Kargil showed once again that deterrence does not firmly protect disputed areas but does limit the extent of the violence. Indian rear admiral Raja Menon put the larger point simply: 'The Kargil crisis demonstrated that the subcontinental nuclear threshold probably lies territorially in the heartland of both countries, and not on the Kashmir cease-fire line.'"[23]

It would be reaching too far to say that Kargil was South Asia's Cuban Missile crisis, but since the near-war, both nations have established hotlines and other confidence-building measures (such as notification of each side's impending missile tests), exchanged cordial visits of state leaders, and opened transportation and communications links. War seems less likely now than at any point in the past. Some experts worry, however, about the consequences of war, should it occur. It would not be thousands that would die, but millions. Michael Krepon, one of the leading American experts on the region and its nuclear dynamics, notes:

> Despite or perhaps because of the inconclusive resolution of crises, some in Pakistan and India continue to believe that gains can be secured below the nuclear threshold. How might advantage be gained when the presence of nuclear weapons militates against decisive end games? Pakistan has previously answered this question by resorting to unconventional methods. If Indian press reports are to be believed, New Delhi is now contemplating the answer of limited war. Each answer reinforces the other,

and both lead to dead ends. If the means chosen to pursue advantage in the next Indo-Pakistan crisis show signs of success, they are likely to prompt escalation, and escalation might not be easily controlled. If the primary alternative to an ambiguous outcome in the next crisis is a loss of face or a loss of territory, the prospective loser will seek to change the outcome.[24]

Many share Krepon's views both in and out of South Asia. Indian scholar P. R. Chari, for example, further observes:

[S]ince the effectiveness of these weapons depends ultimately on the willingness to use them in some situations, there is an issue of coherence of thought that has to be addressed here. Implicitly or explicitly an eventuality of actual use has to be a part of the possible alternative scenarios that must be contemplated, if some benefit is to be obtained from the possession and deployment of nuclear weapons. To hold the belief that nuclear weapons are useful but must never be used lacks cogency.[25]

A quickly escalating crisis over Taiwan is another possible scenario in which nuclear weapons could be used, not accidentally as with any potential U.S.-Russian exchange, but as a result of miscalculation. Neither the United States nor China is eager to engage in a military confrontation over Taiwan's status, and both sides believe they could effectively manage such a crisis. But crises work in mysterious ways—political leaders are not always able to manipulate events as they think they can, and events can escalate very quickly. A Sino-U.S. nuclear exchange may not happen even in the case of a confrontation over Taiwan's status, but it is possible and should not be ignored.

Recent advocacy by some in the United States of new battlefield uses for nuclear weapons and for a program to replace all existing nuclear warheads with a new design could lead to fresh nuclear tests, and possibly lower the nuclear threshold, i.e., the willingness of leaders to use nuclear weapons. The five nuclear weapon states recognized by the Non-Proliferation Treaty have not tested since the signing of the Comprehensive

Nuclear Test-Ban Treaty in 1996, and, until North Korea's October 2006 test, no state had tested since India and Pakistan did so in May 1998. If the United States again tested nuclear weapons, then political, military, and bureaucratic forces in several other countries would undoubtedly pressure their governments to follow suit. Indian scientists, for example, are unhappy with the inconclusive results of their 1998 tests. Indian governments now resist their demands for new tests for fear of the damage they would do to India's international image. It is a compelling example of the power of international norms. New U.S. tests would collapse that norm, trigger tests by India, then perhaps China, Russia, and other nations. The Nuclear Test-Ban Treaty, widely regarded as a pillar of the nonproliferation regime, would crumble, possibly bringing down the entire regime.

NEW NUCLEAR NATIONS AND REGIONAL CONFLICTS

For some scholars and officials, the addition of new nations to the nuclear club is as natural and inevitable as population growth. Kenneth Waltz argues that "nuclear weapons will nevertheless spread, with a new member occasionally joining the club. . . . Someday the world will be populated by fifteen or eighteen nuclear-weapon states."[26]

Monterey Institute expert William Potter says this view is shared by many in the Bush administration. "Principle one" for many officials, he says, is "that nuclear proliferation is inevitable, at best it can be managed, not prevented."[27] Currently, however, there are only two countries of serious concern. If the nuclear programs in North Korea and Iran can be checked, then prospects for halting and reversing proliferation globally improve dramatically. If they are not checked, then they may start a momentum that tips neighboring countries over the nuclear edge.

The danger is *not* that either North Korea or Iran would use nuclear weapons to attack the United States or other countries. These states, like others before them, likely view nuclear weapons as a means to defend themselves, as symbols of national pride and accomplishment, or as bargaining chips to accomplish other goals. (For more on why countries want nuclear weapons, see chapter 3.) Their leaders, like the leaders of other states, would be deterred from using nuclear weapons in a first strike against the United States or its allies by the certainty of swift and massive retaliation. Nor are new nuclear states, as discussed above, likely to consciously proliferate to terrorists, even if such states are in dire need of hard currency exports, like North Korea, or if they have aided terrorist groups in the past, as in the case of Iran.

But what a state like Iran might see as a defensive move would provoke dangerous reactions from other states in the region. A nuclear reaction chain could ripple through a region and across the globe, triggering weapon decisions in several, perhaps many, other states. Such developments would weaken Iran's own security, not increase it. The spread of nuclear weapons to multiple states throughout an already tense region could bring increased rivalry, greater friction, and quite possibly nuclear catastrophe.

This is the danger President Kennedy warned of in 1963:

> I ask you to stop and think for a moment what it would mean to have nuclear weapons in so many hands, in the hands of countries large and small, stable and unstable, responsible and irresponsible, scattered throughout the world. There would be no rest for anyone then, no stability, no real security, and no chance of effective disarmament. There would only be the increased chance of accidental war, and an increased necessity for the great powers to involve themselves in what otherwise would be local conflicts.[28]

Several countries in the Middle East that are capable of pursuing their own nuclear weapon programs or otherwise acquiring nuclear weapons might decide to do so if Iran "goes nuclear." These states include Saudi Arabia, Egypt, and Turkey. Saudi Arabia might seek to purchase nuclear weapons from Pakistan, whose nuclear program Saudi money helped finance. Or Saudi leaders could take a nuclear shortcut by inviting Pakistan to station nuclear weapons on its territory.

This would be completely legal under existing treaties in the same way that the United States bases several hundred nuclear weapons at air bases within the territory of non–nuclear weapon states in Europe.

Other countries have at least the basic facilities and capabilities to mount a nuclear weapons program, albeit not without significant political and economic consequences. Egypt and Turkey could probably manufacture enough nuclear material to produce a nuclear weapon within a decade of launching such an effort. It is possible that the Middle East could go from a region with one nuclear weapon state (Israel), to one with two, three, or five such states within a decade—with all the tensions of the existing political and territorial disputes still unresolved.

This is not an inevitable outcome, however. Iran's continued pursuit of nuclear fuel cycle (particularly uranium enrichment and plutonium separation) capabilities does not need to end with nuclear dominos falling. The ongoing diplomacy involving Iran, the European Union, the IAEA, and increasingly the United States, Russia, and China likely holds the key to the region's nuclear future. If a creative compromise can be struck and diplomacy wins out, then the reaction chain might work in reverse, encouraging negotiations on the long-standing U.S. goal of a Middle East free of nuclear weapons—including Israel.

Northeast Asia has also had long-held regional animosities—between China and Taiwan, China and Japan, North Korea and South Korea, North Korea and Japan, and Japan and South Korea. Only China currently has an established nuclear capability in the region. The United States' nuclear umbrella—the promise that the United States would come to the defense of South Korea and Japan—has helped to convince those states to forgo nuclear weapons for now.

North Korea's October 2006 test plunged the region into crisis, prompting fears of an arms race. Two paths opened up. One would reverse the program, building on progress in the six-party diplomacy between North Korea, the United States, South Korea, Japan, China, and Russia, most notably the September 2005 joint statement that the North would give up its nuclear program in exchange for security assurances and nuclear and non-nuclear energy aid. If, however, North Korea joins China in the nuclear club, then the other states may sense that the nonproliferation momentum in the region has shifted. If they then begin to question America's commitment to their security, each would feel enormous pressure to "go nuclear." As Vice President Dick Cheney said in March 2003, "the idea of a nuclear-armed North Korea . . . [will] probably set off an arms race in that part of the world, and others, perhaps Japan, for example, may be forced to consider whether or not they want to readdress the nuclear question."[29] Whereas in the Middle East it might take a decade or more to reach five nuclear states, Northeast Asia could see five nuclear-armed adversaries in half that time.[30]

South Korea and Taiwan are both technically advanced societies with the infrastructure necessary to launch a full-scale nuclear effort. Both flirted with nuclear weapon programs (South Korea in the 1970s and Taiwan once in the late 1960s and 1970s and again in the late 1980s). Japan, meanwhile, would have to amend its constitution to pursue a nuclear weapons program. Still, Tokyo's civilian stockpile of weapon-usable plutonium, currently enough to make hundreds of nuclear warheads, could be converted to military uses in a matter of weeks or months. Ariel Levite of the Israeli Atomic Energy Commission has argued that Japan's "standby nuclear capability" allows it "to remain within a few months of acquiring nuclear weapons."[31] South Korea has long referred to Japan as an "associate member of the nuclear club."[32]

The Risk of Regime Collapse

The longest-term, but most severe, nuclear threat we face today is the prospect that the entire international nonproliferation regime could collapse. This set of treaties, cooperative efforts, and international commitments has held for over thirty-five years and performed better than almost anyone would have predicted in the 1950s and 1960s. Its disintegration would be devastating.

It is difficult, if not impossible, to convince other states to give up nuclear weapon ambitions or adhere to nonproliferation norms when immensely powerful nuclear weapon states reassert the importance of nuclear weapons to their own security. The United States and the NATO alliance, for example, routinely issue declarations asserting the vital role that nuclear weapons play in U.S. and European security. If the most powerful military nations in the world say that nuclear weapons are necessary for their security, why should a weaker military power conclude that they are not? It is a bit like parents trying to convince their children not to smoke, when they each have a two-pack a day habit and are constantly extolling the pleasures of smoking.

The UN secretary-general's High-Level Panel on Threats, Challenges and Change, which included international security experts from around the world, including Brent Scowcroft, emphasized the threat of regime collapse in 2004:

> Almost 60 states currently operate or are constructing nuclear power or research reactors, and at least 40 possess the industrial and scientific infrastructure which would enable them, if they chose, to build nuclear weapons at relatively short notice if the legal and normative constraints of the Treaty regime no longer apply. . . . The non-proliferation regime is now at risk because of lack of compliance with existing commitments, withdrawal or threats of withdrawal from the Treaty on the Non-Proliferation of Nuclear Weapons to escape those commitments, a changing international security environment and the diffusion of technology. *We are approaching a point at which the erosion of the non-proliferation regime could become irreversible and result in a cascade of proliferation.*[33] (emphasis added)

The health of the regime depends on the performance and resolve of the key state supporters of the regime. If U.S. and Russian nuclear arsenals remain at disproportionately high levels, if they and other nuclear weapon states modernize their arsenals with new weapons and expensive missiles, submarines, and bombers, then many nations will conclude that the weapon states' promise to reduce and eventually eliminate these arsenals has been broken. Non-nuclear states may therefore feel released from their pledge not to acquire nuclear arms.

The example and performance of the nuclear weapon states is one—but not the major—factor threatening the regime. Pressures are also rising from "below," from new states trying to get these weapons. If the nuclear crises in Iran and North Korea go unresolved and regional arms races commence, then states that would not otherwise consider a nuclear option may begin to do so. Non-nuclear states may feel that the protection provided to them under the NPT is eroding and that the only effective path to self-defense is through nuclear arms.

The Non-Proliferation Treaty is also severely threatened by the development in several states of facilities for the enrichment of uranium and the reprocessing of plutonium. Although each state asserts that these are for civilian use only, supplies of these materials potentially put each of these countries "a screwdriver's turn" away from weapons capability. This greatly erodes the confidence that states can have in a neighbor's non-nuclear pledge. While the political commitments of Japan not to develop nuclear weapons, for example, are accepted now, tensions in the region could change how its neighbors view the "virtual arsenal" that Japan's stocks of plutonium provide.

Additionally, there appears to be growing acceptance of the nuclear status of Pakistan and India, with each country accruing prestige and increased attention from leading nuclear weapon states, including the United States. When President Bush proposed in 2005 to bolster U.S.-India ties by overturning treaty and legal bans on sales of nuclear reactors, fuel and technology to India, a bipartisan group of experts, in a letter to Congress, warned,

> Non-nuclear-weapon states have for decades remained true to the original NPT bargain and forsworn nuclear weapons and accepted full-scope IAEA safeguards in return for access to peaceful nuclear technology under

strict and verifiable control. Many of these states made this choice despite strong pressure to spurn the NPT and pursue the nuclear weapons path. They might make a different choice in the future if non-NPT members receive civil nuclear assistance under less rigorous terms.[34]

Some now say, "So what?" Even a nuclear Iran or North Korea, they argue, could also be absorbed into the international system without serious consequence. Kenneth Waltz says, "In asking what the spread of nuclear weapons will do to the world, we are asking about the effects to be expected if a larger number of relatively weak states get nuclear weapons. If such states use nuclear weapons, the world will not end."[35]

For example, if a state like Brazil, which has developed and recently expanded its uranium enrichment capability and which aspires to great power status, sees the acceptance of nuclear weapons in Pakistan and India (and perhaps eventually in North Korea and Iran), then it may come to believe that its international position would not be harmed, but in fact helped, by possession of nuclear weapons.

Then-CIA Director George Tenet warned of this ripple effect in his 2003 testimony before the Senate Select Committee on Intelligence: "The desire for nuclear weapons is on the upsurge. Additional countries may decide to seek nuclear weapons as it becomes clear their neighbors and regional rivals are already doing so. The 'domino theory' of the 21st century may well be nuclear."[36]

This is not just an academic argument. Most nations would continue to eschew nuclear weapons, if only for technological and economic reasons, but countries as diverse as Turkey and South Korea, Egypt and Ukraine, Japan and Syria, Saudi Arabia and Brazil, or South Africa and Indonesia could decide that nuclear weapons are necessary to improving their security or status. There is a real possibility, under these conditions, of a system-wide collapse of the nuclear nonproliferation regime. If it were to occur it could bring the world back to the brink of annihilation for the first time in some twenty years.

The Bush administration came into office in 2001 with high hopes that a dramatic change in U.S. policy could reduce all these risks. They brought with them policies they believed would chart a fundamentally new direction in U.S. nuclear policy and in so doing would increase national security and decrease the chances of new states or terrorist groups threatening the country with nuclear weapons. The next chapter examines the consequences of their policy choices.

CHAPTER SIX

THE NEW U.S. POLICY

Since 1945, American nonproliferation policies have relied on a combination of international agreements, alliance systems, and security commitments. In the jargon of international relations theorists, this means that for most of the nuclear age policies and programs have been based on a liberal internationalist view of the world, coupled with a realist understanding of national behavior and the importance of military force.

Liberal internationalists believe that conflicts between states can be permanently reduced through international institutions and democratic alliances. This view, shared by most U.S. presidents in the twentieth century, provides an explanation for why democratic states do not go to war with each other, a tendency that scholars call the "democratic peace."[1] Unlike realism's unending conflict, liberal internationalism holds that relations between states can be regulated such that one state's gain is not another's loss; all can prosper together through international cooperation. Philosopher Immanuel Kant imagined a world of "rational beings who together require universal laws for their survival."[2] Woodrow Wilson is the U.S. president most often associated with promoting this vision. Today, liberal internationalists would point to the sixty years of peace enjoyed by modern Europe after centuries of bloody strife as a model of the prosperity and tranquility that can be achieved through democratic political and economic integration.

Few governments implement policies guided purely by any one international theory, however. Instead, they combine approaches. The European peace, of course, is backed by formidable military assets, both European and American. German writer Josef Joffe has called the U.S. military "Europe's pacifier."[3] Nonproliferation treaties are similarly bolstered by a commitment to enforce their rules. American nonproliferation strategy has historically been part liberal internationalist—relying on institutions and agreements that regulate, restrict, and prevent the spread of nuclear weapons—and part realist—emphasizing defense assets, alliances, and commitments.

Despite the overall success of this approach, its failures have been heavily criticized in recent years. For these critics, the 183 countries that do not have nuclear weapons are outweighed by the few nations that are trying to acquire them. They argue for new, more aggressive policies directed against these selected states. This is more than merely shifting the emphasis between the two components of the combined approach described above.

For example, in 1998 a group of experts wrote to President Clinton to urge him to take direct action to remove Iraqi dictator Saddam Hussein from power. The group included Paul Wolfowitz, Donald Rumsfeld, John Bolton, Richard Perle, Elliott Abrams, and William Kristol. They described what they saw as the failure of traditional international approaches and in the process ran down a list of the various institutions they no longer found to be reliable instruments of U.S. policy:

> The policy of "containment" of Saddam Hussein has been steadily eroding over the past several months. . . . [W]e can no longer depend on our partners in the Gulf War coalition to continue to uphold the sanctions or to punish Saddam [Hussein] when he blocks or evades UN inspections. Our ability to ensure that Saddam Hussein is not producing weapons of mass destruction, therefore, has substantially diminished. Even if full inspections were eventually to resume, which now seems highly unlikely, experience has shown that it is difficult if not impossible to monitor Iraq's chemical and biological weapons production. . . . As a result, in the not-too-distant future we will be unable to determine with any reasonable level of confidence whether Iraq does or does not possess such weapons.[4]

Most of these thinkers were associated with the "neocon-servative" school. Neoconservatives have combined different elements of realism, liberal internationalism, and idealism to develop a new direction for U.S. foreign policy. They believe in the "democratic peace" espoused by liberal internationalists but substantially mistrust international institutions. In pursuit of freedom and security, they favor a more assertive use of military force than traditional realists. Rather than simply manage the world, they favor using the U.S. military as a tool to transform it. Thus, the experts argued in their letter:

> The only acceptable strategy is one that eliminates the possibility that Iraq will be able to use or threaten to use weapons of mass destruction. In the near term, this means a willingness to undertake military action as diplomacy is clearly failing. In the long term, it means removing Saddam Hussein and his regime from power.[5]

Though many of these thinkers assumed high government positions after the elections of 2000, it was not until the attacks of September 11, 2001, that they were able to profoundly change the course of American anti-proliferation policy. In the wake of the attacks, the Bush administration reassessed proliferation threats to U.S. security. In early 2002, Assistant Secretary of State for Non-Proliferation John Wolf noted, "The President has said that halting proliferation is not one of many objectives of U.S. foreign policy; it is a central framing element."[6] But the new strategy to combat these dangers emphasized fundamentally different methods from the past.

Eliminating Regimes, Not Arsenals

Many officials in the Bush administration believed that the entire process of negotiating and implementing nonprolif-eration treaties was both unnecessary and harmful to U.S. national security interests. They argued that some of the treaties, such as the Comprehensive Nuclear Test-Ban Treaty, the Anti-Ballistic Missile Treaty, and the Landmine Treaty, restrict necessary armaments, thus weakening the principal nation that safeguards global peace and security. Other treaties, such as the Chemical Weapons Convention and the Biological Weapons Convention, promote a false sense of security as some nations sign, then cheat on the agreements. Multilateral meetings were often seen as opportunities for the global Lilliputians to gang up on the American Gulliver.

For example, John Bolton, then a scholar at the American Enterprise Institute, said in 1999 that the Clinton administration suffered from a "fascination with arms control agreements as a substitute for real nonproliferation of weapons of mass destruction."[7] Gary Schmitt, an analyst at the neoconservative Project for the New American Century, said more directly, "Conservatives don't like arms control agreements for the simple reason that they rarely, if ever, increase U.S. security. . . . The real issue here, and the underlying question, is whether the decades-long effort to control the proliferation of weapons of mass destruction and the means to deliver them through arms control treaties has in fact worked." He contended that it was no longer "plausible to argue that our overall security was best served by a web of parchment accords, and not our own military capabilities."[8]

The perceived failures of the treaty regime led the Bush team to demand more flexibility in its options to combat proliferation. Although the administration remained committed to export controls and strengthening the IAEA, the core strategy became using direct military means to eliminate threats they believed obvious. This view held that preventive war, even waged unilaterally, must be considered a valid and necessary response to certain threats. The United States must, in other words, "defend against the threat *before* it is unleashed" (emphasis added).[9]

This action-oriented approach was detailed in two key documents—*The National Security Strategy of the United States of America* (September 2002) and *National Strategy to Combat Weapons of Mass Destruction* (December 2002).[10] The latter, detailing the new plan, called it "a fundamental change from the past."[11] The *National Security Strategy* emphasized the direct application of U.S. military, economic, and political power: "The United States possesses unprecedented—and unequaled—strength and influence in the world. . . . The great strength of this nation must be used to promote a balance of power that favors freedom." Thomas Donnelly, an analyst at the American Enterprise Institute, explains, "The task for the United States is nothing less than the preservation and expansion of today's Pax Americana, the extension of the 'unipolar moment' for as long as possible."[12]

Proliferation was seen as part of this larger, global struggle, not as an end in itself. The primary challenge to continued American supremacy, they argued, was the proliferation of nuclear, biological, and chemical weapons to states or groups hostile to the United States. In this view, there was bad proliferation and good proliferation. Whereas previous presidents treated the spread of these weapons as the core problem and sought their elimination through treaties, the Bush administration saw the threat as a small number of states, particularly the nexus of these states, weapons, and terrorists. Meanwhile, nuclear weapons in the hands of responsible states, that is, the United States and its allies, were seen as necessary instruments for preserving peace and security. Whereas previous presidents would cite, as President Bill Clinton did, the grave threat to the nation "from the *proliferation of nuclear, biological, and chemical weapons,*"[13] President Bush said in his 2003 State of the Union address, "The gravest danger facing America and the world is *outlaw regimes that seek and possess nuclear, chemical, and biological weapons*" (emphasis added). Bush in effect changed the focus from "what" to "who." The new strategy sought the elimination of regimes rather than weapons, in the belief that the U.S. could determine which countries were responsible enough to have nuclear weapons and which ones were not. American power, not multilateral treaties, would enforce this judgment.

Strategy documents and speeches detailed "three pillars" of anti-proliferation policy: traditional nonproliferation agreements, counter-proliferation (including anti-missile systems and military action), and consequence management (responding to the use of nuclear, biological or chemical weapons).[14] Yet most of the effort and funding flowed to the second pillar. In 2001, the government spent approximately $9 billion on counter-proliferation efforts (mostly for anti-missile weapons), compared to $1.5 billion each for nonproliferation and consequence management efforts. By the end of 2005, counter-proliferation funding had increased astronomically with programs to try to intercept ballistic missiles funded at $9–10 billion annually and the war in Iraq, launched in an effort to disarm Saddam Hussein, climbing over $300 billion. Funding for traditional nonproliferation efforts, including all diplomatic activity and cooperative threat reduction programs, remained steady at $1.5 billion.

The Successes of the New Policy

The new approach had been expected to yield dramatic results. Under Secretary of State John Bolton said in 2004, "The Bush administration is making up for decades of stillborn plans, wishful thinking, and irresponsible passivity. After many years of hand-wringing with the vague hope to find shelter from gathering threats, we are now acting decisively. We will no longer accept being dispirited by difficult problems that have no immediate answer."[15]

By 2006, the Bush administration had achieved a number of nonproliferation successes. Libya's announcement in December 2003 that it would abandon decades of work on nuclear and chemical weapons and missile programs was an unqualified triumph. This diplomatic victory was a net plus for the administration even though it actually differed from the preferred U.S. strategy. With Libya, the United States changed a regime's behavior, not the regime. America agreed to guarantee Libya's security, restore full diplomatic relations, and drop all sanctions against the country in exchange for the end of its nuclear weapon, chemical weapon, and long-range-missile programs. Although Libyan President Muammar Qaddafi undoubtedly considered U.S. military actions in Iraq, economic and prestige factors appear to have been the dominant forces in his decision to abandon decades of largely fruitless efforts to acquire nuclear weapons (see chapter 4).

There were other significant successes that supporters of the new approach point to as indicators of its viability. Information provided by Libyan officials (and Iranian admissions to IAEA inspectors) led to the public disclosure of the A.Q. Khan network.[16] Led by the United States, the United Nations Security Council in 2004 adopted UN Resolution 1540, committing all nations to adopt laws to strengthen their export control regimes and to criminalize illegal trade in biological, chemical, and nuclear weapon–related technologies. U.S. and Russian nuclear arsenals continued to decrease and relations between the two former adversaries remain constructive. In 2002, President Bush and Russian President Vladimir Putin signed the Strategic Offensive Reduction Treaty to draw down U.S. and Russian deployed, strategic nuclear arsenals to between 1,700 and 2,200 by the end of 2012. Furthermore, progress had been made on efficient implementation of nuclear security and nonproliferation programs in the former Soviet Union, even if those programs could still use more attention and funding.[17] In 2004, the U.S. Department of Energy established the Global Threat Reduction Initiative (GTRI), an umbrella program to unite ongoing efforts to secure and remove highly enriched uranium from research reactors and other civilian nuclear facilities around the world.

Many countries began cooperating in the Proliferation Security Initiative (PSI) to interdict illegal trade in weapon components. According to Secretary of State Condoleezza Rice, PSI has already been responsible for at least eleven interdictions of goods related to nuclear and ballistic missile programs.[18] In November 2005, Robert Joseph, the undersecretary of state for arms control and international security stressed the importance of PSI, telling a Washington conference, "PSI has transformed how nations act together against proliferation. . . . [It] is not a treaty-based approach involving long, ponderous negotiations that yield results only slowly, if at all. Instead it is a true partnership."[19] There is also greater willingness on the part of some states to enforce nonproliferation commitments. The right combination of force and diplomacy could yet result in negotiated solutions to the North Korean and Iranian programs. And prospects for peacefully resolving regional conflicts may have increased with the growing movement for democracy in the Middle East and Central Asia.

The Failures of the New Policy

The most significant and direct application of the new approach to nonproliferation was the war with Iraq. It was the world's first nonproliferation war, a battle fought primarily over the perceived need to prevent the acquisition or transfer of nuclear, biological, and chemical weapons. More than anything else, the war with Iraq would determine the fate of the new strategy. By the end of 2005, it had become clear that the war had failed to accomplish the administration's objectives.

The war in Iraq manifested three key problems. First, the premise of the war was wrong. Postwar analysis has proved that the war was unnecessary. Saddam Hussein did not have any weapons that could have threatened America. The administration itself concluded by the end of 2004 that Iraq had ended all its nuclear, chemical, and biological programs between 1991 and 1995 and did not have stockpiles of these weapons.[20] Second, the war demonstrated the naïveté of the underlying strategy. Intended to be the prototype for a new, assertive policy that would eliminate bad proliferation at its source, the war proved to be many times more difficult and costly than predicted. Though there was heady talk in Washington in the spring and summer of 2003 of moving on to Tehran, Damascus, and even Pyongyang,[21] as the Iraqi insurgency grew and reconstruction faltered, few believed that the United States should undertake other preventive wars.

Third, in order to rally support for the invasion of Iraq, administration officials presented the public with a false choice: war or acceptance of a growing Iraqi threat. While this framed the issues to the benefit of those who sought war, there was an effective alternative. International mechanisms were working and could have thwarted the limited threat posed by Saddam's regime. With a UN Security Council united by President Bush's diplomatic efforts in the fall of 2002, an intrusive inspection regime was showing results. Although senior U.S. officials belittled the United Nations inspectors before the war and discredited their work, UN sanctions and inspections, in fact, had been more effective than most realized in disarming Iraq after the 1991 war. In 2002 and 2003, the inspectors were finding what little there was to find.[22] If they had been allowed to continue their work for just a few more weeks, inspectors believe, they could have shown that Iraq did not have active weapons programs.[23] This is particularly true of the nuclear program, the hardest program to hide and the one most used to justify the need for immediate military action.

U.S. officials had justified the war as necessary to disarm Saddam Hussein, establish a new model for counter-proliferation, and replace existing international security mechanisms. But by March 2006, 57 percent of Americans had concluded that the war was a mistake, according to a Gallup poll. Former national security advisor Zbigniew Brzezinski summarized the ripple effect many saw from the Iraq invasion and the selective approach to nonproliferation:

America's ability to cope with nuclear nonproliferation has also suffered. The contrast between the attack on the militarily weak Iraq and America's forbearance of the nuclear-armed North Korea has strengthened the conviction of the Iranians that their security can only be enhanced by nuclear weapons."[24]

In addition to the war in Iraq, there were ten key failures of the new proliferation policy:

• The danger of nuclear terrorism may have increased. U.S. intelligence officials concluded in February 2005 Senate testimony that American policy in the Middle East has fueled anti-U.S. feeling and that the Iraq War has provided jihadists with new recruits who "will leave Iraq experienced in and focused on acts of urban terrorism."[25] After the Iraq invasion, terrorist attacks rose globally and al Qaeda grew in influence and adherents.[26] At the same time, weapons and materials are being secured more slowly than expected. The amount of nuclear material secured in the two years after 9/11 was at best equal to the amount secured in the two years before 9/11.[27] Former CIA Director Porter Goss said in his February 2005 Senate testimony that he could not assure the American people that some of the material missing from Russian nuclear sites had not found its way into terrorist hands.[28]

• Iran accelerated its nuclear efforts—whether peaceful or not—and the United States lacked a coherent plan for how to stop the program. Most of the construction and development of Iranian nuclear facilities has occurred since 2000, including the opening of plants to produce uranium gas, the first successful operation of a centrifuge cascade to enrich uranium, and the construction of a vast facility to house over 50,000 centrifuges.

• North Korea also accelerated its program, possibly increasing fivefold its amount of bomb material. Since 2002, North Korea ended the freeze on its plutonium program, claimed to have reprocessed the plutonium into weapons, withdrew from the NPT, and tested a nuclear device.

• Though the A. Q. Khan nuclear black market was disrupted in 2004, failure to do so earlier had allowed Iran, Libya, and possibly North Korea to acquire key components for nuclear weapons production. The failure to get more cooperation from the government of Pakistan (which used the network for its own nuclear imports) made it difficult to determine if the network had been shut down completely or simply had gone further underground.

• More nations declared their intentions to develop the ability to enrich uranium for nuclear reactor fuel—the same technologies can be used to enrich uranium for nuclear bombs.[29] U.S. proposals to curtail these technologies failed to win any significant support.

• The process of negotiating reductions in U.S.-Russian nuclear arsenals came to a sudden end with the 2002 Moscow Treaty. The administration declared that it would not negotiate any further reductions in Russian long-range, strategic weapons and would not begin negotiations to reduce Russian short-range tactical weapons planned by the Clinton administration. The reductions themselves proceeded at a slower pace than previous administrations had planned.[30]

• Administration proposals to research and possibly develop new nuclear weapons coupled with new doctrines

justifying nuclear weapons use against even non-nuclear targets, encouraged other nations, such as Russia and France, to
develop similar plans and encouraged the view that nuclear
weapons should be an essential component of a nation's security program.

• Concern grew that the entire nonproliferation regime
was in danger of a catastrophic collapse. The NPT Review
Conference of May 2005 ended acrimoniously, failing to act
upon the consensus of the majority of states for stronger
nonproliferation and disarmament efforts or to adopt any of
the dozens of useful suggestions proposed by many of the
nations present.

• President Bush's decision to reverse U.S. policy toward
India and begin selling sensitive nuclear technology seemed
to reward India's nuclear proliferation. The action seemed a
de facto recognition of India as a nuclear-weapon state, with
all the rights and privileges reserved for those states that have
joined the NPT. This raised concerns that other states, such
as Pakistan and Israel, might demand the same status and
that others might opt out of the NPT to pursue their own
nuclear plans.

• A core part of the counter-proliferation strategy realized
little progress. From 2000 to 2005, the United States spent
almost $50 billion on anti-missile systems without realizing
any substantial increase in military capability. The anti-missile system under construction in Alaska is widely regarded
as ineffective.[31]

By the beginning of 2006, a broad, bipartisan consensus had developed that the failures of the new approach
outweighed the benefits. Georgetown University School of
Foreign Service Dean Robert Gallucci eloquently summarized the benefits of the previous nonproliferation strategies before the Senate Foreign Relations Committee in
April 2006:

> Most analysts believe that fifty years of non-prolifera-
> tion policy has something to do with explaining why the
> spread of nuclear technology has not led to the prolifera-
> tion of nuclear weapons, why we live in a world of eight or

nine nuclear weapons states, rather then eighty or ninety.
A key part of that policy has been our support for an international norm captured in the very nearly universally
adhered to Nuclear Non-Proliferation Treaty (NPT). The
norm is simple: in the interest of international security, no
more states should acquire nuclear weapons. . . . Certainly the fact that we have eight or nine states with nuclear
weapons rather than only the original five, means that the
norm has not held perfectly well. But it has had substantial force in the face of widespread acquisition of critical
nuclear technologies, and that has been of vital importance to America's security. Simply put, the Administration now proposes to destroy that norm.

Gallucci focused on the drawbacks of the U.S.-India deal,
and the damage the deal could do to global nonproliferation efforts:

The damage will be done to the non-proliferation norm
by *legitimatizing* India's condition, by exempting it from
a policy that has held for decades. And we would do this,
we assert less than honestly, because of its exceptionally
good behavior. . . . [I]f we do this deal, ask how we will
avoid offering a similar one to Brazil or Argentina if they
decide on nuclear weapons acquisition, or our treaty ally
South Korea. Dozens of countries around the world have
exhibited good behavior in nuclear matters, and have the
capability to produce nuclear weapons but choose not to,
at least in part, because of the international norm against
nuclear weapons acquisition reinforced by a policy we
would now propose to abandon. . . . If we do this, we will
put at risk a world of very few nuclear weapons states, and
open the door to the true proliferation of nuclear weapons
in the years ahead.[32]

Council on Foreign Relations President Richard Haass, the
former State Department director of policy planning for President Bush, criticized the reliance on regime change: "The uncertainties surrounding regime change make it an unreliable
approach for dealing with specific problems such as a nuclear

weapons program in an unfriendly state. . . . Regime change cannot be counted on to come quickly enough to remove the nuclear threat now posed by [North Korea and Iran]."[33]

For some, the greatest failure of the new approach was its belief that it could indefinitely maintain a global double standard. This, they felt, tainted American credibility. Representative John Spratt (D-SC), a leader on defense issues in the Congress, said, "My greatest concern is that some in the administration and in Congress seem to think that the United States can move the world in one direction while Washington moves in another; that we can continue to prevail on other countries not to develop nuclear weapons while we develop new tactical applications for such weapons and possibly resume nuclear testing."[34]

Similarly, former assistant secretary John Wolf, after leaving the State Department, said that he while he supported many administration policies, he was worried by the current U.S. approach to nonproliferation. "The [Non-Proliferation] treaty fails if it differentiates or if members try to differentiate between good states who can be trusted with nuclear weapons and all others. We have never been further from the treaty's goals and we are moving in the wrong direction. . . . It's been fashionable recently to talk a lot about counter-proliferation, but that's really a defensive concept. Nonproliferation done right is bigger. . . . In the end, I think you get a better result."[35] Wolf shared Spratt's concerns about programs for new nuclear weapons and new nuclear missions: "One set of concerns relates to the Department of Energy's program to research a new penetrator warhead," he said. "Far more worrisome though is the proposed change in weapons doctrine that envisions using nuclear weapons for WMD pre-emption." Pointing to the risks of preemptive attack illustrated by the Iraq War, he noted that many officials believed Iraq had chemical and biological weapons, "Suppose instead some had argued to use nuclear weapons pre-emptively, and suppose we had. What would have been the implications of doing so and being wrong? Whoops is not a good enough response."[36]

IAEA Director General Mohamed ElBaradei believes that the American emphasis on nuclear superiority and military force may, in fact, increase insecurity: "In the wake of the

Cold War, many of us were hopeful for a new global security regime, a regime that would be inclusive, effective, and no longer dependent on nuclear weapons. But regrettably, we have made little or no progress." ElBaradei argues that a main objective for international security in the twenty-first century should be to establish a system "that would make the use of force—including the use of nuclear weapons—less likely as a means of conflict resolution."[37]

Conclusion

Some believe that the current strategy, or some modified variation, could still prove its worth. However, a combination of approaches would seem to offer the best chance of success—a comprehensive strategy that combines the best elements of the U.S.-centric, force-based approach with the traditional multilateral, treaty-based approach.

The European Union is moving in this direction and has crafted a joint nonproliferation strategy that includes tying all EU trade agreements to the observance of nonproliferation treaties and norms:

> The EU policy is to pursue the implementation and universalisation of the existing disarmament and nonproliferation norms. . . . If the treaty regime is to remain credible, it must be more effective. The EU will place particular emphasis on a policy of reinforcing compliance with the multilateral treaty regime. . . . We have a wide range of instruments available [to fight proliferation]: multilateral treaties and verification mechanisms, nationally and internationally-coordinated export controls, cooperative threat reduction programmes; political and economic levers (including trade and development policies); interdiction of illegal procurement activities and, as a last resort, coercive measures in accordance with the UN charter. [38]

But this integration is incomplete. The United States must still play the leading role in these efforts, and it may sometimes be necessary to resort to military force outside the United Nations. Such enforcement mechanisms should be in support of the treaty regime, not a replacement for it. The final chapter of this book details how this synthesis could be achieved. But first, the next chapter takes stock of the substantial gains made over the past few decades, giving some confidence that publics and policy makers can build on these successes, fortify the nonproliferation regime by taking the steps necessary to prevent nuclear terrorism, restrain potential new nuclear states, and secure and reduce existing state arsenals.

CHAPTER SEVEN

The Good News
About Proliferation

After wading through the history, theory, dangers, challenges and failures of proliferation policy, most readers could be excused for feeling a bit depressed. Don't be. There is quite a bit of good news about the prospects for reducing the threats from nuclear weapons. Many experts and political officials substantially underestimated the success achieved by previous officials working with the formidable tools provided by the nonproliferation regime. While today's threats are serious, wise policy choices in the past have contained and even eliminated similar threats. Prudent policy choices in the future can do the same. Most importantly, we have a pretty good idea of what those government policies should be.

The policies should follow two guiding principles. First, focus the greatest government resources on the most serious threats: preventing nuclear terrorism, blocking the emergence of new nuclear states, reducing the dangers from existing arsenals, and fortifying the nonproliferation regime. Second, our policies should minimize the proliferation drivers while maximizing the proliferation barriers.

Policies to minimize the drivers would reduce the security factors driving states to acquire nuclear weapons, reduce the prestige associated with these weapons, weaken the domestic nuclear proponents and the salience of the issue in domestic politics, and reduce the scientific appeal of nuclear technology. Policies to maximize the barriers would increase the political cost of violating the global nonproliferation norm, increase the difficulties of getting the requisite nuclear technology, and raise the direct and indirect costs of acquiring nuclear weapons. Nonproliferation policies should have positive incentives that increase the barriers by, for example, increasing the prestige and status of states that have chosen not to build nuclear bombs, providing security guarantees to states eschewing nuclear programs, and committing the leading states to greater efforts in those regions where unresolved conflicts give rise to proliferation imperatives.

Often the biggest obstacle to solving a problem is convincing one's self that a solution is possible. At a time when there is tremendous nuclear pessimism in the world, it is heartening to realize that there is also a great deal of good news. This chapter summarizes some of the positive trends discussed in the book and adds a few more. It then turns to policy in greater detail.

Fewer Nuclear Weapons and Programs

The number of nuclear weapons in the world has been cut in half over the past twenty years, from a Cold War high of 65,000 in 1986 to about 27,000 today. These stockpiles will continue to decline for at least the rest of this decade. There are now far fewer countries that have nuclear weapons or weapon programs than there were in the 1960s, '70s, or '80s. In the 1960s, 23 countries had weapons, were conducting weapons-related research, or were discussing the pursuit of weapons, including Australia, Canada, China, Egypt, India, Japan, Norway, Sweden, Switzerland and West Germany. Today, 8 countries have weapons (China, France, India, Israel, Pakistan, Russia, United Kingdom, and the United States) with North Korea a possible ninth. Iran may be pursuing a weapons program under the guise of peaceful nuclear power, but no other nation is believed to be doing so.

More countries have given up nuclear weapons or weapons programs in the past 15 years than have started them. These were not easy cases:

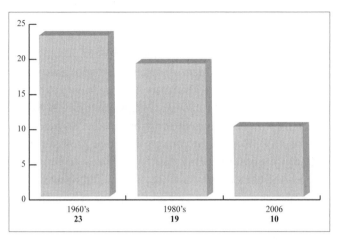

FIGURE 7.1. COUNTRIES WITH NUCLEAR WEAPONS OR PROGRAMS
George Perkovich, Jessica T. Mathews, Joseph Cirincione, Rose Gottemoeller, Jon B. Wolfsthal, *Universal Compliance: A Strategy for Nuclear Security* (Carnegie Endowment for International Peace, March 2005), p. 19.

- Belarus, Kazakhstan, and Ukraine inherited thousands of nuclear weapons after the collapse of the Soviet Union. Within a few years, they were convinced to give them up and join the nuclear Non-Proliferation Treaty (NPT) as non–nuclear weapon states.
- The apartheid government in South Africa, on the eve of transition to majority rule in 1993, announced that it had destroyed its six secret nuclear weapons. Nelson Mandela could have reversed that decision, but he concluded that South Africa's security would be better served in a region where no state had nuclear weapons than in one with a nuclear arms race.
- Similarly, civilian governments in Brazil and Argentina in the 1980s stopped the nuclear weapon research that military juntas had started. Both nations have since joined the NPT.
- We now know with great certainty that United Nations inspection and dismantlement programs ended Iraq's nuclear weapon program in 1991.
- In December 2003, Libya became the most recent nation to abandon a secret program.

The NPT itself is widely considered one of the most successful security pacts in history, with every nation of the world a member except for Israel, India, Pakistan, and North Korea. Most of the 183 member states that do not have nuclear weapons believe what the treaty says: we should eliminate nuclear weapons. Most of the American public agrees. An Associated Press poll in March 2005 showed that 66 percent of Americans believe that no country should be allowed to have nuclear weapons, including the United States. In fact, when asked if the United States and its allies should be allowed to have nuclear weapons and all other nations prevented from doing so, only 13 percent agreed—though that is essentially what U.S. policy is today.

In September 1996, President Bill Clinton signed the Comprehensive Nuclear Test-Ban Treaty, finally concluding the work Presidents Dwight Eisenhower and John Kennedy had begun. Clinton called the treaty "our commitment to end all nuclear tests for all time—the longest-sought, hardest-fought prize in the history of arms control. It will help to prevent the nuclear powers from developing more advanced and more dangerous weapons. It will limit the possibilities for other states to acquire such devices."[1] Even though the U.S. Senate declined to ratify the treaty, since its signing only Pakistan and India had broken the new norm, testing weapons in May 1998. They then pledged to refrain from tests. Over 176 nations have now signed the treaty and 132 have ratified it as of April 2006. For eight years—the longest period in the atomic age—no nuclear weapons had exploded anywhere on, above, or below earth, until North Korea's October 2006 test. Restoring this moratorium will make it more difficult for any other nation to shatter it.

FEWER BALLISTIC MISSILES

There is more good news. The ballistic missile threat that dominated national security debates in the late 1990s was greatly exaggerated. The danger that any nation could strike the United States with this nuclear "bolt-out-of-the-blue" is declining by most measures:

- There are far fewer long-range missiles capable of hitting the United States today than there were ten or twenty years ago. By the beginning of 2006, the total number of such missiles in the world had decreased by 67 percent from the number deployed in 1987.[2]
- There are also far fewer intermediate-range missiles that could threaten our allies. Thanks to Reagan-era arms control treaties, these missiles have been all but eliminated. The United States and Russia no longer deploy them, and with only 12 Chinese missiles of this range left in the world, the global stockpile has declined by a remarkable 98 percent from Cold War levels.
- There are regional threats from the programs that remain, largely in the Middle East, South Asia, and Korea, but even here there is some good news. The number of states with ballistic missile programs has decreased from the number with such programs during the Cold War. By 2005, Argentina, Brazil, Egypt, South Africa, and, most recently, Libya, had all abandoned their efforts.
- Today, the nations that are pursuing long-range ballistic missile development are smaller, poorer, and less technologically advanced than those that had ballistic missile programs fifteen years ago.
- Even with the medium-range missile programs of Iran, Israel, India, North Korea, Pakistan, and Syria, the threat today is a limited one that is confined to a few countries whose political evolution will be the determining factor in whether they emerge as, or remain, threats to global security.[3]

Fewer Biological and Chemical Weapons

In just over three decades biological and chemical weapons moved from essential components of major powers' national defense programs to evil weapons that no civilized nation should possess. Though still a serious terrorist threat, these weapons have been largely eliminated from state arsenals.

In 1969, President Richard Nixon began the unilateral dismantlement of the U.S. biological weapons stockpile, which then had enough viruses, bacteria, and toxins to kill every man, woman, and child and most food crops in the world. Nixon negotiated the Biological Weapons Convention banning these weapons, now signed by 171 nations. While some significant nations remain outside the treaty and some nations may retain biological weapons despite their signature on the pact, we are down to a handful of countries of concern.[4]

In the late 1980s, a U.S. Army program to begin a new generation of chemical weapons prompted one of the most divisive national security debates of that era. The plan was to add to the existing arsenal a new weapon—the so-called Bigeye bomb—that would combine two chemicals in flight to form a deadly nerve agent that would kill on contact. The Army said it was essential to national security; if they did not have a response in kind to the chemical warfare capabilities of the Warsaw Pact, soldiers would die. Votes on whether to produce this weapon split the Congress in half.

In 1991, President George H. W. Bush resolved the debate by declaring that no one should have chemical weapons. He began negotiations for the Chemical Weapons Convention, banning all such weapons. The treaty now has 180 members, and most adhere to its rules. The United States is destroying the 30,000 tons of chemical weapons built during the Cold War, while Russia is destroying its 40,000 tons. A few significant countries, including Israel, Syria, and Egypt, remain outside the treaty and likely still have chemical weapons.[5] But, importantly, no country admits to having these weapons. There is no national pride or international prestige associated with chemical or biological weapons. They are taboo.

A New Attitude

Can the same happen to nuclear weapons? These weapons are embedded more deeply in national arsenals and psyches than chemical or biological weapons ever were, but that does not mean they are a permanent part of national identity. Brown University scholar Nina Tannenwald says:

Today the sense that nuclear weapons are illegitimate is fundamental to the future of the nonproliferation regime. A prohibition regime cannot be sustained over the long haul by sheer force or coercion or physical denial. It requires an internalized belief among its participants that the prohibited item is illegitimate and abhorrent and that the prohibitions must apply to all.[6]

We may be seeing the beginning of just such a trend. Many political and military leaders recognize the limited military utility of weapons whose use would kill thousands of innocent civilians. "I think the time is now for a thoughtful and open debate on the role of nuclear weapons in our country's national security strategy," Congressman David Hobson (R-OH) said in February 2005. "It's been 15 years since the end of the cold war, and in my opinion, the Department of Energy's weapon-complex decision making is still being driven by the nuclear weapons structure put in place over the past 50 years."[7] Hobson's point is supported by the research of Federation of American Scientists' expert Ivan Oelrich. "If we search for missions for nuclear weapons, we can always find them," he says, "but if we search for weapons to fulfill military missions then we will only rarely light upon nuclear weapons as the best solution."[8] Of the fifteen missions currently proposed for U.S. nuclear weapons by the administration's 2002 Nuclear Posture Review (the document that provides overall guidance and direction for the nuclear forces and doctrine), Oelrich concluded that only one mission requires keeping U.S. strategic nuclear forces near their present levels: "The U.S. arsenal today looks much as it would if a disarming first strike against Russia were still its dominant mission."[9] (The Nuclear Posture Review is discussed in more detail below.)

Hobson, a solid Midwest conservative, chaired the subcommittee of the House Appropriations Committee that funds nuclear weapon programs. He led the effort to block funding for the administration's proposed "nuclear bunker buster," a new nuclear weapon designed to go after conventional targets such as underground shelters. He convinced the House and Senate to eliminate the funding to research this new weapon in 2004 and 2005, essentially ending the program.

General Eugene Habiger told an international conference in November 2005 that the United States and Russia could quickly reduce their enormous arsenals to 600 total warheads each.[10] Habiger was commander in chief of the U.S. Strategic Command in the 1990s—a man who had his finger on the buttons that could have launched thousands of warheads. Former secretary of defense Robert McNamara, sitting next to Habiger on the same panel, went further. He called the current U.S. and NATO nuclear policies "insane." He said they were "illegal, immoral, militarily unnecessary, and destructive of the nonproliferation regime—it's time to change them." McNamara advocates greatly reducing the arsenals and then working to eliminate the weapons completely, just as countries have done with chemical and biological weapons.[11]

Several expert studies recommend quickly reducing the U.S. force down to a total of 1,000 warheads, with 500–600 deployed and the remainder held in reserve.[12] There is, in fact, broad agreement across the political spectrum that U.S. nuclear forces could be reduced from thousands to hundreds without harming national security. Former National Security Council and Defense Department official Franklin Miller (who played a key role in U.S. nuclear policy for the past two decades) said in November 2005, "It's my personal belief that the levels of U.S. strategic weapons can and should decline further than those allowed in the Treaty of Moscow. I would hope that the administration takes steps in the next year or so to produce that."[13] Former Reagan and Bush administration official Richard Perle said, "I see no reason why we can't go well below 1,000. I want the lowest number possible, under the tightest control possible. . . . The truth is we are never going to use them. The Russians aren't going to use theirs either."[14]

THE FUTURE OF PROLIFERATION POLICY

The bureaucratic and political obstacles to implementing these changes are formidable; not just globally but nationally. They will require not just a change on the part of other nations, but changes in U.S. policy as well. A change in U.S. policy, in fact, may be the prerequisite to implementing a global transformation. At the risk of sounding like a self-help book, we cannot change the world until we change ourselves. For it is in the United States that the prestige, security, and domestic drivers for nuclear weapons remain the strongest and the barriers the weakest.

In the United States, perhaps more than in any other country, the atom is tied directly to the national ego. For many political leaders, it is inconceivable that the United States would give up the weapon we invented. With a heightened sense of security threats, diminishing any military program smacks some as unilateral disarmament—even though nuclear weapons have nothing to do with preventing terrorism and no proposal requires the United States to reduce alone.

National intelligence estimates no longer seem to examine the connection between U.S. policy and other nations' proliferation. If one were to do so, analysts would almost certainly find the same relationship today that intelligence agencies found in the 1950s and 1960s. As the 1961 NIE concluded, while most countries still have powerful international and domestic reasons for not pursuing nuclear weapons, "growing pessimism as to the likelihood of any realistic disarmament agreement could in some cases . . . tend to undermine opposition to the acquisition of a national nuclear capability."[15] In the twenty-first century, the findings of the 1961 study still apply: "many of these countries will probably continue to improve their overall capabilities in the nuclear field and develop their present peaceful programs with one eye cocked to the future possibility that they may eventually decide to develop an operational nuclear capability independently."[16]

With the end of the Cold War, many officials and experts thought the two superpowers would and could rapidly dismantle their now-obsolete nuclear war-fighting capabilities. However, even though many senior officials in the Clinton administration shared Habiger's perspective, there was little change in the U.S. nuclear posture. Georgetown University professor Janne Nolan said that during the 1994 Nuclear Posture Review,

There was no high-level, sustained commitment given to considering, let alone implementing, fundamental change.

It started out as a very ambitious effort to scrub all of the assumptions of both declaratory and operational doctrine, to examine whether we needed a triad [nuclear weapons on bombers, missiles, and submarines], why we needed to continue to rely on prompt counterforce, and so on. For many reasons, the review ended up as a pallid, little document that was not briefed around for very long and that essentially ratified the status quo.[17]

Officials meant well, but they were not prepared for the resistance they encountered. They floated serious reform proposals, says Nolan. "In the end, however, the NPR collapsed from bureaucratic inertia and the absence of presidential leadership."[18]

In this century—just as in the last—the issue is still a political football that some use to buttress their own security credentials or to attack others as "weak on defense." Democrats are particularly vulnerable to such attacks and often, as during the Clinton administration, try to adopt policies that will shield them from political damage.[19] This dynamic is unlikely to change. Frances FitzGerald, in her penetrating study of the Reagan presidency and the Star Wars program, *Way Out There in the Blue*, notes, "For those who made their careers as defense experts it was never totally safe to be on the left of a strategic debate, and in a time when the country was in a conservative mood, it was downright dangerous."[20]

During the Bush administration, a heightened sense of national insecurity and the rise into key policy positions of experts with decidedly hawkish views on nuclear weapons produced a Nuclear Posture Review in 2002 that closely mirrored recommendations produced by neoconservative think tanks before the election. In summary, the highly controversial new posture, still in effect today,

- validated the reductions agreed upon by the United States and Russia in 1997;
- advocated development of a new generation of strategic nuclear weapons for the next fifty years;
- advocated new designs for new types of nuclear weapons;

- advocated new uses for nuclear weapons against non-nuclear threats;
- funded programs to shorten the time required to begin testing new nuclear weapon designs; and
- increased significantly the funding for and capacity of nuclear weapons production facilities.[21]

The review reversed the general deemphasis on nuclear weapon of the previous decade and reasserted the necessity and desirability of nuclear weapons for a broad range of existing and possibly new missions. The review explicitly discussed planning for using weapons on China, North Korea, Syria, Iraq, Iran, Libya, and other countries.[22]

Positions endorsed by this review have since been adopted by other states, including Russia, which reasserted its policy of using nuclear weapons against non-nuclear threats, and France, whose president, Jacques Chirac, said in January 2006 said his country would use its nuclear weapons to counter any state that might resort "to terrorist means."[23] The United Kingdom, with the smallest arsenal of the five nuclear weapon states recognized by the NPT, is beginning a debate on the future of its submarine-based force. It will cost over a hundred billion dollars to replace the current fleet. Officials seem to be influenced by U.S. views and favor preserving the prestige and security the weapons seem to offer. It is possible, however, that budgetary realities and disarmament sentiment could tip the debate the other way and the country could be the first of the five to give up its arsenal, setting a model for the rest of the world.

FORGING A COMPROMISE

With the United States politically divided, with the Western alliance split between the U.S. neoconservativism and European liberal internationalism, and with international institutions either weakened by these divisions or, like the European Union, still too new to assert their authority, it is unlikely that any single approach to international relations will determine policy in this decade. More realistically, officials can strive for a combination of approaches that would balance enforcement of nonproliferation commitments with implementation of disarmament commitments.

In 2005, the Carnegie Endowment published *Universal Compliance: A Strategy for Nuclear Security*, an ambitious report detailing the theory and practical applications of such a comprehensive approach.[24] The experts (including this author) argued, "The new strategic aim of nonproliferation policy should be to achieve *universal compliance* with the norms and rules of a *toughened* nuclear nonproliferation regime."[25] After a two-year process incorporating the best ideas from experts and officials from over twenty nations, the authors presented over 100 recommendations to undermine the drivers and strengthen the barriers to proliferation.

Like the scientists and officials of the 1940s, they understood the magnitude of this task. Carnegie Endowment President Jessica T. Mathews, in presenting the report she coauthored, said:

> What we're urging here is not easily done; we know that. It is not incremental change and it will not come for a low political cost. It is very simply a strategy that recognizes that nuclear proliferation is the greatest security threat the world faces, and which asks and expects the United States government and other governments, nuclear and non-nuclear, to act as though that were indeed true. President Bush has said that we must, in his words, do everything we can to control the spread of nuclear weapons. This is an everything-we-can-do strategy.[26]

The report analyzed how to end the threat of nuclear terrorism by implementing comprehensive efforts to secure and eliminate nuclear materials worldwide and to stop the illegal transfer of nuclear technology. The strategy would prevent new nuclear weapon states by increasing penalties for withdrawal from the NPT, enforcing compliance with strengthened treaties, and radically reforming the nuclear fuel cycle to prevent states from acquiring dual-use technologies for uranium enrichment or plutonium reprocessing. The threat from existing arsenals would be reduced by shrinking global stockpiles, curtailing research on new nuclear weapons, and taking weapons off hair-trigger alert status. Finally, greater efforts would be devoted to resolving the regional conflicts that fuel proliferation and to bringing the three nuclear weapon states outside the NPT (India, Pakistan, and Israel) into conformance with an expanded set of global nonproliferation norms.

The key to implementing these and other innovations will be convincing each side in the current proliferation policy divide to accept parts of the other's approach. Those who believe that international security is best achieved through multilateral institutions must accept that they have to spend as much time enforcing treaties as they do collecting signatures on them. Those who believe that maintaining absolute U.S. superiority is the only reliable defense strategy must recognize that international institutions and laws are essential to U.S. legitimacy and security. As *Weekly Standard* contributing editor Robert Kagan says, "The United States can neither appear to be acting only in its self-interest, nor can it, in fact, act as if its own national interest were all that mattered."[27] British Prime Minister Tony Blair put it more directly: "If America wants the rest of the world to be part of the agenda it has set, it must be part of their agenda, too."[28]

Some elements of this compromise approach began creeping into U.S. policy in 2005, as Secretary of State Condoleezza Rice slowly but steadily changed the strategy toward North Korea to take into consideration the positions of South Korea, China, and Russia and began actual negotiations with the North Koreans within the structure of the six-party talks. This was a quiet, but dramatic reversal. As the *New York Times* somewhat caustically editorialized, "[F]or four years, the Bush administration put more creative energy into name-calling than into serious talks. The main result was that the North moved four years further along toward being able to threaten its neighbors with nuclear weapons."[29] In mid-2005, U.S. rhetoric toward North Korea softened, the U.S. initiated several bilateral meetings, and U.S. officials were allowed to depart from prepared texts and engage in a genuine give-and-take with their Korean counterparts.

The new approach resulted in a September 2005 breakthrough when the government of North Korea formally committed to give up all nuclear weapons and existing nuclear programs and to return to the Non-Proliferation Treaty in exchange for a nonaggression pledge from the United States and economic and energy aid. The chief U.S. negotiator at the talks, Assistant Secretary of State Christopher Hill, praised the agreement as a "win-win situation." (Indeed, all successful negotiations have to be so. The parties must be able to leave the table declaring victory and return to their countries and peoples with tangible achievements.) The declaration was only a partial victory, however, and tough negotiations remained, including assuring that North Korea, after breaking previous pledges, would honor this one, and negotiating the verification and sequencing of the dismantlement of the North Korean facilities and provision of aid. It was possible that hard-liners in both capitals could kill the deal with a reversion to the posturing of the previous four years. By February 2006, this appeared to be exactly what transpired, when new demands from Washington piled resolution of North Korea's counterfeiting operations on top of an already overloaded negotiating cart. The results were apparently what these officials sought—the talks collapsed. By October 2006, the talks were still in limbo when North Korea exploded its nuclear test.

The failure of a U.S. policy with both North Korea and Iran underscores the need for a new, synthesized approach to resolve the three most difficult problems confronting us today: the risk of nuclear terrorism, the thin line separating the production of civilian nuclear power and the production of nuclear weapons, and the emergence of new nuclear states. The final chapter details what such a strategy would look like.

CHAPTER EIGHT

Nuclear Solutions

As we have seen in the previous chapter, nuclear force levels in the world are likely to decline steadily over the next decade and these reductions may well accelerate. As these numbers go down, it is likely that senior officials will be more willing to take weapons off hair-trigger alert, thus reducing the chance of accidental or unauthorized launch. The general movement of policy seems to be in that direction. There are three problems, however, that are more difficult to resolve. They require forging a consensus of expert opinion, focusing the attention of senior officials, securing the necessary funding, and, above all, securing presidential leadership. None of these problems can be solved from the bottom up. The president of the United States and leaders of the other nuclear weapon states and other key countries must be committed to working together on these core issues. If they are so committed, then the lessons learned from the sixty-year history of nuclear weapons and theories developed from that history provide us with a robust set of policy options for solving the three most difficult nuclear threats: terrorism, technology, and new weapon states.

Solving Problem Number One: Preventing Nuclear Terrorism

It is common sense that national security policy should be oriented toward the main danger to the United States and other nations. Today, that does not come from a nation intentionally attacking with nuclear weapons. Even a nuclear-armed North Korea or Iran would know that the use of any weapon would be regime suicide. The most urgent threat is a terrorist attack, and the number one goal should be to ensure that any such attack is non-nuclear.

Given the difficulties of a terrorist acquiring or making a nuclear bomb, the actual risk of such an attack is still low.[1] But it is not zero, and the consequences would be enormous. Hurricane Katrina provided some idea of what it would mean to have a U.S. city disappear from the national grid. Many, in fact, compared the storm to Hiroshima. But Hiroshima was much worse. The bomb, small by today's standards, killed 140,000 people and destroyed or damaged 70,000 of the 76,000 buildings in the city.

As with the known risk to New Orleans, the government response to the nuclear threat has been inadequate. Former Senator Sam Nunn says, "American citizens have every reason to ask, 'Are we doing all we can to prevent a nuclear attack?' The answer is 'No, we are not.'"[2] Congressman David Hobson agrees: "If we really believe a nuclear 9/11 is the most serious thing facing us, then we haven't even begun to scratch the surface."[3] The danger was obvious to many even at the very beginning of the nuclear age. Historians Kai Bird and Martin Sherwin write, "Asked in a closed Senate hearing room 'whether three or four men couldn't smuggle units of an [atomic] bomb into New York and blow up the whole city,' [Manhattan Project Director J. Robert] Oppenheimer responded, 'Of course it could be done, and people could destroy New York.'"[4]

It is now possible to shore up the nuclear security dams and levees that can prevent this ultimate disaster. A broad expert consensus already exists on the core elements of such a plan: secure all weapon-usable materials (highly enriched uranium and plutonium) against theft or diversion; end the production of these materials; end the use of these materials in civilian research, power reactors, and naval reactors; and eliminate the large surplus stockpiles of these materials held by the United States, Russia, and other nations.[5]

This is why most experts agree with Sam Nunn:

The most effective, least expensive way to prevent nuclear terrorism is to secure nuclear weapons and materials at the source. Acquiring weapons and materials is the hardest step for the terrorists to take, and the easiest step for us to stop. By contrast, every subsequent step in the process is easier for the terrorists to take, and harder for us to stop. . . . That is why homeland security and the defense against catastrophic terrorism must begin with securing weapons and fissile materials in every country and every facility that has them.[6]

Theft of Russian nuclear material is not just a theoretical threat. As Matthew Bunn and Anthony Wier write, ". . . broken alarms still do not get fixed, security forces often go without adequate body armor and communications equipment, and more."[7] As of the end of 2004, only some 26 percent of nuclear material outside of weapons had been protected with "comprehensive" security upgrades.[8]

Many of the programs to secure these materials are now in place. Lacking is the high-level political commitment and adequate funding to fully implement them. That is, though these are tough problems and there are often national bureaucratic obstacles to overcome, these programs work. As numerous independent studies have found, they need presidential leadership to energize them.

For example, since 1991, Congress has funded significant technical and financial assistance to Russia under the Nunn-Lugar programs to help Moscow secure stored nuclear warheads, to guard warheads in transport, and to improve tracking and accounting procedures. Two of these are a joint program between Russia and the United States to dispose of 34 tons of plutonium (enough for more than 6,000 nuclear bombs) and a program to convert highly enriched uranium to low-enriched uranium for sale to an American nuclear energy corporation. This latter program, dubbed "Megatons to Megawatts," now powers one out of ten lightbulbs in the United States. The U.S. has bought 500 tons of highly enriched uranium from Russia, extracted from disassembled warheads. Half of the this amount has been mixed with natural uranium in Russia, and shipped to the United States, where it is converted into fuel rods that account for half the nuclear power produced in this country, or 10 percent of the total electricity generated every year. It works, it is free to the American taxpayer, and it could quickly be accelerated. The program could fairly easily quickly convert and ship the remaining tons of weapons-grade uranium and buy up an additional 500 tons from Russian warheads, rather than continue at its current pace.

There are also programs under way to eliminate or secure all the dangerous nuclear material outside of Russia. The program could achieve a global cleanout of these vulnerable sites in dozens of nations in the next four years, instead of the ten years currently planned, if the president so desired. Most of the work is fairly straight forward, but often it requires maneuvers worthy of *Mission: Impossible*. Here are three examples:

- November 1994: 581 kilograms of weapon-usable uranium were secreted out of Kazakhstan to the United States in a top-secret operation codenamed "Project Sapphire." Racing against the impending winter blizzards and possible attempts by terrorists or Iranians to obtain this highly valuable material, U.S. and Kazakh technicians repackaged the HEU into 1,300 steel containers.[9] All materials were then loaded onto two Air Force C-5 transport planes and whisked away to Oak Ridge National Laboratory in Tennessee.[10] This massive undertaking was the first operation of its kind under the Nunn-Lugar program and was only possible because Khazakh President Nursultan Nazarbayev trusted the United States enough to call for help in removing the fissile materials, having built up this level of trust through a host of cooperative projects.[11]

- August 2002: Two bombs worth (48 kilograms) of weapon-grade uranium were repatriated from a research reactor at the Vinca Institute in Serbia to a Russian processing plant. The secret nighttime operation was funded jointly by the United States and the Nuclear Threat Initiative (NTI), a private organization started by Sam Nunn and CNN founder Ted Turner. While the United States funded the actual material transport, NTI provided $5 million for environmental cleanup, without which Serbia refused the transfer.[12] The cooperation between government and private organizations holds promise for future progress. Project Vinca could become a prototype for future cooperative efforts.

• September 2005: After midnight, a heavily armed special police force led a cargo truck from the Czech Technical University in Prague to a waiting Russian cargo plane. The truck carried 14 kilograms of weapons-grade uranium.[13] The Prague airlift was the eighth successful repatriation of fissile material to Russia from low-security civilian facilities under the recently created U.S. Global Threat Reduction Initiative (GTRI). Its mission is to specifically "identify, secure, recover and/or facilitate the disposition of high-risk, vulnerable nuclear and radiological materials around the world that pose a threat to the United States and the international community."[14] Approximately 122 kilograms of HEU, enough to make about five bombs, have been safely transferred from Serbia, Romania, Bulgaria, Libya, Uzbekistan, the Czech Republic, and Latvia.[15] GTRI continues its work towards complete repatriation of Russian- and U.S.-origin fissile material and is also working to upgrade security at targeted facilities and support conversion of research test reactors from running on highly enriched uranium to low-enriched uranium.[16]

With increased funding and presidential commitment, all these efforts could be accelerated to secure or eliminate the vast majority of nuclear weapons and materials by 2010.[17] The final report of the 9/11 Public Discourse Project (an extension of the 9/11 Commission) gave the U.S. government failing grades in this area. Commission Chairman Thomas Kean questioned why more high-level attention hadn't been given to preventing nuclear terrorism: "Why isn't the President talking about securing nuclear materials? . . . The President should make this goal his top national security priority."[18] This would make it nearly impossible for a terrorist group to threaten any nation with the "ultimate catastrophe."[19] As former Assistant Secretary of Defense Ashton Carter puts it, "We *can* envision the eradication of nuclear terrorism."[20]

Solving Problem Number Two: Preventing Nuclear Fuel Rods from Becoming Nuclear Bombs

The core problem with the spread of nuclear technology is not nuclear reactors; it is what goes into and comes out of the reactors. The same facilities that enrich uranium to low levels for fuel can be used to enrich uranium to high levels for bombs. The same facilities that reprocess spent reactor fuel rods for disposal can be used to extract plutonium for weapons.

Over forty countries have nuclear reactors. Very few of them make their own fuel. They purchase it from one of the six countries that make the fuel or from the one existing international consortium, the Uranium Enrichment Company (URENCO). China, France, Japan, Pakistan, Russia, and United States are the only countries that currently enrich uranium in significant quantities. Germany, the Netherlands and the United Kingdom together produce fuel in facilities owned jointly by URENCO.

Today, the fuel problem is growing more serious as several new nations seek fuel production capabilities and as the technological barriers to acquiring them shrink. Iran is the most urgent example of this larger problem. The Iranian government insists that Iran needs to develop nuclear power and indigenous fuel cycle capabilities. Many countries are understandably suspicious that the program is a cover for obtaining the technologies needed to make nuclear weapons. As several experts point out, it does not make economic sense for any nation to build its own indigenous enrichment and reprocessing facilities if its national nuclear power output is less than 25,000 megawatts.[21] Iran, however, insists that it must forge ahead with enrichment plants even though it has yet to put its first 1,000-megawatt reactor into operation.

In addition to Iran, Brazil plans to open an enrichment facility in this decade and other countries, such as South Korea and Ukraine have indicated interest in developing their own facilities. Japan's new reprocessing plant at its $20 billion Rokkasho-mura facility will add to the mountains of plutonium it has already reprocessed in European plants.

From the very beginning of the nuclear age, scientists and policy makers tried to control the production of fuel. Scientists believed in 1945 that the rationing of uranium ores could be the simplest way to control nuclear technology (see chapter 1). Under an international agreement, uranium would be accounted for, and there would be a check on the conversion of natural uranium into fissile material, they argued. Thus, the plan Bernard Baruch presented in 1946 sought to establish an International Atomic Development Authority that would own and control all "dangerous" elements of the nuclear fuel cycle, including all uranium mining, processing, conversion, and enrichment facilities.

President Dwight D. Eisenhower picked up parts of these ideas in his Atoms for Peace Program in 1953. In the decades that followed, there were several major efforts that either studied or recommended the creation of multinational fuel supply centers. These included the International Nuclear Fuel Cycle Evaluation, the United Nations Conference for the Promotion of International Co-operation in the Peaceful Uses of Nuclear Energy, and the Committee on Assurances of Supply.

There is again today broad agreement that a comprehensive nonproliferation solution must include the reform of the ownership and control of the means of producing fuel for nuclear reactors. Proposals for doing so have been advanced by President George Bush, IAEA Director-General Mohamed ElBaradei, Russian President Vladimir Putin, and by leading nongovernmental experts.

All these proposals seek to end the further production of materials for use in nuclear weapons and stop—at least temporarily—construction of new facilities for enriching uranium or separating plutonium. Some propose that all such enrichment or separation take place only in facilities owned and operated by multinational entities, others seek tougher export controls to prevent the development of new fuel factories, others propose new contractual and commercial means of control. But all recognize that preventing new nations such as Iran or Brazil from entering the uranium enrichment business will require more than a country-specific approach.

On February 11, 2004, President Bush said:

> The world must create a safe, orderly system to field civilian nuclear plants without adding to the danger of weapons proliferation. The world's leading nuclear exporters should ensure that states have reliable access at reasonable cost to fuel for civilian reactors, so long as those states renounce enrichment and reprocessing. Enrichment and reprocessing are not necessary for nations seeking to harness nuclear energy for peaceful purposes.[22]

Little progress has been made in furthering President Bush's proposed reform, in part due to a lack of U.S. follow-up, and in part to wide resistance to the needed changes. There are concerns among developing nations that a supplier cartel would unduly restrict their access to nuclear technology and a broader reluctance among non–nuclear weapon states to accept more stringent nonproliferation obligations when nuclear weapon states are seen as failing in their commitments to disarmament.

For example, while the Bush proposal would stop nuclear production capabilities from being built in new states, his plan would not stop the continued production of weapon-usable materials by states that already have such plants. This seems to perpetuate an unfair two-tier system. In addition to the existing divide of states that have nuclear weapons and states that do not, it seems to add a new distinction between states allowed to have fuel facilities and states that are not. Iranian officials have seized on this apparent discrimination with some success. They insist that they—and all states—have a right to this technology.

ElBaradei agrees with Bush's assessment of the problem. "The wide dissemination of the most proliferation-sensitive parts of the nuclear fuel cycle . . . could be the 'Achilles' heel' of the nuclear non-proliferation regime," he warned in March 2004. He disagrees with Bush, however, in how the problem could be solved: "It is important to tighten control over these operations, which could be done by bringing them under some form of multilateral control, in a limited number of regional centers."

ElBaradei offered a three part solution:

> First, it is time to limit the processing of weapon-usable material (separated plutonium and high-enriched uranium) in civilian nuclear programmes, as well as the production of new material through reprocessing and enrichment, by agreeing to restrict these operations exclusively to facilities under multinational control. . . .
>
> Second, nuclear-energy systems should be deployed that, by design, avoid the use of materials that may be applied directly to making nuclear weapons. . . . This is not a futuristic dream; much of the technology for proliferation-resistant nuclear-energy systems has already been developed or is actively being researched. . . .
>
> Third, we should consider multinational approaches to the management and disposal of spent fuel and radioactive waste.[23]

An expert panel on the nuclear fuel cycle reported back to the IAEA director-general in 2005, identifying possible multilateral approaches to fuel cycle reform and analyzing the benefits and difficulties of each arrangement.[24] ElBaradei is committed to advancing this agenda but has yet to attract the support needed to implement any of these suggestions.

A first step to building the needed consensus could be a new international arrangement that would guarantee fuel cycle services (supply and disposal of fuel) to states that do not possess domestic capabilities. Such a mechanism would have to provide a credible international guarantee of fresh reactor fuel and removal of spent fuel at prices that offer an economic incentive to the recipient state. Such an arrangement would reduce, if not eliminate, the economic or energy security justification for states to pursue their own fuel cycle facilities, and in so doing would test states' commitment to a non-weapons path. States that turn down reliable and economically attractive alternatives to costly new production facilities would engender suspicion of their intentions, inviting sanctions and other international pressures. The EU proposed such an arrangement as part of the solution to the Iranian crisis. This could serve as the prototype for a new global deal.

In January 2005, Russian President Vladmir Putin proposed the creation of a global infrastructure "to offer nuclear fuel cycle services, including [uranium] enrichment under the control of the IAEA" to all countries, provided that they observe the nonproliferation regime.[25] "Its backbone element will include a network of centres providing services in nuclear fuel cycle, including uranium enrichment, and they will be controlled by the International Atomic Energy Agency and will operate on the basis of nondiscriminatory access," Putin said.[26]

Promising non–nuclear weapon states access to nuclear technology was critical to forging the grand bargain that allowed the Non-Proliferation Treaty to enter into force. Today, any efforts to restrict or deny access to that technology (especially when many in the West are calling nuclear power essential to solving the world's energy shortages and reducing the greenhouse effect from carbon emissions) are resisted by states unwilling to cede any ground on their access to nuclear technology, particularly when they believe that other existing nonproliferation obligations, including those associated with disarmament, are going unimplemented. Meanwhile, states with nuclear fuel capabilities are reluctant to place them under international control.

An innovative possibility for bridging the gap was advanced by John Deutch, Arnold Kanter, Ernest Moniz, and Daniel Poneman in a 2005 *Survival* article. They have proposed perhaps the most developed commercial idea, what they call an "Assured Nuclear Fuel Services Initiative":

> Countries that do not currently possess uranium enrichment or plutonium-reprocessing facilities would agree not to obtain any such facilities or related technologies and materials for an extended period of time. By the same logic, countries that do possess such facilities would agree not to provide them, or related equipment or technology, to countries that do not. In exchange, during this period they would receive, on attractive terms, guaranteed cradle-to-grave fuel services—specifically, fresh nuclear fuel supply and spent fuel removal—under an agreement signed by all those governments in a position to provide such services. The IAEA would apply safeguards to any

fuel-cycle activities covered by the agreement in addition to its traditional safeguard duties on the reactors in the user states. Fuel-service transactions themselves, however, would be between commercial entities negotiating commercial contracts.[27]

The authors believe their proposal could work because it is based on economic incentives, not strictly political ones. They appeal to the nuclear power industry to realize that failure to reform the fuel cycle will lead inevitably to a country making the leap from civilian nuclear power to military nuclear weapons—with devastating consequences for the industry:

> The Assured Nuclear Fuel Services Initiative offers something for everyone. Nuclear supplier states would obtain revenues and increased confidence in avoiding a proliferation incident in a third country whose actions could put the large and potentially growing fleet of nuclear power stations in operation around the world at risk (a "proliferation Chernobyl"). User states would obtain cost-effective, guaranteed access to nuclear fuel and guaranteed relief from the burden of dealing with nuclear waste management. And the world would gain an added measure of safety from the risk of weapons proliferation that the spread of inherently dangerous fuel-cycle facilities would bring.[28]

Only high-level attention to this difficult issue can forge the international agreement necessary to pick among these various options. The United States should be the natural leader of this effort, but this will require a departure from current priorities. It will mean placing reform of the fuel cycle as a top national security priority, joining with the urgent task of securing weapon-usable fissile materials.

SOLVING PROBLEM NUMBER 3: PREVENTING NEW STATES

Most of the news, debate and discussion of nonproliferation problems have focused in recent years on the two or three states suspected of developing new weapon programs. In part, this is because the overthrow of these governments, particularly in the Middle East, has overlapped with other political and security agendas. The war in Iraq was only partially about eliminating Saddam Hussein's weapons capability, though that was the major justification for the war. As former Deputy Secretary of Defense Paul Wolfowitz famously admitted, "For bureaucratic reasons we settled on one issue, weapons of mass destruction, because it was the one reason everyone could agree on."[29]

The crises with Iran and North Korea are serious, but proliferation problems cannot be solved one country at a time. As the Carnegie study notes:

> Attempting to stem nuclear proliferation crisis by crisis—from Iraq, to North Korea, to Iran, et cetera—ultimately invites defeat. As each deal is cut, it sets a new expectation for the next proliferator. Regime change by force in country after country is neither right nor realistic. The United States would bankrupt and isolate itself, all the while convincing additional countries that nuclear weapons would be their only protection. A more systematic approach that prevents states within the NPT from acquiring the nuclear infrastructure needed to produce nuclear weapons is the only real sustainable option.[30]

While the specifics and politics vary from country to country, a comprehensive, multidimensional approach is needed for all the threats we face from new nations acquiring weapons. Iran, by far the most difficult of the cases, can serve as a model of how such an approach could work.

Think for a moment about what it will take to convince the current or future Iranian government to abandon plans to build between six and twenty nuclear power reactors and all the facilities needed to make and reprocess the fuel for these reactors. Plans to do so predate the Islamic Republic. The United States, in fact, provided Iran with its first research reactor in the late 1960s (it is still operating at the University of Tehran) and encouraged Iran in its nuclear pursuits. In the 1970s this encouragement included agreement by senior officials such as Henry Kissinger, Donald Rumsfeld, Paul Wolfowitz, and Richard Cheney that Iran could develop indigenous facilities for enriching uranium and for reprocessing the spent fuel from nuclear reactors. Then-ruler Shah Reza Pahlavi developed plans to build 22 nuclear power reactors with an electrical output of 23,000 megawatts. Iran's current leaders say they are merely continuing these plans.

Whatever its true intentions, it will not be easy to convince Iran that while it could proceed with construction of power reactors, the country must abandon construction of fuel-manufacturing facilities. It will likely require both the threat of sanctions and the promise of the economic benefits of cooperation.

This is the package of carrots and sticks that made up the negotiations between the European Union and Iran. Calibrating the right balance in this mix is difficult enough, but the package itself is probably not sufficient to seal a deal. In 2005 and early 2006, the hard-line government of President Mahmoud Ahmadinejad further complicated the issue with its harsh rhetorical insistence on proceeding with the nuclear plans and pointed threats to Israel. While the rhetoric may eventually fade, at the core, Iran or any country's reasons for wanting its own fuel cycle capabilities are similar to the reasons some countries want nuclear weapons: security, prestige and domestic political pressures. All of these will have to be addressed in order to craft a permanent solution.

Part of the security equation can be addressed by the prospect of a new relationship with the United States that ends regime change efforts. Iran would need some assurances that agreements on the nuclear program could end efforts by the United States and Israel to remove the current regime. The United States has told North Korea that it has no hostile intentions toward the state and that an end to that country's program would lead to the restoration of diplomatic relations. Similar assurances will be needed for Iran. But there is also a regional dimension. Ending the threat from an Iranian nuclear program will require placing the Iranian decision in the context of the long-standing U.S. goal of a Middle East free of nuclear weapons. It will be impossible for a country as important as Iran to abstain permanently from acquiring the technologies for producing nuclear weapons—at least as a hedge—if other countries in the region have them (the dynamic noted by the 1961 National Intelligence Estimate decades ago). Iran's leaders will want some assurances that there is a process under way that can remove what they see as potential threats from their neighbors, including Israel. For domestic political reasons, they will want to present their nuclear abstinence as part of a movement toward a shared and balanced regional commitment.

Many readers might throw up there hands at this point. "Israel, give up its nuclear weapons? Impossible!" But such nuclear-free zones have been created in other regions which, though not as intensely contested as the Middle East, still had to overcome substantial rivalries and which saw the abandonment of existing programs (in South America) and the dismantlement of actual weapons (in Africa and Central Asia). Little diplomatic effort has been put behind the declared U.S. policy in recent years—certainly nothing on the scale of the effort Republican and Democrats needed to create the nuclear Non-Proliferation Treaty and its support mechanisms in the 1960s and 1970s.

Ridding the region of nuclear weapons will, of course, be difficult, but it is far better than the alternative of a Middle East with not one nuclear power (Israel) but two, three, or four nuclear weapon states—and with unresolved territorial, religious, and political disputes. The latter is a recipe for nuclear war. The key issue is to get the process going, so that states in the region can have some viable alternative to the pessimistic view that the Middle East will never be nuclear free. A distinguished group of twenty nuclear experts representing a cross-section of national and political views recommended in 2005 that part of the solution to a "nuclear-ready Iran" was to encourage Israel to initiate a "Middle East nuclear restraint effort" that would begin by shutting down the Israeli production reactor at Dimona. Israel, the group convened by the Nonproliferation Policy Education Center said, should then show that it was willing to take further steps, including dismantling all its fissile-producing facilities and handing over control of its weapons-usable fissile material to the IAEA, as long as other states in the region did the same.[31]

In order for this plan or any similar plan to succeed, there will have to be a concurrent effort to change fundamentally the way nuclear fuel is produced and reprocessed. Doing so would satisfy a nation's security considerations that it does not have to build its own facilities in order to have a secure supply of fuel for its reactors. Some Iranians see the current negotiations as a new effort by the West to place them, once again, in a dependent relationship. This time the West would not control their oil, they say, but the energy of the future, nuclear fuel. Iran, indeed any nation, will not permanently acquiesce to a discriminatory regime that adds to the existing inequality—allowing some countries to have nuclear weapons while others cannot—by now allowing some countries to make nuclear fuel while others cannot.

As detailed in the previous section, reforming the current system will require overcoming billions of dollars worth of corporate and national investments and core national commitments to the present methods of producing and disposing of nuclear fuel. Thorough reform, however, is the only sure way to prevent more and more nations from acquiring the technology that can bring them—legally—right up to the threshold of nuclear weapons capability.

The key is to begin moving in this direction. A first step could be crafting with Iran a compromise agreement that would allow some processing of uranium to take place inside Iran, for example converting uranium to the gas used in centrifuges, but shipping the gas to Russia for enrichment and fabrication into fuel rods.[32] The Iranian government could declare that it was using Iranian uranium to fuel Iranian reactors, but the world would have kept Iran from constructing the facilities that would bring it close to weapons capability. This interim step could hold for several years as a more permanent fuel supply regime was constructed.

Finally, these discussions must take place in a world where nuclear weapons are being devalued as measures of security, status, and technical achievement. Just as it is fruitless for parents to try to convince their children not to smoke while they are reveling in a two-pack-a-day habit, it will be impossible for other nations to refrain permanently from acquiring nuclear weapons while they remain the currency of great power status. As the Carnegie authors concluded, "The core bargain of the NPT, and of global nonproliferation politics, can neither be ignored nor wished away. It underpins the international security system and shapes the expectations of citizens and leaders around the world."[33]

Breaking the nuclear habit will not be easy, but there are ways to minimize the unease some may feel as they are weaned away from dependence on these weapons. The United States and Russia account for over 95 percent of the world's nuclear weapons. The two nations have such redundant nuclear capability that it would not compromise any vital security interests to quickly reduce down to General Habiger's recommended level of 600 total warheads each. Further reductions and the possibility of complete elimination could then be examined in detailed papers prepared by and for the nuclear weapon states. If accompanied by reaffirmation of the ban on nuclear testing, removal of all weapons from rapid-launch alert status, establishment of a firm norm against the first use of these weapons, and commitments to make the reductions in weapons irreversible and verifiable, the momentum and example generated could fundamentally alter the global dynamic.

Such an effort would hearken back to the early Truman proposals that coupled weapons elimination with strict, verified enforcement of nonproliferation. Dramatic reductions in nuclear forces could be joined, for example, with reforms making it more difficult for countries to withdraw from the NPT (by clarifying that no state may withdraw from the treaty and escape responsibility for prior violations of the treaty or retain access to controlled materials and equipment acquired for "peaceful" purposes).[34] It would make it easier to obtain national commitments to stop the illegal transfer of nuclear technologies and reform the fuel cycle. The reduction in the number of weapons and the production of nuclear materials would also greatly decrease the risk of terrorists acquiring such materials.

CONCLUSION

Ultimately, reducing the risks from nuclear weapons in the twenty-first century cannot be just a military or nuclear energy strategy. At the beginning of the nuclear age, it was already clear that unless we solved the underlying political conflicts that encourage some states to seek security in nuclear arms, we would never prevent nuclear competition. Oppenheimer said, "We must ask, of any proposals for the control of atomic energy, what part they can play in reducing the probability of war. Proposals which in no way advance the general problem of the avoidance of war, are not satisfactory proposals."[35]

Thus, nuclear-weapon-specific efforts should be joined by focused initiatives to resolve conflicts in key regions. A quick look at the map should make clear that nuclear weapons have not spread around the world uniformly. It has not been like a drop of ink diffusing evenly in a glass of water. Vast areas of the world—entire continents—are nuclear-weapon free. There are no nuclear weapons in South America, Africa, Australia, or Southeast Asia. Rather, the states of proliferation concern are in an arc of crisis that flows from the Middle East through South Asia up to Northeast Asia. In other words, the concern is in regions where unresolved territorial, political, and religious disputes give rise to the desire to gain some strategic advantage by acquiring nuclear weapons.

Countries have given up nuclear weapons and programs in the past only when these disputes have been resolved. The pattern of the past should be the template for the future. Avoiding nuclear war in South Asia requires continuing the progress in normalizing relations between India and Pakistan, achieving a permanent resolution of the Kashmir issue, and assuring that China's rise is, indeed, peaceful. Ridding the Middle East of nuclear weapons and new nuclear programs requires normalization of relations between Israel and other regional states and groups based on a just resolution to the Israeli-Palestinian conflict.

Ending all war may be a utopian dream, but we have made more progress in the past two decades than most people realize. Since the end of the Cold War, and in large part because of the end of the surrogate struggles that competition engendered, there has been a steady decline in regional conflicts. The 2005 *Human Security Report*, an independent study funded by five countries and published by Oxford University Press, recorded a 40 percent decline in deadly conflicts from 1992 to 2003.[36] The report noted that there was an 80 percent decline in both the deadliest conflicts—those with 1,000 or more battle deaths—and in the number of genocides and other mass slaughters of civilians. How did this happen? "In the late 1980s, Washington and Moscow stopped fueling 'proxy wars' in the developing world, and the United Nations was liberated to play the global security role its founders intended," Andrew Mack, the director of the project, concluded. "Freed from the paralyzing stasis of Cold War geopolitics, the Security Council initiated an unprecedented, though sometimes inchoate, explosion of international activism designed to stop ongoing wars and prevent new ones."[37]

As this record of success becomes more widely recognized, it may become possible to convince national leaders to devote more effort to resolving the conflicts in Korea, South Asia, and the Middle East. Resolution of some of these may come more quickly than most imagine. Others will take more time, but as history teaches us, it is the direction in which we are moving that informs national attitudes and shapes each state's security decisions. The more arrows we can get pointed in the right direction, the easier it becomes to make progress on all fronts.

Former U.S. State Department official Robert Einhorn and former Defense Department official Kurt Campbell note that the wisdom of societies and states that have gone without nuclear weapons is reinforced by "a world in which the goals of the NPT are being fulfilled—where existing nuclear arsenals are being reduced, parties are not pursuing clandestine nuclear programs, nuclear testing has been stopped, the taboo against the use of nuclear weapons is being strengthened, and in general, the salience of nuclear weapons in international affairs is diminishing."[38]

There is every reason to believe that in the first half of this century the peoples and nations of the world will come to see nuclear weapons as the "historic accident" Mohamed ElBaradei says they are. It may become clearer that nations have no need for the vast destructive force contained in a few kilograms of enriched uranium and plutonium. These weapons still appeal to national pride but they are increasingly unappealing to national budgets and military needs. It took just sixty years to get to this point in the nuclear road. If enough national leaders decide to walk the path together, it should not take another sixty to get to a safer, better world. We may finally be able to correct the one mistake Einstein thought he made.

AFTERWORD

THE SHAPE OF THINGS TO COME

Significant developments in the proliferation of nuclear weapons took place in late 2006 and 2007, after this book was finalized for publication. This afterword, added for the paperback edition, surveys these events, both perilous and promising. Overall, the trends since the publication of the original edition confirm the basic concepts developed in the preceding pages:

- The proliferation of nuclear weapons is not inevitable.
- The spread of nuclear weapons increases the risks of catastrophe rather than providing security or stability.
- The current strategy focused on regime change as the cure for proliferation has failed to solve the core problems and has made many problems worse.
- The best solutions are ones that systematically reduce proliferation drivers and increase proliferation barriers.
- A consensus to adopt such a comprehensive new strategy is developing.

THE PERILS OF PROLIFERATION

As if to highlight the dangers of a strategy that narrows the proliferation problem to one of hostile regimes seeking nuclear weapons, the assassination of former prime minister and opposition leader Benazir Bhutto in December 2007 and the intensification of the political crisis in Pakistan brought into sharp relief the fact that the most immediate nuclear threat facing the United States and other countries comes not from Iraq, Iran, or North Korea, but from unsecured nuclear arsenals in any country, with Pakistan at the top of the list. With an unstable military dictatorship, enough material for 60–120 nuclear bombs, strong Islamic fundamentalist influences in the military and intelligence services, and armed Islamic fundamentalist groups—including Al Qaeda—operating within its territory, Pakistan is arguably the most dangerous country on earth.

Despite the Bush administration's intense focus on Iraq and Iran over the past six years, it is in Pakistan where Osama bin Laden may have his best chance of getting a nuclear weapon. Pakistan could turn overnight from a major, non-NATO ally of the United States into the world's worst nuclear nightmare. Pakistani officials say the weapons and weapon materials are secure, guarded by the most trusted military units. Most experts assume that these claims are correct, but they cannot independently verify the number of nuclear weapons in Pakistan, their locations, or their security. Increased unrest could split the military or distract the troops guarding the weapon materials, providing an opening for a raid by an organized radical group, perhaps with inside help.

Even before the Bhutto assassination, Jihadists had stepped up their attacks on Pakistani military facilities. Ominously, these include several of the military bases housing nuclear-related facilities. On November 1, 2007, a suicide bomber killed eight Air Force personnel and wounded 40 others at Sargodha Air Force Base in the Punjab region, home of Pakistan's Air Force Central Command and the military headquarters for control of their nuclear arsenal.[1] On December 10, 2007, another suicide bomber attacked a bus filled with 35 children of Pakistani Air Force officers at the Kamra Air Force Base in Peshawar province that includes facilities and an ordnance complex likely associated with the storage and maintenance of Pakistani nuclear weapons.[2]

This dangerous situation developed over years and goes beyond the mistakes of the current nonproliferation strategy (discussed below). Past Democratic and Republican administrations have constantly placed proliferation and democracy concerns second to other geopolitical aims.

Officials who regarded Pakistan as an ally needed to rout Soviet troops (and later the Taliban) from Afghanistan, or wanted the country as a balance to India or China, then looked the other way as Pakistani scientist A. Q. Khan developed a network to import technology and materials for Pakistan's nuclear weapons program, even when he began exporting the technology to other countries. The nuclear chickens may be coming home to roost, reminding everyone that nuclear weapons are a danger wherever they exist and terrorists who are intent on acquiring them will go to the most vulnerable sites, regardless of the political orientation of the state.

Chaos in Pakistan also counters the argument that nuclear weapons are a stabilizing force, as discussed in the preface to this book and on pages 100–102. Whatever role nuclear weapons may play in discouraging war between India and Pakistan would be more than offset by terrorists stealing nuclear materials from Pakistan's nuclear laboratories or a radical Islamic fundamentalist regime coming to power and gaining control of Pakistan's entire nuclear arsenal. The latter does not seem likely, but then few predicted the 1979 Iranian revolution. As former Soviet president Michael Gorbachev wrote in January 2007, "It is becoming clearer that nuclear weapons are no longer a means of achieving security; in fact, with every passing year they make our security more precarious."[3]

The year 2007 also dramatically demonstrated the danger of accidental or unauthorized use of weapons in existing state arsenals. On August 29, 2007, the U.S. Air Force lost track of the equivalent of 60 Hiroshima bombs for 36 hours as a B-52 bomber flew across the country with 6 nuclear missiles tucked under its wings. Unknown to the air crews, the missiles were each armed with a 150-kiloton nuclear warhead, ten times the size of the bomb that destroyed Hiroshima.

The Air Force has not flown nuclear weapons on bombers for 40 years and has not even practiced loading these weapons on them for 17 years. The live bombs were put on by accident. Most experts had thought it impossible that anyone could get past the half-dozen security checks designed to prevent the unauthorized use of the most dangerous weapons on earth.

Yet *Washington Post* reporter Joby Warrick disclosed that the loaded bomber "sat on the tarmac overnight without special guards, protected for 15 hours by only the base's exterior chain-link fence and roving security patrols."[4] To its credit, the Air Force disciplined the officers and crews involved. But if the country with the most sophisticated nuclear security system in the world could lose six hydrogen bombs, what could happen in other countries? How secure are the estimated 15,000 weapons in Russia? Or the highly enriched uranium and plutonium—enough for hundreds of thousands of weapons—scattered in hundreds of buildings in over 40 countries?

The United States made significant cuts in its nuclear stockpile in 2007, but through accounting, not actual dismantlement. On December 18, 2007, the administration announced plans to reduce the nuclear stockpile by "nearly 50 percent" by the end of 2007. Officials did this by declaring that 5,150 warheads would no longer be part of the reserve force. They have been tagged for eventual dismantlement, though it is not clear when this will be accomplished. The United States took apart approximately 1,800 warheads a year during the 1990s, but the process has slowed to a crawl with only an estimated 100 warheads disassembled in 2007.

Thus, at the beginning of 2008, the United States maintained an estimated 5,400 nuclear warheads. Of these, 4,075 were operationally deployed—3,575 on strategic delivery vehicles (missiles, submarines, and bombers) and 500 for nonstrategic missions (cruise missiles and bombs)—with about 1,260 additional warheads held in reserve.[5] Several programs to improve the capabilities of the nuclear force continued. The entire Minuteman III missile force is undergoing a multibillion-dollar overhaul focusing on replacing the aging warheads with even more powerful ones. Production of new nuclear weapons also began for the first time in 15 years, with Los Alamos National Laboratory producing replacement cores for the W88 warhead used on the submarine-launched Trident II missiles.[6]

REVERSING PROLIFERATION IN NORTH KOREA

Some of the most hopeful news of the year came from an unlikely source—North Korea. At the beginning of 2008, despite delays and disagreements, U.S. scientists were in North Korea taking apart the reactor that had produced enough plutonium for an estimated 6–12 bombs, most of it during the past five years.

It has been a long and difficult road. The agreement that had frozen North Korea's plutonium production program for eight years and suspended its missile tests for four years unraveled in 2002. This was partially the result of the disclosure that North Korea had likely cheated on the agreement by secretly importing equipment for uranium enrichment but primarily the result of a decision by U.S. officials to use the cheating as justification for killing a deal they never liked. As Vice President Cheney summed up the policy, "We don't negotiate with evil; we defeat it."[7]

As the failures of this approach grew evident (North Korea restarted its reactor and began pumping out plutonium), pragmatists in the administration led by Secretary of State Condoleezza Rice slowly nudged the policy back into negotiations, culminating in a September 2005 agreement in the six-party talks to end the nuclear program in exchange for economic assistance and security assurances. Hard-line officials immediately torpedoed the deal by imposing sanctions on North Korean bank accounts. The North Koreans reacted by walking out of the talks and then in July 2006 tested a long-range missile—that exploded soon after launch—and in October its first nuclear weapon, which fizzled but sent shock waves around the world (see pp. 137–138).

After an extensive struggle among his officials, President Bush shifted to direct negotiations with a despised foe. It worked. By February 2007, the renewed six-party talks had reinstated the September 2005 agreement, supplemented by a step-by-step implementation sequence. U.S. scientists joined teams of international experts in Yongbyon to disable the plutonium production reactor. The year 2008 could see the full disclosure and dismantlement of the nuclear program and the beginning of normalization of U.S.-North Korean relations.

The shift was part of an overall swing in the administration (and in the country as a whole) toward a centrist pragmatism. The *Washington Post* concluded "the fist-shaking that characterized much of the first six years of the Bush administration's North Korea policy has been replaced by a dogged insistence on negotiations and by offers of aid and other concessions—contingent on verified moves to get rid of nuclear facilities."[8] Opponents of the negotiations tried to derail the agreement throughout the year. Former UN ambassador John Bolton called it a "bad deal,"[9] while the editors of the *National Review* asked: "When exactly did Kim Jong Il become trustworthy?"[10] and the editors of the *Wall Street Journal* dubbed it "Faith-based nonproliferation."[11]

In part, the split on the North Korean deal and its implications reflect ideological positions. Liberals see negotiated agreements as the preferable way to resolve even the most intractable disputes. Conservatives, and their more aggressive neoconservative allies, tend to see arms control treaties as a trap, promoting the illusion of security that can only be guaranteed by American military might. Some feared it would also set a precedent for negotiations with Iran, upsetting their plans for military action to topple the regime in Tehran.[12] A closer look at the various elements contributing to this apparent nonproliferation success with North Korea provides a clearer understanding of both the policy reversal and the broader policy trends.

The first element was the situation of North Korea itself. A poor, isolated country that produces little save fear and tyranny, it was in a weak strategic position. The multilateral sanctions and economic incentives clearly played a part in the decision of the Korean leadership to compromise.

Second was the unanimity of the other five nations in the six-party talks. All five wanted to stop a nuclear-armed North Korea from emerging. Their tactics differed, but they were united in their efforts to stop Pyongyang from trying to perfect the flawed nuclear device it tested in October 2006. That unity extended to the unanimous declaration of the Security Council condemning North Korea and imposing sanctions on the regime after its October nuclear test.

The third element contributing to the shift was the more assertive role played by China. The October 9 test surprised and angered China, upsetting its greater strategic plans. China does not want North Korea destabilizing its borders or provoking Japan, and that is just what happened after the test. Japan started a public debate over whether they should get their own nuclear weapons—the last thing China wants. State Counselor Tang Jiaxuan, China's third-highest ranking official, quickly visited Pyongyang to deliver a message asserting China's displeasure directly to North Korean leaders. China cannot dictate North Korea's actions, but the pressure brought a halt to North Korean nuclear tests and an agreement to return to negotiations. China also convinced the United States to come to the table, choreographing talks in Beijing that produced the first of several breakthrough bilateral sessions.

Fourth was the power shift in Congress as a result of the November 2006 elections. The Democratic control of Congress flipped the pressures on the Bush administration, with immediate effect. Shortly after the elections, at a November House International Relations Committee hearing still under Republican rule, members led by Rep. Tom Lantos (D-CA) hammered Undersecretary of State Nicholas Burns over the failed administration policy, cajoling him into engaging in direct talks with North Korea.

Fifth was the change in Defense Department leadership. Donald Rumsfeld, an ardent opponent of direct negotiations with North Korea, resigned as defense secretary, and was replaced by pragmatist Robert Gates, who is more inclined to engage in the direct negotiations previously seen as appeasement. Vice President Dick Cheney alone among the senior ranks remained opposed to dealing with Pyongyang—and he was distracted with the trial of his former aide Scooter Libby, which threatened to implicate him in a scandal that had exposed a covert CIA agent's identity.

Sixth, the political fortunes of the president of the United States had deteriorated. In the end, it was the president's call: deal or no deal. Formerly, President Bush lined up with Cheney, Rumsfeld, and UN Ambassador Bolton, but with these officials gone and badly in need of some success for his beleaguered administration, the president tilted toward pragmatism. North Korea was one of the few possibilities for a foreign policy victory during the remainder of his term.

Finally, the intelligence agencies also retracted a bit of false intelligence that had seemed to justify breaking the agreement with North Korea in 2002. North Korea was not operating a factory to enrich uranium or as intent on acquiring weapons as once claimed. A CIA report to Congress of November 19, 2002, asserted the agency had "recently learned that the North is constructing a plant that could produce enough weapons-grade uranium for two or more nuclear weapons per year when fully operational—which could be as soon as mid-decade."[13] This finding, according to one press report, appears to have been made only after senior officials, including former deputy secretary of defense Paul Wolfowitz, intervened to overrule dissenting views and presented the sketchy evidence as conclusive proof.[14]

On February 27, 2007, Joseph DeTrani, the North Korea coordinator for the director of national intelligence, told the Senate Armed Services Committee that while they still had "high confidence" that some procurement had taken place (parts for an estimated 20 centrifuges), the assessment that North Korea was constructing a plant to pump out dozens of weapons was made at only the "mid-confidence level."[15] In other words, disagreement existed among the agencies. Imported aluminum tubes, U.S. officials now believe, were intended for other purposes (the tubes Iraqis imported before the war, turned out to be for rockets, not centrifuges); and there was no evidence of plant construction, operation, or enrichment.[16]

All these events led to an agreement that overcame the considerable difficulty of dealing with North Korean dictator Kim Jong-Il's "hermit kingdom." Suspicions still run high on both sides, full North Korean compliance is not assured and there are delays, but the overall progress is encouraging. Responding to a personal letter from President Bush in December 2007, North Korean officials confirmed that they would stick to the deal if America did the same. Despite efforts by neoconservatives to derail the agreement by using everything from the September 2007 Israeli attack on Syria to the December election of Lee Myung-bak as South Korea's new president, all signs are that Bush is staying on the negotiations track. With persistence and the steady pressure provided by converging strategic realities in Northeast Asia, this time the deal might hold.

THE DEATH OF THE BUSH DOCTRINE

The success of the North Korea negotiations was part of a broader movement away from the regime change policy of the previous years. At the end of 2007, *Newsweek* summed up the conventional wisdom on U.S. nuclear policy with an arrow pointing down and the tag line "Busy with no-nukes Iraq and Iran, while nuclear Pakistan melts down." Crude but correct, this was magazine-speak for the consensus view of proliferation experts: the policy of preventative war that began with the invasion of Iraq and that some wanted to continue to Syria and Iran had diverted attention and resources to secondary dangers while exacerbating existing nuclear threats. By focusing on and ineffectively dealing with states that someday might develop nuclear weapons, officials had allowed crises to develop that could put nuclear weapons in the hands of terrorists in weeks.

The year 2007 may come to be viewed as the year the Bush Doctrine died. This policy, described in chapter 6, held that the greatest danger to U.S. national security came from the nexus of hostile regimes, terrorists, and nuclear technology. It posited that regime change was the answer to proliferation and that the military should be the leading tool of statecraft. Few believe that to be true today, given the experiences of the wars in Iraq and Afghanistan, the failures of intelligence in Iraq, Iran, and North Korea, and the turmoil in Pakistan.

The decisive end to this doctrine may have come not in the streets of Baghdad but from the conclusions of a stunning National Intelligence Estimate (NIE) examining Iran's nuclear program released in November 2007.

Just a month before, President George Bush had warned that the continuation by Iran of its nuclear weapons program could trigger a global war: "So I've told people that if you're interested in avoiding World War III, it seems like you ought to be interested in preventing them from having the knowledge necessary to make a nuclear weapon."[17] The president's policy, begun nearly six years earlier when he had declared Iran part of the "axis of evil," seemed alive and well. His comments fanned the hopes of neoconservatives and the fears of pragmatists that the president would support a military attack on Iran.

On December 3, however, a new assessment representing the unanimous opinion of all 16 U.S. intelligence agencies concluded that Iran had ended its dedicated nuclear weapons work four years earlier, in 2003. In an abrupt reversal of previous estimates (most recently in 2005), the intelligence agencies concluded that "Tehran's decision to halt its nuclear weapons program suggests it is less determined to develop nuclear weapons than we have been judging since 2005," adding, "We do not know whether [Iran] currently intends to develop nuclear weapons."[18]

The NIE presented a far more nuanced picture of both the nuclear program and the Iranian government's intentions than previous estimates, directly contradicting the one-dimensional portrait painted by many conservatives, including those in the White House. The estimate conformed to the views of many independent experts. I concluded in early 2006 that Iran did not have a crash program to build a nuclear bomb[19] and wrote later that year:

> Based on what we now know, it is unlikely that Iran has a large, secret nuclear weapons program, though U.S. officials and many journalists talk as if they do. Rather, most evidence indicates that Iran has now embarked on a significant effort to acquire legally and openly all the technologies necessary for a nuclear power program, technologies that would enable it to also produce a nuclear weapon sometime in the next decade were it to decide to do so.
>
> While it seems very likely that Iran did conduct weapons-related activities in the past, including possible acquisition of weapon designs and some limited research experiments, it also appears that the weapons work has ended, or, at least been suspended. . . . The evidence of past weapons work is largely circumstantial, but compelling. . . . This research seems to have slowed after the end of the Iran-Iraq war, proceeding in fits and starts during the 1990s. The major efforts seem to have turned to the publicly acknowledged programs, including resumption

of construction of the reactor at Bushehr . . . and the construction of the uranium conversion facility at Isfahan
with Chinese help.

With the exposure in late 2002 of Iran's third major effort, the secret construction of uranium-enrichment facilities at Natanz, Iran was forced to allow International
Atomic Energy Agency (IAEA) inspectors access to most
facilities and records. The IAEA work has now given us
an extensive look at both the history and extent of the
program. It may also have led to Iran's current strategy:
Cooperate with the inspections enough to provide information on current efforts, block investigations that could
expose past, embarrassing weapons work, negotiate limits on the program that allow the assistance the country
needs to both build power reactors and develop enrichment and reprocessing capabilities.[20]

The most significant finding in the NIE was not its judgment on the nature of the nuclear program but its judgment
on the nature of the regime. After years of persistent arguments for war with Iran, the intelligence community now
made the case for diplomatic engagement.

The case for military strikes was based in large part on
the idea that Iran was lead by mad mullahs that could not
be deterred and that posed as grave a threat as that of Nazi
Germany. "If Iran is to be prevented from developing a
nuclear arsenal," argued *Commentary* editor Norman Podhoretz, "there is no alternative to the actual use of military
force—any more than there was an alternative to force if Hitler was to be stopped in 1938."[21] *Washington Post* columnist
Charles Krauthammer said Iran was led by "religious fanatics
seized with an eschatological belief in the imminent apoca-
lypse and in their own divine duty to hasten the End of Days.
The mullahs are infinitely more likely to use these weapons
than anyone in the history of the nuclear age."[22] John Bolton
warned, "When you have a regime that would be happier in
the afterlife than in this life, this is not a regime that is subject
to classic theories of deterrence. Retaliation for them, which
would obliterate their society, doesn't have the same negative
connotations for their leadership."[23]

The Iran NIE destroyed that caricature. "Tehran's decisions," according to the report, "are guided by a cost-benefit approach rather than a rush to a weapon irrespective of the political, economic, and military costs." The assessment pointed the way to a new U.S. policy: "Some combination of threats of intensified international scrutiny and pressures, along with opportunities for Iran to achieve its security, prestige, and goals for regional influence in other ways, might—if perceived by Iran's leaders as credible—prompt Tehran to extend the current halt to its nuclear weapons program." [24]

Similarly, with Center for American Progress senior analyst Andrew Grotto, I had argued in a March 2007 report on Iran, *Contain and Engage*, that current U.S. policies "fall short of fundamentally changing Iran's cost/benefit calculus."[25] The report concluded:

> The international community must constantly remind Iran of the potential benefits as well as the continued and escalating costs of its failure to comply with its nonproliferation obligations. Rather than pursue the faint hope that the organization of coercive measures will force Iran's capitulation, our contain and engage strategy couples the pressures created by sanctions, diplomatic isolation and investment freezes with practical compromises and realizable security assurances to encourage Iran onto a verifiable, non-nuclear weapons path.[26]

Robert Kagan, a leading neoconservative analyst and a fierce proponent of the war with Iraq, was quick to adjust to the post-NIE realities. He argued that with the military option gone and the ability to impose sanctions weakened, the time had arrived to talk directly to Tehran.

> The Bush administration cannot take military action against Iran during its remaining time in office, or credibly threaten to do so, unless it is in response to an extremely provocative Iranian action. A military strike against suspected Iranian nuclear facilities was always fraught with risk. For the Bush administration, that option is gone. . . . With its policy tools broken, the Bush administration can

sit around isolated for the next year. Or it can seize the initiative, and do the next administration a favor, by opening direct talks with Tehran. [27]

Finally, the NIE represented a significant move toward reestablishing the professionalism and integrity of the threat-assessment process. This process had been badly warped by the establishment of alternative intelligence operations in the Department of Defense by former senior officials Donald Rumsfeld, Steven Cambone, and Douglas Feith, with the support of Vice President Cheney. Bypassing the established intelligence agencies, their Office of Special Plans and related groups had fed alternative—and false—intelligence directly to the White House in support of coercive policies directed toward Iraq, North Korea, and Iran. These officials brought great pressure on the agencies to agree with their views.

The report may signal that the conservative new directors of national intelligence and the Central Intelligence Agency are insulating their analysts from the political pressures responsible for the previously distorted assessments. The report will also allow U.S. policymakers and the American public to engage in realistic debate over Iran's uranium enrichment program, which without a doubt poses a significant challenge to U.S. interests in the Middle East and elsewhere.

A COMPREHENSIVE APPROACH

Reversing the spread of nuclear weapons cannot be achieved in a vacuum. As we approach the end of the first decade of the twenty-first century, any serious policy approach must start with an appreciation for the difficult situation confronting such an effort. The *New York Times* concluded on the last day of 2007:

> Out of panic and ideology, President Bush squandered America's position of moral and political leadership, swept aside international institutions and treaties, sullied America's global image, and trampled on the constitutional pillars that have supported our democracy through

the most terrifying and challenging times. These policies have fed the world's anger and alienation and have not made any of us safer.[28]

But it is not all bleak. Although strong anti-American currents are swirling around the world and real enemies will use them to harm the United States, there remains, says *Foreign Policy* editor Moisés Naim, an equally strong international demand for the United States to play a larger role in world affairs:

> Of course, the America that the world wants back is not the one that preemptively invades potential enemies, bullies allies or disdains international law. The demand is for an America that rallies other nations prone to sitting on the fence while international crises are boiling out of control; for a superpower that comes up with innovative initiatives to tackle the great challenges of the day, such as climate change, nuclear proliferation and violent Islamist fundamentalism. The demand is for an America that enforces the rules that facilitate international commerce and works effectively to stabilize an accident-prone global economy. Naturally, the world also wants a superpower willing to foot the bill with a largess that no other nation can match.[29]

The next president will have to marshal all the international help possible. George Perkovich, vice president of the Carnegie Endowment for International Peace, was one of the authors of *Universal Compliance* (cited on pp. 136–137 and 153–154), a study published in 2005 that argues for a strategy based on the principle that nations that possess nuclear weapons must show that tougher nonproliferation rules not only benefit the powerful but also constrain the powerful. He updated the report in June 2007, saying:

> Events of the past two years have deepened this conviction. Terrorists and hostile regimes attempting to acquire or use nuclear weapons can be stopped only by coordinated international efforts to strengthen and enforce rules.

To obtain this cooperation, the states that hold nuclear weapons for status and security must provide much greater equity to those that do not.

This strategic imperative is difficult for the United States, Russia, France, the United Kingdom, China, India, Pakistan, and Israel to accept, but they will face a much more dangerous world if they do not. If their intentions are not clearly to seek a world without nuclear weapons, a number of other states will seek equity through proliferation, while a greater number will look the other way, thinking that the original nuclear weapon states deserve the competition.[30]

One example is the race that has now begun among Arab countries to match Iran's nuclear capabilities. In 2007, almost a dozen Muslim nations declared their interest in developing nuclear energy programs. This unprecedented desire for nuclear power is all the more disturbing because it is paired with the unseemly rush of salesmen to supply the coveted technology.

While U.S. officials were reaching a new agreement with India in 2007 that dismantled nuclear-proliferation barriers in order to sell nuclear technology to that nation, President Nicolas Sarkozy of France signed a deal with Libya on nuclear cooperation between the two countries and agreed to help the United Arab Emirates launch a civilian nuclear program that will begin with the construction of two nuclear power reactors in the tiny state. Indicating that this could be just the beginning of a major sales-and-supply effort, Sarkozy declared his interest in helping both Saudi Arabia and Egypt build nuclear reactors and said that the West should trust Arab states with nuclear technology.[31] Sarkozy had a point: no one can deny Arab states access to nuclear technology, especially since they are acquiring it under existing international rules and agreeing to inspections by officials of the International Atomic Energy Agency. But is this new interest really about meeting demands for electric power and desalinization plants?

There is only one nuclear power reactor in the entire Middle East—the one under construction in Bushehr, Iran.

(Israel has a research reactor, as do several other Middle Eastern states.) In all of Africa, there are only two, both in South Africa. Suddenly, after multiple energy crises over the 63 years of the nuclear age, the countries that control over one-fourth of the world's oil supplies are investing in nuclear power programs. This is not about energy; it is a nuclear hedge against Iran.

King Abdullah of Jordan admitted as much in a January 2007 interview: "The rules have changed on the nuclear subject throughout the whole region. . . . After this summer everybody's going for nuclear programs." He was referring to the war in Lebanon during the summer of 2006 between Israel and Hezbollah, perceived in the region as evidence of Iran's growing clout. Other leaders are not as frank in public, but convey similar sentiments in private.

Egypt and Turkey, two of Iran's main rivals, are leading the nuclear surge. Both have flirted with nuclear weapons programs, and both have announced ambitious plans for the construction of nuclear power reactors. Not to be outdone, Saudi Arabia and the five other members of the Gulf Cooperation Council (Bahrain, Kuwait, Oman, Qatar, and the United Arab Emirates) at the end of 2006 "commissioned a joint study on the use of nuclear technology for peaceful purposes." In January 2007, Algeria and Russia signed an agreement on nuclear development, with France, South Korea, China, and the United States also jockeying for nuclear sales to this region. Syria announced that it, too, wants to explore nuclear power, as did Jordan and Morocco. In early 2008, Abu Dhabi solicited bids from several large French companies to buy two modern, third-generation nuclear reactors.[32] In early 2008, Turkey gently dropped the other nuclear shoe, quietly sending feelers to gauge American reaction to its planned construction of a uranium-enrichment center—the same type of operation that the United States opposes in Iran.[33]

Finally, the Arab League provided an overall umbrella for these initiatives when, at the end of its summit meeting in March 2007, it "called on the Arab states to expand the use of peaceful nuclear technology in all domains serving continuous development." Perhaps these states are truly motivated to join the "nuclear renaissance" promoted by the nuclear power

industry and to counter global warming. But the main message to the West from moderate Arab and Muslim leaders
seems political, not industrial or ecological. "We can't trust
you," they are saying. "You are failing to contain Iran and we
need to prepare."

To counter this surge, nations that sell nuclear technology
should be just as energetic in promoting the resolution of regional conflicts as they are in promoting their products. They
should work seriously to create a guaranteed source of fuel
for any new reactors, if they proceed, either by the construction of multinational uranium-enrichment facilities in the
Middle East (favored by Saudi Arabia), or another area (suggested by Russia) or by the establishment of a "virtual fuel"
bank, an idea proposed by Mohammad ElBaradei, director
general of the IAEA. This would require building the unity of
the United States, western Europe, Russia, and the regional
states to effectively contain the Iranian program. Finally, it
means that engaging with Tehran is even more crucial to halt
not only the Iranian nuclear program, but also those that will
soon start to materialize to counter it.

MOVEMENT TOWARD A
NEW STRATEGY ACCELERATES

Prospects for the adoption of policies aimed to stop the proliferation of nuclear weapons increased during 2007, as the
world entered a period of rapid political transition. By early
2009, four of the five permanent members of the United Nations Security Council (France, the United Kingdom, the
United States, and Russia) will have new leaders who were
elected since mid-2007. Other key states, including Iran and
Israel, may as well, while Germany, Italy, Australia, South
Korea, and Japan have already elected new executives. International organizations, too, will refresh their leadership,
with a new secretary general now installed at the United Nations and possibly a new director general of the International
Atomic Energy Agency in 2009.

Rarely have the political stars realigned so dramatically.
The photo of the participants in the G8 summit in 2009 will

likely not include a single leader who was present at the 2006 summit, save for Prime Minister Stephen Harper of Canada. This is a unique opportunity to advance new policies that can dramatically reduce and even eliminate many of the dangers that have kept political leaders and security officials worried about a nuclear 9/11.

Stepping up to the challenge, several leading candidates for the presidency of the United States offered sweeping proposals for nuclear security in 2007 and 2008. On the Republican side, former governor Mitt Romney had the most to say on the issue. Before suspending his campaign, he promised he would appoint a senior ambassador to lead efforts to prevent nuclear terrorism, including accelerating and expanding efforts to secure global nuclear stockpiles to the "gold standard." He also favored creating an international fuel bank to back up commercial supplies and criminalizing nuclear trafficking to equate it with genocide and war crimes. Senator John McCain (R-AZ) devoted just one paragraph to proliferation in a *Foreign Affairs* article that focused on stricter export controls, harsher punishments for proliferators, and increased budgets for nuclear inspections.[34]

On the Democratic side, former Senator John Edwards (D-NC), Governor Bill Richardson (D-NM), and Senator Barack Obama (D-IL) promised to lead efforts not just to reduce but to eliminate nuclear weapons. Obama had the most developed plan, based in part on his work with Senator Richard Lugar (R-IN) and a bill he introduced with Senator Chuck Hagel (R-NE). In a speech delivered in October 2007, he endorsed a plan to secure all loose nuclear materials during his first term as president; negotiate dramatic reductions in U.S. and Russian nuclear stockpiles; negotiate a verifiable global ban on the production of fissile materials; create an international nuclear fuel bank; increase funding for IAEA inspections and safeguards; seek a global ban on all intermediate-range missiles; and increase the current warning time that keep thousands of nuclear warheads ready to launch within 15 minutes, reducing the risk that the weapons would be used by accident or misperception.

Senator Hillary Clinton (D-NY) promised similar presidential attention to preventing nuclear terror and to shrinking global arsenals. In an article published in *Foreign Affairs* at the end of the year, Clinton lamented the failure to build on the profound international unity created after the 9/11 attacks. She promised that she will not let her opportunity slip away, pledging to negotiate an end to the nuclear programs in Iran and North Korea; secure all loose nuclear materials during her first term; establish a nuclear fuel bank; negotiate an accord to verifiably reduce U.S. and Russian arsenals; and, significantly, seek Senate approval of the nuclear test ban by 2009, the tenth anniversary of the Senate's initial rejection of the treaty. This last step, Senator Clinton said, "would enhance the United States' credibility when demanding that other nations refrain from testing."[35]

Summarizing this trend among the Democratic candidates, former National Security staff member Ivo Daldaar and former Arms Control and Disarmament Agency director John Holum, two top advisors to Obama, wrote that the key was for the next administration to make the commitment to the elimination of nuclear weapons the "organizing principle of [its] nuclear weapons policies":

> There is much that the United States can do to lift the dark nuclear shadow over the world. It can sharply reduce its nuclear stockpile to 1,000 weapons or less, if Russia agrees to go down to the same level. It can eliminate tactical nuclear weapons to underscore that it understands that a nuclear weapon is a nuclear weapon, no matter its size, yield, range, or mode of delivery. It can agree never to produce highly enriched uranium and plutonium for weapons purposes, and accept the need for intrusive verification if other states agree to end such production as well. It can commit never again to test a nuclear device, and ratify the Comprehensive Test Ban Treaty.

Compared with existing policies, this set of initiatives would be like night and day. There is and likely will be some conservative opposition to these plans. In October 2007, in reaction to an effort by Senator Carl Levin (D-MI), chairman of the Senate Armed Services Committee, to condition the production of the so-called Reliable Replacement Warhead on a sense of the Senate provision that the nuclear test ban treaty should be ratified, Senator Jon Kyl (R-AZ) circulated a letter, signed by 38 senators, who successfully opposed the provision.[36] Republican presidential candidates did not address these issues in detail in 2007, but seem to have kept their positions close to this conservative line, with several candidates during the Republican debates endorsing the possible use of nuclear weapons against Iran.

However, in Congress there was some Republican support for these new policies, as demonstrated by the legislation (SR 1977) introduced by Senators Obama and Hagel, which would authorize the policies detailed by Obama in his speech, plus others. Most significantly, the bill would continue "the United States moratorium on nuclear test explosions, initiating a bipartisan process to achieve ratification of the Comprehensive Test Ban Treaty, working to secure ratification by other key countries, and fully supporting United States commitments to fund the international monitoring system to help detect and deter possible nuclear explosions by other countries." The legislation also specifically endorsed "pursuing and concluding an agreement to verifiably halt the production of fissile materials for nuclear weapons."

Senators Dianne Feinstein (D-CA) and Susan Collins (R-ME) also cooperated on SR 1914, the Nuclear Policy and Posture Review Act of 2007, requiring that a comprehensive nuclear weapons policy and posture review be submitted to Congress by the administration and prohibiting funding for any new nuclear warhead development until such reviews were completed. Their bill would require that the review examine "the role of nuclear forces in United States military strategy, planning and programming" and the "policy requirements and objectives for the United States to maintain a safe, reliable and credible nuclear deterrence posture," among other issues. Similar legislation passed in the House and was added to the defense authorization bill by the chairwoman of the House Armed Services Committee's Subcommittee on Strategic Forces, Representative Ellen Tauscher (D-CA). It includes a provision creating an independent commission to examine U.S. nuclear policy.

The year 2007 ended with bipartisan congressional actions that generally had the effect of blocking the production of new types of nuclear weapons and the construction of antimissile bases in Europe, reducing funding for these antimissile programs overall, mandating a new nuclear policy review, and providing funding for an international fuel bank.

The final factor in the movement toward a new policy is the critical role of nongovernmental organizations. Many groups in 2007 were working to provide the policies that new national leaders could adopt. "With this leadership change," former United Nations under-secretary-general for disarmament affairs Jayantha Dhanapala told a February 2007 conference in New York, "it is for us in civil society to try to urge new perspectives and new opportunities for them to seize so that we all make the right choices at the right time."[37]

Analysts at over a dozen institutes at the beginning of 2008 were perfecting just such proposals and promoting their ideas at conferences and in reports, testimonies, blogs, interviews, and films. There is broad agreement in progressive and moderate policy circles on what must be done, as demonstrated by the report "Reducing Nuclear Threats and Preventing Nuclear Terrorism," released in October 2007 by a group of former officials and military officers. The group was composed of more than 30 senior experts, including Madeleine Albright, Graham Allison, Samuel Berger, Wesley Clark, Thomas Daschle, Michèle Flournoy, Robert Gallucci, William Perry, John Podesta, Susan Rice, John Shalikashvili, Wendy Sherman, and me. The report proposed a consensus strategy for reducing all the nuclear threats—one that would work seriously and systematically to prevent a nuclear 9/11, stop new states from going nuclear, deter any state from launching a nuclear strike on the United States, and restore American leadership to the broad network of nations willing to work toward reducing nuclear perils.[38]

Key recommendations include many of the steps noted earlier, plus developing conventional weapons that would eliminate any need to resort to nuclear weapons in response to nonnuclear attacks, delaying the production of any new types of nuclear weapons until there is a comprehensive nuclear policy review, determining that any antimissile systems actually work before deploying them, and postponing plans for antimissile bases in Europe until there is a reliable assessment of the threat and the technology.

All these efforts are propelled by a bipartisan appeal from Republicans George Shultz and Henry Kissinger and Democrats William Perry and Sam Nunn that was published in their January 4, 2007, *Wall Street Journal* op-ed, "A World Free of Nuclear Weapons." During 2007 and 2008, these four veteran Cold Warriors developed their article into an ongoing campaign with conferences, testimonies, publications, and efforts to enlist the support of all former secretaries of state and defense. They want the United States to recommit to the vision of eliminating nuclear weapons and marry that vision to an action plan that includes steep reductions in nuclear arsenals, the ratification of the test ban treaty, and taking all weapons off hair-trigger alert. They thus created substantial political space for many officials to embrace more ambitious agendas than they had.

Nancy Reagan sent a personal letter of endorsement to the group's conference in October 2007, and California governor Arnold Schwarzenegger provided a dramatic speech, read by former secretary of state Shultz when the governor was prevented from attending by a wild fire emergency. He said, in part:

> The words that this audience knows so well, the words that President Kennedy spoke during the Cold War, have regained their urgency: "The world was not meant to be a prison in which man awaits his execution." Here in California we still have levees that were built a hundred years ago. These levees are an imminent threat to the well-being of this state and its people. It would be only a matter of time before a disaster strikes. But we're not waiting until such a disaster.
>
> We in California have taken action to protect our people and our economy from devastation. Neither can this nation nor the world wait to act until there is a nuclear disaster. . . . You have a big vision, a vision as big as humanity—to free the world of nuclear weapons. . . . I want to help. Let me know how I can use my power and

influence as governor to further your vision. Because my heart is with you. My support is firm. My door is open.

On January 15, 2008, the four published a new op-ed, announcing that their initiative had garnered the support of seven former secretaries of state, five former secretaries of defense, and five former national security advisers—almost everyone still living who had served in these posts since the Kennedy administration. The list includes Madeleine Albright, Richard V. Allen, James A. Baker III, Samuel R. Berger, Zbigniew Brzezinski, Frank Carlucci, Warren Christopher, William Cohen, Lawrence Eagleburger, Melvin Laird, Anthony Lake, Robert McFarlane, Robert McNamara and Colin Powell. (Kissinger and Powell served as both national security advisers and secretaries of state.)

Thus, for the first time since the initial efforts of the Truman administration in the 1940s and the nonproliferation programs of the Kennedy administration in the 1960s, a serious movement to eliminate nuclear weapons has developed not from the political left but from the bipartisan, moderate middle. This promises to give the movement greater political importance and policy relevance than previous efforts—even the broad-based Nuclear Freeze Movement of the 1980s—had. It may be possible for the first time since the beginning of the Cold War to move seriously toward the elimination of nuclear weapons. It is not clear if the goal can be reached, but the process alone could secure long-sought nuclear security goals.

CONCLUSION

These reports and efforts are harbingers of a new policy moment. There is a greater chance to achieve dramatic, historic change in global nuclear policy now than at any other time in the past 15 years. Those involved in these policy initiatives believe that a world with an increasing number of nuclear weapon states is not inevitable. Neither is a nuclear attack by terrorists. Both can be prevented, but only if their prevention becomes an overriding national priority and only with strong U.S. leadership in international threat reduction and nonproliferation efforts.

The prospects of that developing over the next few years are already encouraging. The next president of the United States—whether a Republican or Democrat—will likely have a decidedly different nonproliferation policy than the failed strategy attempted over the past few years. There are already signs that other governments are willing to develop and promote new initiatives, such as the remarkable speech delivered in June 2007 by Margaret Beckett, then the British foreign secretary, at the Carnegie International Nonproliferation Conference—at that time the most dramatic reaffirmation of the goal of elimination of nuclear weapons presented by any senior official of a state that possesses nuclear weapons. This speech was approved by incoming prime minister Gordon Brown and provided both vision and practicality. Beckett said, in part:

> When it comes to building this new impetus for global nuclear disarmament, I want the UK to be at the forefront of both the thinking and the practical work; to be, as it were, a disarmament laboratory. As far as new thinking goes, the International Institute of Strategic Studies is planning an in-depth study to help determine the requirements for the eventual elimination of all nuclear weapons. We will participate in that study and provide funding for one of their workshops focusing on some of the crucial technical questions in this area. The study and subsequent workshops will offer a thorough and systematic analysis of what a commitment to a world free of nuclear weapons means in practice.[39]

Achieving a world free from nuclear weapons is—as even the most ardent proponents admit—a daunting task. By marrying this vision to pragmatic steps, however, it should be possible to implement measures that can restore the lost momentum of previous years; concretely reduce the risks of nuclear terrorism, nuclear war, and nuclear use; and both rebuild the global consensus to prevent the emergence of nuclear weapon states and drastically reduce the arsenals of the current weapon states. As Foreign Secretary Beckett said: "My commitment to that vision, truly visionary in its day, of a world free of nuclear weapons is undimmed. And although we in this room may not see the end of that road, we can take those first further steps down it. For any generation that would be a noble calling. For ours, it is a duty."

Beckett's call was picked up by Prime Minister Gordon Brown in a January 21, 2008, address in India:

> We must send a powerful signal to all members of the international community that the race for more and bigger stockpiles of nuclear destruction is over. The expiry of the remaining US-Russia arms deals, the continued existence of these large arsenals, the stalemates on a fissile material cut-off treaty and the Comprehensive Test Ban Treaty must all be addressed.
>
> And let me say today Britain is prepared to use our expertise to help determine the requirements for the verifiable elimination of nuclear warheads. And I pledge that in the run-up to the Non Proliferation Treaty review conference in 2010 we will be at the forefront of the international campaign to accelerate disarmament amongst possessor states, to prevent proliferation to new states, and to ultimately achieve a world that is free from nuclear weapons.[40]

At the beginning of 2008, the outlines of a transformational nuclear policy were emerging. To many it seemed that the policy deadlocks of the past few years could be broken. Few of those engaged in the efforts were certain of success, but all were committed. Some were veterans of previous campaigns; others, new recruits. They were all ready to follow the entreaty of Shakespeare's Henry V, "Once more unto the breach, dear friends, once more."

NOTES

PREFACE

1. For the most comprehensive and widely cited example of this debate, see Scott D. Sagan and Kenneth N. Waltz, *The Spread of Nuclear Weapons: A Debate Renewed* (New York: Norton, 2003).

2. Statistics referenced by Siegfried Hecker in remarks to the Carnegie International Non-Proliferation Conference (November 8, 2005), available at http://www.carnegieendowment.org/static/npp/2005conference/presentations/Talk_Of_Nation_2.pdf.

3. See John Mearsheimer, "Back to the Future," *International Security* 15, no. 1 (Summer 1990).

4. At the November 2005 Carnegie International Non-Proliferation Conference in Washington, D.C., former secretary of defense Robert McNamara said that during the Cuban Missile Crisis, "President Kennedy lucked out. . . . We didn't believe the nuclear danger was anywhere close to what we learned 29 years later. We lucked out." See remarks by Robert McNamara at the Carnegie International Non-Proliferation Conference November 8, 2005, available at http://www.carnegieendowment.org/static/npp/2005conference/presentations/Talk_Of_Nation_2.pdf.

5. Matthew Bunn, "The Demand for Black Market Fissile Material" (updated June 2005), available at http://www.nti.org/e_research/cnwm/threat/demand.asp.

6. Charles D. Ferguson and William C. Potter, *The Four Faces of Nuclear Terrorism* (Monterey, Calif.: Monterey Institute for International Studies, 2004), p. 3.

7. Mohamed ElBaradei, "Remarks at IAEA Nobel Peace Prize Ceremony 2005" December, 10 2005, available at http://www.iaea.org/NewsCenter/Statements/2005/ebsp2005n020.html.

1. BUILDING THE BOMB

1. Letter from Albert Einstein to Franklin Roosevelt (August 2, 1939), available at http://www.dannen.com/ae-fdr.html.
2. The Frisch/Peierls Memoranda of March 1940, in Robert Serber, *The Los Alamos Primer* (Berkeley: University of California Press, 1992), pp. 79–88.
3. Frisch/Peierls Memoranda, p. 82.
4. Frisch/Peierls Memoranda, p. 81.
5. McGeorge Bundy, *Danger and Survival* (New York: Random House, 1988), pp. 25–26.
6. Cited in Richard Rhodes, *The Making of the Atomic Bomb* (New York: Simon & Schuster, 1986), p. 369.
7. Robert S. Norris, *Racing for the Bomb* (South Royalton, Vt.: Steerforth Press, 2002,), p. x.
8. Rhodes, *The Making of the Atomic Bomb*, p. 448.
9. Gerard J. DeGroot, *The Bomb: A Life* (Cambridge, Mass.: Harvard University Press, 2005), p. 37.
10. Serber, *The Los Alamos Primer*, p. 3.
11. The speed of light in a vacuum is 186,282 miles per second or 299,792 kilometers per second. The squares of these are 34,700,983,524 and 89,875,243,264.
12. "The Bomb Goes Public," The Manhattan Project, Making the Atomic Bomb Part V: The Atomic Bomb and American Strategy. Atomic Archive, available at http://www.atomicarchive.com/History/mp/p5s14.shtml.
13. Serber, *The Los Alamos Primer*, p. 11. Each fission occurs in about 10^{-8} seconds.
14. Serber, *Los Alamos Primer*, p. 57.
15. Norris, *Racing for the Bomb*, p. 363.
16. Ibid., p. 364.
17. The plutonium core inside modern warheads has been estimated to have a radius of approximately 5cm. See Steve Fetter, Valery A. Frolov, Oleg F. Prilutsky, and Roald Z. Sagdeev, "Appendix A: Fissile Material and Weapon Design," *Science & Global Security,* vol. 1 (1990): 225–302.
18. David Holloway, *Stalin and the Bomb: The Soviet Union and Atomic Energy 1939–1956* (New Haven: Yale University Press), p.117
19. Notes of the Interim Committee Meeting, Thursday, May 31, 1945, available at the Truman Presidential Museum and Library, http://www.trumanlibrary.org.
20. Norman Polmar and Thomas B. Allen, "Invasion Most Costly," *Proceedings, U.S. Naval Institute* 121, 8 (August 1995): 51–56.
21. J. Samuel Walker, "Recent Literature on Truman's Atomic Bomb

Decision," *Diplomatic History* 29, no. 2 (April 2005). See also J. Samual Walker, "The Decision to Use the Bomb: A Historiographical Update," in Michael J. Hogan, ed., *Hiroshima in History and Memory* (Cambridge, England: Cambridge University Press, 1996).

22. Gar Alperovitz, *Atomic Diplomacy: Hiroshima and Potsdam,* revised and expanded edition (East Haven, Conn.: Pluto Press, 1985), pp. 19, 287. See also Gar Alperovitz, *The Decision to Use the Bomb and the Architecture of an American Myth* (London: HarperCollins, 1995).

23. See for example Martin Sherwin, *The Atomic Bomb and the Grand Alliance* (New York: Knopf, 1975), pp. 194, 220–238.

24. Barton J. Bernstein, "The Atomic Bombings Reconsidered," *Foreign Affairs* 74, no. 1 (January 1995): 135.

2. CONTROLLING THE BOMB

1. These and other citations are from "Report of the Committee on Political and Social Problems," Manhattan Project Metallurgical Laboratory, University of Chicago, June 11, 1945 (Franck report). See also Jane Vaynman, "Nuclear Time Capsule," Carnegie Endowment proliferation analysis, June 2, 2005, available at http://www.carnegieendowment.org/npp/publications/index.cfm?fa=view&id=17023.

2. Len Weiss presents an excellent detailed history of these proposals in "Atoms for Peace," *Bulletin of the Atomic Scientists* 59, no. 6 (November/December 2003), pp. 34–44.

3. Cited in David Holloway, *Entering the Nuclear Arms Race: The Soviet Decision to Build the Atomic Bomb 1939–1945* (Washington, D.C.: Wilson Center, 1979), p. 41.

4. Lawrence S. Wittner, *One World or None: A History of the World Disarmament Movement Through 1953* (Palo Alto: Stanford University Press, 1990), p. 254.

5. David Holloway, *Stalin and the Bomb* (New Haven and London: Yale University Press, 1994), p.133.

6. Holloway, *Stalin and the Bomb,* p. 94.

7. Harry S. Truman, *Memoirs,* vol. 1, *Year of Decisions* (Garden City, N.Y.: Doubleday, 1955), p. 416.

8. Holloway, *Stalin and the Bomb,* p. 122.

9. Cited in Holloway, *Stalin and the Bomb,* p. 132.

10. The most significant information, particularly the implosion bomb design, came from Klaus Fuchs, a German-born British physicist working at Los Alamos. See Thomas B. Cochran, Robert S. Norris, and Oleg A. Bukharin, *Making the Russian Bomb: From Stalin to Yeltsin* (Boulder, Colo.: Westview Press, 1995), p. 15.

11. Holloway, *Stalin and the Bomb,* 220. The U.S. project took four years and nine months, from October 1941, when Roosevelt decided to pursue the atomic bomb, to the July 1945 Trinity test. Russia took four years from the start of the full-scale industrial project in August 1945 to the test in August 1949.

12. From *Sto sorok besed s Molotovym: iz dnevnika F. Chueva* (Moscow: Terra, 1991), cited in David Holloway, *Stalin and the Bomb,* p. 164.

13. Conant to Stimson, January 22, 1947, Stimson Papers, box 154, folder 18, cited in Martin J. Sherwin, "How Well They Meant," *Bulletin of the Atomic Scientists* 41, no. 7 (August 1985): 14.

3. RACING WITH THE BOMB

1. Whereas fission bombs are limited in destructive yield by the ability to keep the uranium or plutonium cores compressed as the force of the fission reactions blows them apart, fusion bombs use the heat of a fission bomb to fuse atoms of hydrogen together. The yield of these thermonuclear devices is limited only by the amount of fuel (deuterium or tritium compounds) that can be packaged in the warhead.

2. Barton J. Bernstein, "Truman and the H-Bomb," *Bulletin of the Atomic Scientists* (March 1984): 13.

3. Ibid.

4. Albert Einstein, "Arms Can Bring No Security," *Bulletin of the Atomic Scientists* 6, no. 3 (March 1950): 71.

5. In advanced nuclear designs, the power of the primary itself is often "boosted" by placing deuterium and tritium within the atomic device. These materials are typically injected as a gas into the center of the uranium or plutonium before the nuclear chain reaction is initiated. As the chain reaction begins to release energy, some of the energy compresses and heats these lighter atoms, causing then to fuse together. These thermonuclear reactions release additional energy and neutrons, and the neutrons cause additional fission reactions, thereby accelerating the ongoing fission chain reaction, increasing the energy output and efficiency of the boosted device.

6. David Fischer, *History of the IAEA* (Vienna: International Atomic Energy Agency, 1997), p. 32.

7. Stephen Ambrose, *Eisenhower the President* (New York: Simon & Schuster, 1984), p. 104.

8. President Eisenhower, "Address Before the General Assembly of the United Nations on the Peaceful Uses of Nuclear Energy," December 8, 1953, in Congressional Research Service, *Nuclear Proliferation Factbook* (Washington, D.C.: Library of Congress, 1994), p. 15.

9. Ibid.

10. Bertrand Goldschmidt, in Joseph F. Pilat, Robert E. Pendley, and Charles K. Ebinger, eds., *Atoms for Peace: An Analysis after 30 Years* (Boulder, Colo.: Westview Press, 1985), pp. 111, 117.

11. Leonard Weiss, "Atoms for Peace," *Bulletin of the Atomic Scientists* 59, no. 6 (November/December 2003): 41.

12. Of these sixteen, they assessed five as "likely" to do so.

13. John F. Kennedy, "Address Before the General Assembly of the United Nations," September 25, 1961, available at http://www .jfklibrary.org/Historical+Resources/Archives/Reference+Desk/ Speeches/JFK/003POF03UnitedNations09251961.htm.

14. John F. Kennedy, "Face-to-Face: Nixon-Kennedy," Vice President Richard M. Nixon and Senator John F. Kennedy, Third Joint Television-Radio Broadcast, October 13, 1960, available at http://www .jfklibrary.org/60-3rd.htm.

15. Ibid.

16. Arthur Schlesinger Jr., "Bush's Thousand Days," *Washington Post*, April 24, 2006.

17. Robert McNamara, *In Retrospect* (New York: Times Books, 1995), p. 341.

18. Though the U.S. nuclear arsenal continued to grow through the first half of the 1960s, the rate of growth was significantly slower.

19. John F. Kennedy, "Address Before the General Assembly."

20. Richard Nixon, "Remarks at a Ceremony Marking the Ratification and Entry Into Force of the Treaty on the Non-Proliferation of Nuclear Weapons," March 5, 1970, available at http://www .nixonfoundation.org/clientuploads/directory/archive/1970_pdf _files/1970_0070.pdf.

21. Glenn Seaborg, *Stemming the Tide: Arms Control in the Johnson Years* (Lexington, Mass.: Lexington Books, 1971), pp. 355–56.

22. George Bunn, "The NPT and Options for its Extension in 1995," *Nonproliferation Review* (Winter 1994), available at http://cns.miis .edu/pubs/npr/vol01/12/bunn12.pdf.

23. David Fischer, *Stopping the Spread of Nuclear Weapons: The Past and the Prospects* (London: Routledge, 1992), pp. 6–7.

24. Director of Central Intelligence, "National Intelligence Estimate 100–2-58," July 1, 1958 (approved for release July 2004), p. 2.

25. Director of Central Intelligence, "National Intelligence Estimate Number 4–3-61," September 21, 1961, p. 9.

26. The Gilpatric Committee was formally titled the "President's Task Force on Preventing the Spread of Nuclear Weapons."

27. Seaborg, *Stemming the Tide*, p. 141.

28. George Bunn, "The World's Nonproliferation Regime in Time," *IAEA Bulletin* 46, no. 2 (2004).

29. Glenn T. Seaborg, *Kennedy, Khrushchev, and the Test Ban* (Berkeley: University of California Press, 1981), p. 276.

30. Seaborg, *Kennedy, Khrushchev, and the Test Ban,* p. 278.

31. "Atom Treaty Hit Again by Thurmond," *Washington Post,* February 11, 1969.

32. "Stennis Criticizes A-Treaty," *Washington Post,* February 28, 1969.

33. Paul Boyer, *Fallout* (Columbus: Ohio State University Press, 1998).

34. Natural Resources Defense Council, Table of Global Nuclear Weapons Stockpiles 1945–2002, available at http://www.nrdc.org/nuclear/nudb/datab19.asp.

35. Lewis M. Simons, "A-Blast Temporarily Muffles Gandhi Critics," *Washington Post,* May 20, 1974.

36. Thomas Halsted, "The Spread of Nuclear Weapons—Is the Dam About to Burst?" *Bulletin of the Atomic Scientists* 31, no. 5 (May 1975): 8–11.

37. George Perkovich, *India's Nuclear Bomb* (Berkeley: University of California Press, 1999), p. 190.

38. Perkovich, *India's Nuclear Bomb,* p. 191.

39. Christopher Clary, "Dr. Khan's Nuclear Wal-Mart," *Disarmament Diplomacy* (March/April 2004), available at http://www.acronym.org.uk/dd/dd76/76cc.htm.

40. Richard Perle, *Newsweek,* February 18, 1983, as cited in Frances FitzGerald, *Way Out There in the Blue: Reagan, Star Wars, and the End of the Cold War* (New York: Simon & Schuster, 2000), p. 179.

41. Cited in FitzGerald, *Way Out There in the Blue,* p. 88.

42. FitzGerald, *Way Out There in the Blue,* p. 109.

43. Gerard J. DeGroot, *The Bomb* (Cambridge: Harvard University Press, 2005), p. 307.

44. Irving Kristol, "It Wasn't Inevitable," American Enterprise Institute, *On The Issues,* June 2004.

45. Anatoly Dobrynin, *In Confidence* (New York: Times Books, 1995), pp. 482, 495, cited in Lawrence Wittner, *Toward Nuclear Abolition,* vol. 3 of *The Struggle Against the Bomb* (Palo Alto: Stanford University Press, 2003), p 308.

46. *New York Times,* October 28, 1992, cited in Wittner, *Toward Nuclear Abolition,* p. 308.

47. Joseph Cirincione, Jon Wolfsthal, and Miriam Rajkumar, *Deadly Arsenals: Nuclear, Biological and Chemical Threats* (Washington, D.C.: Carnegie Endowment for International Peace, 2005), p. 8.

48. The ten countries known to have nuclear weapons or believed to be seeking them are the United States, Russia, Great Britain, China, France, India, Pakistan, Israel, North Korea, Iran.

49. The eleven countries with ballistic missiles that can travel more than 1,000 kilometers are China, France, India, Iran, Israel,

North Korea, Pakistan, Russia, Saudi Arabia, United Kingdom, United States.

4. Why States Want Nuclear Weapons— and Why They Don't

1. Britain, China, France, India, Israel, Pakistan, Russia, and the United States all have nuclear weapons. North Korea claims to have a "nuclear deterrent." Iran claims that its nuclear program is for peaceful purposes only, though many suspect that it is intended to produce weapons.

2. Director of Central Intelligence, "Nuclear Weapons and Delivery Capabilities of Free World Countries Other Than the US and UK," National Intelligence Estimate Number 4-3-61 (September 21, 1961), available at http://www.gwu.edu/~nsarchiv/NSAEBB/NSAEBB155/.

3. Thomas Hobbes, *Leviathan*, ed. by C. B. MacPherson (Baltimore: Penguin, 1968), pp. 186, 188.

4. *Renmin Ribao* (*People's Daily*), October 22, 1964, cited in John Wilson Leis and Xue Litai, *China Builds the Bomb* (Palo Alto: Stanford University Press, 1988), p. 2.

5. Jaswant Singh, "Against Nuclear Apartheid," *Foreign Affairs* (September/October 1998): 42.

6. Secretary of State George P. Shultz, quoted in Scott Sagan, "Why Do States Build Nuclear Weapons? Three Models in Search of a Bomb," *International Security* (Winter 1996/97): 57.

7. Richard K. Betts, "Paranoids, Pygmies, Pariahs, and Nonproliferation Revisited," *Security Studies* (Spring/Summer 1993): 100–22. Betts acknowledges that pygmies and paranoids can be threatened by either conventional or nuclear rivals.

8. Waldo Stumpf, "South Africa's Nuclear Weapons Program: From Deterrence to Dismantlement," *Arms Control Today* (December 1995–January 1996): 4.

9. Joseph Cirincione, Jon B. Wolfsthal, and Miriam Rajkumar, *Deadly Arsenals: Nuclear, Biological and Chemical Threats* (Washington, D.C.: Carnegie Endowment for International Peace, 2005), p. 361.

10. Ibid.

11. Betts does not include Israel in this category, though it appears to meet the definition better than any other state.

12. Avner Cohen, *Israel and the Bomb* (New York: Columbia University Press, 1998), p. 10.

13. Ibid., p. 342.

14. Cirincione, Wolfsthal, and Rajkumar, *Deadly Arsenals*, pp. 259–61.

15. James M. Goldgeier and Michael McFaul, "A Tale of Two Worlds: Core and Periphery in the Post-Cold War Era, *International Organization* (Spring 1992): 467–91.

16. Glenn Chafetz, "The End of the Cold War and the Future of Nuclear Proliferation: An Alternative to the Neorealist Perspective," *Security Studies* (Spring/Summer 1993): 133–34.

17. Ibid., p. 129.

18. Zachary Davis, "The Realist Nuclear Regime," *Security Studies* (Spring/Summer 1993): 80.

19. Some scholars, most notably Kenneth Waltz, argue that rival states sharing a common border are more secure with nuclear weapons than without them. Waltz provides an example of this dynamic: "The Soviet Union and the United States, and the Soviet Union and China, were hostile enough; and the latter pair shared a border. Nuclear weapons caused China and the Soviet Union to deal cautiously with each other." Even smaller nuclear powers can establish credible deterrence. Waltz argues that "nuclear weapons lessen the intensity as well as the frequency of war among their possessors. For fear of escalation nuclear states do not want to fight long and hard over important interests—indeed, they do not want to fight at all. Minor nuclear states have even better reasons than major ones to accommodate one another and to avoid fighting." Scott D. Sagan and Kenneth N. Waltz, *The Spread of Nuclear Weapons: A Debate Renewed* (New York: Norton, 2003), pp. 12, 37.

20. Quoted in Chafetz, "The End of the Cold War," p. 136.

21. Jonathan D. Pollack and Mitchell B. Reiss, "South Korea: The Tyranny of Geography and the Vexations of History," in Kurt M. Campbell, Robert J. Einhorn, and Mitchell B. Reiss, *The Nuclear Tipping Point: Why States Reconsider Their Nuclear Choices* (Washington, D.C.: Brookings Institution Press, 2004), p. 261. This case study is based primarily on the research of Pollack and Reiss and of Reiss himself in *Without the Bomb: The Politics of Nuclear Nonproliferation* (New York: Columbia University Press, 1988), pp. 78–108.

22. "Nixon's Acceptance of the Republican Party Nomination for President," August 8, 1968, available at http://watergate.info/nixon/acceptance-speech-1968.shtml.

23. Pollack and Reiss, *Without the Bomb*, p .262.

24. Ibid., p. 263.

25. Cited in Pollack and Reiss, *Without the Bomb,* p. 263.

26. Pollack and Reiss, *Without the Bomb*, p. 107.

27. See Jungmin Kang, Peter Hayes, Li Bin Tatsujiro Suzuki, and Richard Tanter, "South Korea's Nuclear Surprise," *Bulletin of the Atomic Scientists* (January/February 2005): 40–49.

28. Sagan, "Why Do States Build Nuclear Weapons?" p. 73.

29. Ibid., p. 77.

30. Ibid., p. 78.

31. See Wilfrid Kohl, *French Nuclear Diplomacy* (Princeton: Princeton University Press, 1971), p. 150, n. 46.

32. McGeorge Bundy, *Danger and Survival* (New York: Random House, 1988), p. 476.

33. Ibid., p. 502.

34. Lawrence S. Wittner, *Resisting the Bomb,* vol. 2 of *The Struggle Against the Bomb* (Palo Alto: Stanford University Press, 1997), p. 392.

35. Singh, "Against Nuclear Apartheid."

36. Bertrand Russell and Albert Einstein, "The Russell-Einstein Manifesto," July 9, 1955, available at http://www.pugwash.org/about/manifesto.htm.

37. George W. Bush, "Libya Pledges to Dismantle WMD Programs," remarks by the president, December 19, 2003, available at http://www.whitehouse.gov/news/releases/2003/12/20031219–9.html.

38. Mohamed ElBaradei, Statement at the Carnegie International Non-Proliferation Conference, November 7, 2005.

39. Chafetz, "The End of the Cold War," p. 128.

40. Peter R. Lavoy, "Nuclear Myths and the Causes of Nuclear Proliferation," *Security Studies* (Spring/Summer 1993): 198.

41. Sagan, "Why Do States Build Nuclear Weapons?" p. 64.

42. Cirincione, Wolfsthal, and Rajkumar, *Deadly Arsenals,* p. 240.

43. Quoted in Kamal Matinuddin, *The Nuclearization of South Asia* (Oxford: Oxford University Press, 2002), p. 138.

44. Matinuddin, *The Nuclearization of South Asia,* p. 138.

45. Robert S. Norris, Statement at the 2005 Carnegie International Non-Proliferation Conference, November 7, 2005. Statement available at http://www.carnegieendowment.org/static/npp/2005conference/presentations/Nuclear_History_transcript.pdf.

46. Lavoy, "Nuclear Myths and the Causes of Nuclear Proliferation," p. 199.

47. Sagan, "Why Do States Build Nuclear Weapons?" p. 65.

48. Ibid., p. 199.

49. Much of this brief case study relies on the work of George Perkovich in *India's Nuclear Bomb* (Berkeley: University of California Press, 1999) and of Scott Sagan, "Why Do States Build Nuclear Weapons?"

50. Perkovich, *India's Nuclear Bomb,* p. 6. See also Jon B. Wolfsthal, "Asia's Nuclear Dominoes?" *Current History* (April 2003): 172.

51. Perkovich, *India's Nuclear Bomb,* p. 1.

52. Lavoy, "Nuclear Myths and the Causes of Nuclear Proliferation," p. 202.

53. Singh, "Against Nuclear Apartheid."

54. K. Rangaswami, "Leaders Reject Demand for Atom Bomb," *Hindu*, November 9, 1964, p. 1, as cited in Perkovich, *India's Nuclear Bomb*, p. 74.

55. Perkovich, *India's Nuclear Bomb*, p. 74.

56. Sagan, "Why Do States Build Nuclear Weapons?" p. 66.

57. Perkovich, *India's Nuclear Bomb*, p. 152.

58. Neena Vyas, "India: BJP in Govt. to Exercise N-Option," *The Hindu*, January 14, 1998.

59. Perkovich, *India's Nuclear Bomb*, p. 412.

60. For a comprehensive history of these movements, see Lawrence S. Wittner, *The Struggle Against the Bomb*, 3 vols. (Palo Alto: Stanford University Press, 1993–2003).

61. Colin L. Powell, *My American Journey* (New York: Random House, 1995), p. 324.

62. Ibid., p. 540.

63. Ibid., p. 541.

64. Kurt M. Campbell and Tsuyoshi Sunohara, "Japan: Thinking the Unthinkable," in Campbell, Einhorn, and Reiss, *The Nuclear Tipping Point*, p. 219.

65. Ibid., p. 220.

66. Ibid., pp. 221, 229. See also Reiss, *Without the Bomb*, p. 117.

67. Ibid., p. 241. The most foreseeable changes would be to the regional security environment, including a North Korean nuclear weapons test, a Chinese nuclear arms buildup, and/or aggressive Chinese military action.

68. Cited in Richard Rhodes, *The Making of the Atomic Bomb* (New York: Simon & Schuster, 1986), p. 757.

69. Robert S. Norris, Andrew S. Burrows, and Richard W. Fieldhouse, *Nuclear Weapons Databook*, vol. 5, *British, French, and Chinese Nuclear Weapons* (Boulder, Colo.: Westview Press, 1994), p. 19. Also see chapter 1 in this book for details on the role of the British MAUD report in development of the atomic bomb.

70. General Advisory Committee to the U.S. Atomic Energy Agency, "Majority Annex to The GAC Report of October 30, 1949," available at http://www.atomicarchive.com/Docs/Hydrogen/GACReport .shtml. A number of prominent atomic scientists served on the GAC, including, J.Robert Oppenheimer (chairman), James B. Conant, Enrico Fermi, and Isidor Rabi. The report of the commission was presented to David E. Lilienthal, president of the Atomic Energy Commission, which at the time was responsible for developing and controlling nuclear weapons and energy.

71. Cited in Rhodes, *The Making of the Atomic Bomb*, pp. 751–52.

72. Cited in Bradley A. Thayer, "The Causes of Nuclear Proliferation

and the Utility of the Nuclear Nonproliferation Regime," *Security Studies* (Spring 1995): 480.

73. Cited in Bundy, *Danger and Survival* p. 211.

74. Ibid., p. 213.

75. Benjamin Frankel, "The Brooding Shadow: Systemic Incentives and Nuclear Weapons Proliferation," *Security Studies* (Spring/Summer 1993): 40.

76. Peter D. Zimmerman, "Technical Barriers to Nuclear Proliferation," *Security Studies* (Spring/Summer 1993): 348.

77. Michael May, "Nuclear Weapons Supply and Demand," *American Scientist* (November–December 1994): 530.

78. Ibid., p. 531.

79. Mohamed ElBaradei, "The Status of the Nuclear Inspections in Iraq: An Update," presentation to the United Nations Security Council, March 7, 2003, available at http://www.iaea.org/NewsCenter/Statements/2003/ebsp2003n006.shtml.

80. Ken Fireman, "Iraq Weapons Debate: CIA Report Contradicts Administration Assessment," *Newsday*, October 26, 2003.

81. See International Institute for Strategic Studies, *Iran's Strategic Weapons Programmes: A Net Assessment* (London: International Institute for Strategic Studies, 2005). See also David Albright and Corey Hinderstein, "Iran's Next Steps: Final Tests and the Construction of a Uranium Enrichment Plant," Institute for Science and International Security Issue Brief, January 12, 2006, available at http://www.isis-online.org/publications/iran/irancascade.pdf.

82. Mitchell Reiss, *Bridled Ambition: Why Countries Constrain Their Nuclear Capabilities* (Washington, D.C.: Woodrow Wilson Center Press, 1995), p. 66.

83. Reiss, *Bridled Ambition*, p. 67.

84. Jeffrey Chamberlin, "Comparisons of U.S. and Foreign Military Spending: Data from Selected Public Sources," *Congressional Research Service*, January 28, 2004, available at http://www.fas.org/man/crs/RL32209.pdf.

85. William J. Weida, "The Economic Implications of Nuclear Weapons and Nuclear Deterrence," in Stephen I. Schwartz, ed., *Atomic Audit: The Costs and Consequences of U.S. Nuclear Weapons Since 1940* (Washington, D.C.: Brookings Institution Press, 1998), p. 519.

86. Cited in Schwartz, *Atomic Audit*, p. 4.

87. Joseph Cirincione, "Lessons Lost," *Bulletin of the Atomic Scientists* (November 2005): 47. This figure is based on the 1996 estimate in Schwartz, *Atomic Audit*. It has been updated to account for nuclear weapons spending in the past ten years, and has been converted from 1996 dollars to 2006 dollars.

88. Flynt Leverett, "Why Libya Gave Up on the Bomb," *New York Times*, January 23, 2004.

89. Cirincione, Wolfsthal, and Rajkumar, *Deadly Arsenals,* p. 320.

90. Nicola Clark, "Libya Signs Energy Exploration Deal with Shell," *New York Times*, March 26, 2004.

91. Cirincione, Wolfsthal, and Rajkumar, *Deadly Arsenals*, p. 321.

92. Scott MacLeod and Amany Radwan, "10 Questions for Muammar Gaddafi," *Time*, January 30, 2005.

93. Cirincione, Wolfsthal, and Rajkumar, *Deadly Arsenals,* p. 373. See also Reiss, *Bridled Ambition*, pp. 91–92.

94. Reiss, *Bridled Ambition*, pp. 93–105.

95. Ibid., pp. 103, 110.

96. Ibid., p. 111.

97. Ibid., p. 128.

98. Leonard S. Spector with Jacqueline R. Smith. *Nuclear Ambitions* (Boulder, Colo.: Westview Press, 1990), p. 227.

99. Jan Prawitz, "From Nuclear Option to Non-Nuclear Promotion: The Sweden Case," Swedish Institute of International Affairs, Research Report 20, 1995, pp. 13–14.

100. Arjun Makhijani, Stephen I. Schwartz, and William J. Weida, "Nuclear Waste Management and Environmental Remediation," in Schwartz, *Atomic Audit,* p. 355.

101. Reiss, *Bridled Ambition*, p. 322. In 1995, he estimated U.S. environmental costs at $30 billion to $100 billion, and Soviet costs at $300 billion.

102. Sagan, "Why Do States Build Nuclear Weapons?" p. 85.

5. TODAY'S NUCLEAR WORLD

1. Jonathan Schell, *The Fate of the Earth* (Palo Alto: Stanford University Press, 2000), p. 3.

2. Calculations are based on the following deployed strategic warhead totals: 1986 combined total of 22,526 (U.S.—12,314, U.S.S.R.—10,212); 2006 combined total of 8,835 (U.S.—5,021, U.S.S.R.—3,814).

3. Linton Brooks, Richard Lugar, and Sam Nunn, "Examining Nuclear Threats Past and Present" *Talk of the Nation,* National Public Radio broadcast, recorded November 8, 2005, at the Carnegie International Non-Proliferation Conference.

4. Graham Allison, *Nuclear Terrorism: The Ultimate Preventable Catastrophe* (New York: Times Books, 2004), p. 15.

5. Brent Scowcroft, "A Critical Nuclear Moment," *Washington Post*, June 24, 2004.

6. Matthew Bunn, "The Demand for Black Market Fissile Material,"

available at http://www.nti.org/e_research/cnwm/threat/demand .asp.

7. Charles D. Ferguson and William C. Potter, *Four Faces of Nuclear Terrorism* (Monterey, Calif.: Monterey Institute for International Studies, 2004), p. 14.

8. Matthew Bunn and Anthony Wier, *Securing the Bomb 2005: The New Global Imperatives* (Cambridge and Washington, D.C.: Project on Managing the Atom, and Nuclear Threat Initiative, 2005), p. 12.

9. Jessica Stern, *The Ultimate Terrorists* (Cambridge: Harvard University Press, 1999), p. 58.

10. Paul Leventhal and Yonah Alexander, *Preventing Nuclear Terrorism* (Lexington, Mass.: Lexington Books, 1987), p. 9.

11. George W. Bush, State of the Union address, January 29, 2002, available at http://www.whitehouse.gov/news/releases/2002/01/ 20020129 –11.html.

12. "IAEA Illicit Nuclear Trafficking Facts and Figures," available at http://www.iaea.org/NewsCenter/Features/RadSources/Fact_Figures .html. It is important to note here that the database includes all incidents involving "unauthorized acquisition, provision, possession, use, transfer or disposal . . . whether intentional or not, including those that are both successful and unsuccessful."

13. Kimberly McCloud and Matthew Osborne, "WMD Terrorism and Usama bin Laden," Center for Nonproliferation Studies, Monterey Institute of International Studies (2001), available at http://cns.miis .edu/pubs/reports/binladen.htm. See also Bunn, "The Demand for Black Market Fissile Material."

14. Matthew Bunn and Anthony Wier note that only 46 percent of Russia's nuclear material has been secured through U.S.-Russian cooperative programs. However, these security measures have been completed in 75 percent of the sites that house these materials. The U.S. Defense and Energy departments are working to upgrade security at 112 of the estimated 150–210 nuclear weapons storage sites. Of these, 50–60 percent have received "quick fix" or "rapid upgrades," while only 15–20 percent have received their full set of intended security measures. See Bunn and Wier, *Securing the Bomb 2005*, pp. 32–37.

15. David Albright and Kimberly Kramer, "Global Stocks of Nuclear Explosive Materials," Institute for Science and International Security (August 2005).

16. Jack Kelley, "Terrorists Courted Nuclear Scientists," *USA Today*, November 15, 2001.

17. David Albright and Holly Higgins, "A Bomb for the Ummah," *Bulletin of the Atomic Scientists* 59, no. 2 (March/April 2003): 53.

18. Kamran Khan and Molly Moore, "2 Nuclear Experts Briefed Bin Laden, Pakistanis Say," *Washington Post*, December 16, 2001.

19. It is widely accepted that for terrorists seeking to construct a nuclear device, highly-enriched uranium is preferable to plutonium. As explained in chapter 1, there are two basic nuclear weapon designs: the gun type and the implosion type. The gun-type design is the least complex and only uses uranium. So for any terrorist group seeking an improvised nuclear device, it would be easiest to design and construct a gun-type device using highly enriched uranium. For a more detailed explanation, see Ferguson and Potter, *Four Faces of Nuclear Terrorism*, p. 131.

20. Albright and Kramer, "Global Stocks of Nuclear Explosive Materials."

21. Sam Nunn, Speech to the Carnegie International Non-Proliferation Conference, June 21, 2004, available at http://www.ProliferationNews.org.

22. Ibid.

23. Scott D. Sagan and Kenneth N. Waltz, *The Spread of Nuclear Weapons: A Debate Renewed* (New York: Norton, 2003), p. 115.

24. Michael Krepon, "From Confrontation to Cooperation," Stimson Center, 2004, available at http://www.stimson.org/southasia/pubs.cfm?ID = 197.

25. P. R. Chari, "Nuclear Restraint, Nuclear Risk Reduction, and the Security—Insecurity Paradox in South Asia," Stimson Center, January 2000, available at http://stimson.org/southasia/pdf/NRRMChari.pdf.

26. Sagan and Waltz, *The Spread of Nuclear Weapons*, p. 4.

27. William Potter, remarks during panel on "The New Look of U.S. Nonproliferation Policy," Carnegie International Non-Proliferation Conference, 2005, available at www.ProliferationNews.org.

28. John F. Kennedy, "Radio and Television Address to the American People on the Nuclear Test Ban Treaty," July 26, 1963, available at http://www.jfklibrary.org/jfk_test_ban_speech.html.

29. Richard Cheney, remarks on *Meet the Press*, NBC television broadcast, March 16, 2003.

30. For detailed discussions of the nuclear histories, capabilities, and strategic thinking of each of these states, see Kurt M. Campbell, Robert J. Einhorn, and Mitchell B. Reiss. *The Nuclear Tipping Point: Why States Reconsider their Nuclear Choices* (Washington, D.C.: Brookings Institution Press, 2004).

31. Ariel Levite, "Never Say Never Again," *International Security* 27, no. 3 (Winter 2002/03): 59–88.

32. Ibid.

33. "A More Secure World: Our Shared Responsibility," Report of the

Secretary-General's High-Level Panel on Threats, Challenges and Change, United Nations, 2004, pp. 39–40.

34. "Issues and Questions on July 18 Proposal for Nuclear Cooperation with India," letter to U.S. House of Representatives, November 18, 2005, available at http://www.armscontrol.org/pdf/20051118_India_Ltr_Congress.pdf.

35. Sagan and Waltz, *The Spread of Nuclear Weapons*, p. 17.

36. George Tenet, Testimony before Senate Select Committee on Intelligence (2003), available at http://www.caci.com/homeland_security/pres_address/tenet_2–12–03.shtml.

6. The New U.S. Policy

1. See, for example, Bruce Russett, *Grasping the Democratic Peace: Principles for a Post–Cold War World* (Princeton: Princeton University Press, 1994).

2. Immanuel Kant, *Kant's Political Writings*, ed. Hans Reiss and trans. H.B. Nisbet (Cambridge, England: Cambridge University Press 1970), p. 113, cited in Michael W. Doyle, "Liberal Internationalism: Peace, War, and Democracy," available at: http://nobelprize.org/peace/articles/doyle/.

3. Cited in Jack Snyder, "One World, Rival Theories," *Foreign Policy* (November/December 2004): 55.

4. Letter to President Bill Clinton, January 26, 1998, available at http://www.newamericancentury.org/iraqclintonletter.htm.

5. Ibid.

6. John S. Wolf, remarks to the 12th Annual International Arms Control Conference, April 19, 2002, available at www.state.gov/t/np/rls/rm/9635.htm.

7. John Bolton, "A Legacy of Betrayal," *Washington Times,* May 12, 1999.

8. Gary Schmitt, "Memorandum to Opinion Leaders," December 13, 2001, available at http://www.newamericancentury.org/defense-20011213.htm.

9. National Security Council, *National Security Strategy of the United States of America,* September 2002, available at http://www.whitehouse.gov/nsc/nss.html.

10. National Security Council, *The National Security Strategy of the United States of America,* available at http://www.whitehouse.gov/nsc/nss.pdf. National Security Council, National Strategy to Combat Weapons of Mass Destruction, p. 1, available at http://www.whitehouse.gov/news/releases/2002/12/WMDStrategy.pdf.

11. National Security Council, *National Strategy to Combat Weapons of Mass Destruction,* p. 1.

12. Thomas Donnelly, "The Top Ten Questions for the Post-9/11 World," American Enterprise Institute *National Security Outlook,* July 23, 2004.

13. President Bill Clinton, "Continuation of Emergency Regarding Weapons of Mass Destruction," November 12, 1998, White House Statement, available at http://www.fas.org/news/usa/1998/11/98111212_tlt.html.

14. National Security Council, *National Strategy to Combat Weapons of Mass Destruction.*

15. John Bolton, remarks to Chicago Council on Foreign Relations, October 19, 2004.

16. For a chronology of the network see Michael Laufer, "A. W. Khan Nuclear Chronology," Carnegie Proliferation Brief, vol. 7, no. 8, September 7, 2005, available at http://www.carnegieendowment.org/static/npp/Khan_Chronology.pdf.

17. At their February 2005 meeting in Bratislava, Slovakia, Bush and Putin emphasized the importance of protecting nuclear material. In July 2005, the two countries resolved a liability dispute that had been holding up a program to eliminate 68 tons of weapons-grade plutonium.

18. Condoleezza Rice, "Remarks on the Second Anniversary of the Proliferation Security Initiative," May 31, 2005, available at http://www.state.gov/secretary/rm/2005/46951.htm.

19. Under Secretary of State for Arms Control and International Security Robert Joseph, remarks at the Carnegie International Non-Proliferation Conference, November 7, 2005, available at http://www.carnegieendowment.org/static/npp/2005conference/2005_conference.htm.

20. "Comprehensive Report of the Special Advisor to the DCI on Iraq's WMD," September 30, 2004, available at http://www.cia.gov/cia/reports/iraq_wmd_2004/. In its key findings, the report concludes, "Saddam Husayn ended the nuclear program in 1991 following the Gulf war. ISG [Iraqi Survey Group] found no evidence to suggest concerted efforts to restart the program." On Iraq's chemical weapons program, the report states, "ISG judges that Iraq unilaterally destroyed its undeclared chemical weapons stockpile in 1991." On the biological weapons program, it concludes, "ISG judges that Baghdad abandoned its existing BW program [by late 1995] . . . ISG found no direct evidence that Iraq, after 1996, had plans for a new BW program." The report comes to the same conclusion regarding Iraq's Scud missile program: "The Iraq Survey Group (ISG) has uncovered no evidence that Iraq retained Scud-variant missiles . . . after 1991."

21. For example, see Michael A. Ledeen, "Syria and Iran Must Get

Their Turn," *National Post*, April 7, 2003. Ledeen writes, "There is no more time for diplomatic 'solutions.' The United States will have to deal with the terror masters [Iran and Syria], here and now. Iran, at least, offers Americans the possibility of a memorable victory, because the Iranian people openly loath the regime, and will enthusiastically combat it, if only the United States supports them in their just struggle. . . . It's time to bring down the other terror masters." See also R. James Woolsey and Thomas G. McInerney, "The Next Korean War: Using the Military is an Option. Here's How It Can Be Done," *Wall Street Journal*, August 4, 2003. Woolsey and McInerney write, "We must be prepared to win a war, not execute a strike. U.S. and South Korean forces have spent nearly half a century preparing to fight and win such a war."

22. Between October 2002 and March 2003, the UN Monitoring Verification and Inspections Commission (UNMOVIC) found a few old cluster bombs capable of holding chemical weapons and several 155-mm shells containing mustard gas produced over fifteen years earlier. UNMOVIC also supervised the destruction of several dozen al-Samoud II ballistic missiles, which exceeded the allowed range by 30 kilometers.

23. Hans Blix, former executive director of UNMOVIC, told an international nonproliferation conference in June 2004, "A continuation of the inspections, as desired by the majority of members of the Security Council, would have allowed visits to all sites suspected by national intelligence agencies and would have yielded no weapons of mass destruction because there were none. The intelligence agencies, I trust, would have been more impressed with these results than with the information they had, in many cases from defectors who were interested not in inspection, but in invasion." Statement available at http://www.ceip.org/files/projects/npp/resources/2004conference/speeches/blix.htm. In a March 2003 report to the UN Security Council, IAEA Director-General Mohamed ElBaradei came to an equally strong conclusion about the lack of an Iraqi nuclear weapons program: "the IAEA has found to date no evidence or plausible indication of the revival of a nuclear weapons programme in Iraq. . . . The IAEA's detailed knowledge of Iraqi capabilities . . . should enable us, barring exceptional circumstances, within a few months, to provide the Security Council with an objective and through assessment of whether Iraq has revived or attempted to revive its nuclear weapons programme." Statement available at http://www.iaea.org/NewsCenter/Focus/IaeaIraq/wp_res1284.shtml.

24. Zbigniew Brzezinski, "George Bush's Suicidal Statecraft" *International Herald Tribune*, October 13, 2005.

25. Porter J. Goss, "DCI's Global Intelligence Challenges Briefing," Testimony before the Senate Select Committee on Intelligence, February 16, 2005. See also Vice Admiral Lowell E. Jacoby, "Current and Projected National Security Threats to the United States," Testimony before the Senate Select Committee on Intelligence, February 16, 2005.

26. In 2002, the number of "significant" international terrorist incidents was 136; in 2003 it was 175; in 2004, it was 651. See U.S. Department of State, "Patterns of Global Terrorism 2002" and "Patterns of Global Terrorism 2003," available at http://www.state.gov/s/ct/rls/pgtrpt/. See also National Counterterrorism Center, "A Chronology of Significant International Terrorism for 2004," available at http://www.tkb.org/documents/Downloads/NCTC_Report.pdf.

27. Matthew Bunn and Anthony Wier, *Securing the Bomb 2005: The New Global Imperatives* (Cambridge and Washington, D.C.: Harvard University and Nuclear Threat Initiative, May 2005), pp. 30–32. See also "NNSA Expands Nuclear Security Cooperation with Russia," National Nuclear Security Administration Fact Sheet, October 2005, available at http://www.nnsa.doe.gov/docs/factsheets/2005/NA-05-FS03.pdf.

28. "Officials Fear New Terrorist Attacks," Associated Press, February 17, 2005.

29. Brazil, Iran, and South Korea have all announced their intentions to enrich their own uranium. In January 2006, Ukraine likewise expressed interest in domestic uranium enrichment.

30. Presidents Bush and Putin signed the Strategic Offensive Reductions Treaty (SORT) in June 2002. Now, for the first time since the negotiated threat reduction process began with SALT in the early 1970s, there are no plans for additional agreements. Under SORT, both sides are required to reduce their deployed strategic nuclear weapons to between 1,700 and 2,200 by the end of 2012. Under the proposed START III agreement, negotiated by Presidents Clinton and Yeltsin in 1997, each side would have drawn down to similar numbers of deployed strategic nuclear weapons by 2007, five years earlier than envisioned under SORT. START III would also have provided a framework for discussions on reductions in tactical nuclear weapons and dismantlement of warheads. See Joseph Cirincione, Jon Wolfsthal, and Miriam Rajkumar, *Deadly Arsenals: Nuclear, Biological, and Chemical Threats* (Washington, D.C.: Carnegie Endowment for International Peace, 2005), pp. 204–5, 209–11.

31. In September 2004, former Pentagon director of operational test and evaluation, Philip Coyle, told a Washington audience, "The [anti-missile] system being deployed [in Alaska] has no demon-

strated capability against a real attack and is missing most of its major elements." Philip Coyle, "The Problems and Prospects of the New Alaska Missile Interceptor Site: Ten Fallacies About Missile Defense," available at http://www.cdi.org/program/document.cfm ?DocumentID=2484&StartRow=1&ListRows=10&appendURL =&Orderby=D.DateLastUpdated&ProgramID=6&from_ page=index.cfm. In April 2005, a group of twenty-two physicists, including nine Nobel laureates, came to an identical conclusion in a letter to Senator John Warner (R-Va.): "The GMD [Ground-Based Midcourse Defense] system has no demonstrated capability to defense against a real attack, even from a single warhead unaccompanied by countermeasures." The letter is available at http://www .ucsusa.org/global_security/missile_defense/scientists-letter-to -john-w-warner-on-missile-defense.html.

32. Robert L. Gallucci, "The Proposed U.S.-India Nuclear Deal," Testimony before the Senate Foreign Relations Committee, April 26, 2006, hearing on "U.S.-India Atomic Energy Cooperation: Strategic and Nonproliferation Implications."

33. Richard N. Haass, "Regime Change and Its Limits," *Foreign Affairs* (July/August 2005): 70.

34. John M. Spratt, "Stopping a Dangerous Drift in U.S. Arms Control Policy," *Arms Control Today* 33, no. 2 (March 2003).

35. John Wolf, "Addressing Today's Nuclear Nonproliferation Challenges: Iran, North Korea, and the U.S.-India Nuclear Deal," Arms Control Association Press Briefing, September 16, 2005, available at http://www.armscontrol.org/events/20050916 _NuclearNonproliferation.asp.

36. Ibid.

37. Mohamed ElBaradei, "Reflection on Nuclear Challenges Today," lecture to the International Institute for Strategic Studies, London, December 6, 2005, available at http://www.iaea.org/NewsCenter/ Statements/2005/ebsp2005n019.html.

38. Council of the European Union, EU Strategy Against Proliferation of Weapons of Mass Destruction, Brussels, December 10, 2003, p. 6.

7. THE GOOD NEWS ABOUT PROLIFERATION

1. William Clinton, remarks at the 52nd Session of the United Nations General Assembly, New York, September 22, 1997, available at http://clinton4.nara.gov/WH/New/html/19970922–20823.html.

2. In 1987 the Soviet Union deployed 2,380 long-range missiles and China approximately 20. The number declined to 797 by 2006 (777 Russian; 20 Chinese).

3. See Joseph Cirincione, "The Declining Ballistic Missile Threat," *Policy Outlook*, Carnegie Endowment for International Peace, February 2005, available at http://www.carnegieendowment.org/pdf/ The_Declining_Ballistic_Missile_Threat_2005.pdf.

4. See Joseph Cirincione, Jon B. Wolfsthal, Miriam Rajkumar, *Deadly Arsenals: Nuclear, Biological and Chemical Threats* (Washington, D.C.: Carnegie Endowment for International Peace, 2005), pp. 57–82.

5. Ibid.

6. Nina Tannenwald, "The Nuclear Taboo and the Nuclear Nonproliferation Regime," Remarks at Carnegie International Non-Proliferation Conference, Washington, D.C. November 7, 2005, available at http://www.carnegieendowment.org/static/npp/2005conference/ presentations/tannenwald_remarks.pdf.

7. David Hobson, "U.S. Nuclear Security in the 21st Century," Arms Control Association Luncheon Address, Washington, D.C., February 2005, available at http://www.armscontrol.org/ events/20050203_transcript_hobson.asp.

8. Ivan Oelrich, "Missions for Nuclear Weapons after the Cold War," *Occasional Paper No. 3*, Federation of American Scientists (December 2004): 3.

9. Ibid., p. 41.

10. These comments were made as part of a panel aired by National Public Radio show, *Talk of the Nation,* on November 8, 2005 from the Carnegie International Non-Proliferation Conference. The audio is available at: http://www.carnegieendowment.org/static/npp/ 2005conference/2005_conference.htm.

11. Ibid.

12. See for example, Lawrence J. Korb, Caroline P. Wadhams, and Andrew J. Grotto, *Restoring American Military Power: A Progressive Quadrennial Defense Review,* January 2006, available at www .centerforamericanprogress.org. See also Sidney D. Drell and James E. Goodby, *What Are Nuclear Weapons For? Recommendations for Restructuring U.S. Strategic Nuclear Forces*, April 2005, available at http://www.armscontrol.org/pdf/USNW_2005_Drell-Goodby.pdf.

13. Frank Miller, remarks at the Carnegie International Non-Proliferation Conference, November 8, 2004, available at http:// www.carnegieendowment.org/static/npp/2005conference/2005 _conference.htm.

14. John Barry, Evan Thomas and Sharon Squassoni, "Dropping the Bomb," *Newsweek*, June 25, 2001, p. 28.

15. Director of Central intelligence, National Intelligence Estimate Number 4–3–61, "Nuclear Weapons and Delivery Capabilities of

Free World Countries Other Than the US and UK," September 21, 1961, p. 5.

16. Ibid., p. 6.

17. Janne E. Nolan, "Parsing the Nuclear Posture Review: An ACA Panel Discussion," March 2002, available at http://www.armscontrol.org/act/2002_03/panelmarch02.asp.

18. Janne E. Nolan, "Preparing for the 2001 Nuclear Posture Review," Arms Control Today, November 2000, available at http://www.armscontrol.org/act/2000_11/Nolan.asp. For a detailed treatment of the 1994 review, see also Janne Nolan, An Elusive Consensus: Nuclear Weapons and American Security after the Cold War (Washington, D.C.: Brookings Institution Press, 1999).

19. For an example of how this dynamic played out, see Joseph Cirincione, "Why the Right Lost the Missile Defense Debate," Foreign Policy (Spring 1997).

20. Frances FitzGerald, Way Out There in the Blue (New York: Simon & Schuster, 2000), p. 97.

21. For a detailed treatment, see Joseph Cirincione, "A Deeply Flawed Review," Testimony before the Senate Foreign Relations Committee, May 16, 2002, available at http://www.carnegieendowment.org/publications/index.cfm?fa=view&id=988&prog=zgp&proj=znpp.

22. Excerpts from the Nuclear Posture Review are available at http://www.globalsecurity.org/wmd/library/policy/dod/npr.htm.

23. "Chirac Backs Nuclear Force to Counter 'Terrorist' Use of WMD," Bloomberg News, January 19, 2006, available at http://www.bloomberg.com/apps/news?pid=10000085&sid=aBRhHUIymKis&refer=europe.

24. George Perkovich, Jessica Mathews, Joseph Cirincione, Rose Gottemoeller and Jon Wolfsthal, Universal Compliance: A Strategy for Nuclear Security (Washington, D.C.: Carnegie Endowment for International Peace, 2005). Available for download at http://www.CarnegieEndowment.org/strategy.

25. Ibid., p. 33.

26. Jessica T. Mathews, presentation at launch of Universal Compliance, March 3, 2005, available at http://www.carnegieendowment.org/files/UC-transcript1.pdf.

27. Robert Kagan, Of Paradise and Power: America and Europe in the New World Order (New York: Knopf, 2003), p. 154.

28. Special Address by Tony Blair at the Opening Plenary of the World Economic Forum, Davos, Switzerland, January 26, 2005, available at http://www.weforum.org/en/knowledge/KN_SESS_SUMM_13143.

29. "Diplomacy's Fleeting Moment in Korea," *New York Times*, January 3, 2006, p. A18.

8. NUCLEAR SOLUTIONS

1. For an excellent discussion of why nuclear terrorism is unlikely, see Robin M. Frost, "Nuclear Terrorism After 9/11," Adelphi Paper 378, International Institute for Strategic Studies (London: December, 2005).

2. Sam Nunn, "The Day After an Attack, What Would We Wish We Had Done? Why Aren't We Doing It Now?" Testimony by Sam Nunn, co-chairman, Nuclear Threat Initiative, before the 9/11 Public Discourse Project, June 27, 2005, available at http://www.nti.org/c_press/testimony_nunn911commission_062705.pdf.

3. David Ruppe, "Republican Lawmaker Slams Bush Nuclear Plans," *Global Security Newswire*, February 4, 2005, available at http://www.nti.org/d_newswire/issues/2005_2_4.html#88A200EA.

4. Kai Bird and Martin Sherwin, *American Prometheus: The Triumph and Tragedy of J. Robert Oppenheimer* (New York: Knopf, 2005), p. 349.

5. These recommendations are elaborated in George Perkovich Jessica Mathews, Joseph Cirincione, Rose Gottemoeller, and Jon Wolfsthal, *Universal Compliance: A Strategy for Nuclear Security* (Washington, D.C.: Carnegie Endowment for International Peace, 2005), pp. 83–125.

6. Sam Nunn, remarks to the Carnegie International Non-Proliferation Conference, November 14, 2002.

7. Matthew Bunn and Anthony Wier, *Securing the Bomb 2005: The New Global Imperatives*, (Cambridge and Washington, D.C.: Harvard University and Nuclear Threat Initiative, 2005), p. 9.

8. Bunn and Wier, *Securing the Bomb 2005*, pp. 30–33.

9. "Kazakhstan: Project Sapphire," Nuclear Threat Initiative, available at http://www.nti.org/db/nisprofs/kazakst/fissmat/sapphire.htm.

10. Ashton B. Carter and William J. Perry, *Preventive Defense: A New Security Strategy for America* (Washington, D.C.: Brookings Institution Press, 1999), p. 65.

11. Ibid., pp. 66–67.

12. James Dao, "Nuclear Material Secretly Flown From Serbia To Russia for Safety," *New York Times*, August 23, 2002.

13. C. J. Chivers, "Prague Ships Its Nuclear-Bomb Fuel to Russian Storage." *New York Times,* September 28, 2005.

14. "Acceleration of Removal or Security of Fissile Materials, Radiological Materials, and Related Equipment at Vulnerable Sites Worldwide," Interim Report, Unclassified Summary, National Nuclear Security Administration (NNSA, 2005).

15. "Highly Enriched Uranium Transferred to Russia from Czech Republic" U.S. Department of State, September 27 2005.

16. Interim Report, Unclassified Summary, NNSA (2005).

17. The Baker-Cutler report of 2001 recommended that funding for nuclear threat reduction programs in Russia should be tripled in order to meet materials security goals. See Appendix A of Howard Baker and Lloyd Cutler, "A Report Card on the Department of Energy's Nonproliferation Programs with Russia," U.S. Department of Energy Russia Task Force, January 10, 2001, available at http://www.stimson.org/ctr/pdf/BakerCutlerReport2001.pdf.

18. "Opening Remarks of Thomas H. Kean and Lee H. Hamilton, Chair and Vice Chair of the 9/11 Public Discourse Project," November 14, 2005, available at http://www.9-11pdp.org/press/2005-11-14_remarks.pdf.

19. See Graham Allison, *The Ultimate Preventable Catastrophe* (New York: Times Books, 2004).

20. Ashton B. Carter, "Worst People and Worst Weapons," Statement before the 9/11 Public Discourse Project's Hearings on "The 9/11 Commission Report: The Unfinished Agenda," June 27, 2005, available at http://bcsia.ksg.harvard.edu/BCSIA_content/documents/Testimony9-11Commission-6-27-05.pdf.

21. John Deutch, Arnold Kanter, Ernest Moniz, and Daniel Poneman, "Making the World Safe for Nuclear Energy," *Survival* 46, no. 4 (Winter 2004–2005): 69.

22. George W. Bush, "Remarks by the President on Weapons of Mass Destruction Proliferation," February 11, 2004, available at http://www.whitehouse.gov/news/releases/2004/02/20040211-4.html.

23. Mohamed ElBaradei, "Towards a Safer World," *Economist*, October 16, 2003, available at http://www.iaea.org/NewsCenter/Statements/2003/ebTE20031016.shtml.

24. "Multilateral Approaches to the Nuclear Fuel Cycle: Expert Group Report submitted to the Director General of the International Atomic Energy Agency," International Atomic Energy Agency, INFCIRC/640, February 22, 2005.

25. "Putin Proposes Access to Nuclear Energy for All Countries," RIA Novosti, January 25, 2006.

26. "Russia's Nuclear Centre Proposal Solves Global Security Problems," ITAR-TASS, January 25, 2005.

27. Deutch et al., "Making the World Safe for Nuclear Energy," p. 68.

28. Deutch et al., "Making the World Safe for Nuclear Energy," p. 68

29. "Wolfowitz Comments Revive Doubts Over Iraq's WMD," Associated Press, May 30, 2003.

30. Perkovich et al., *Universal Compliance*, pp. 94, 97.

31. Henry Sokolski and Patrick Clawson, eds., *Getting Ready for a*

Nuclear-Ready Iran (Carlisle, Pa.: U.S. Army War College Strategic Studies Institute, 2005), pp. 16–17.

32. Uranium hexafluoride is fed into centrifuges for enrichment, but this compound is too volatile to ship. The uranium, however, could be converted to uranium tetraflouride (on step down in the conversion process) and shipped. This is an expensive, inelegant, but possibly politically acceptable solution.

33. Perkovich et al., *Universal Compliance,* p. 39.

34. See for example, the excellent suggestions made by Sally Horn, a State Department representative to the NPT Review Conference in May 2005, summarized in Joseph Cirincione, "No Easy Out," Carnegie Analysis, May 24, 2005, available at http://www.ProliferationNews.org.

35. J. Robert Oppenheimer, "The International Control of Atomic Energy," *Bulletin of the Atomic Scientists* (June 1946).

36. Andrew Mack, "Peace on Earth? Increasingly, Yes," *Washington Post* December 28, 2005, p. A21.

37. Ibid.

38. Kurt M. Campbell, Robert Einhorn, and Mitchell Reiss, eds., *The Nuclear Tipping Point: Global Prospects for Revisiting Nuclear Renunciation* (Washington, D.C.: Brookings Institution Press, 2004), cited in Universal Compliance, p. 130.

AFTERWORD: THE SHAPE OF THINGS TO COME

1. "Suicide Bomb Hits Pakistani Bus," *BBC News*, November 1, 2007, available at http://news.bbc.co.uk/2/hi/south_asia/7072428.stm.

2. Bill Roggio, "Suicide Attack at Pakistani Nuclear Weapons Complex," *Long War Journal*, December 10, 2007.

3. Mikhail Gorbachev, "The Nuclear Threat," *Wall Street Journal*, January 31, 2007.

4. Joby Warrick and Walter Pincus, "The Saga of a Bent Spear: Six Nuclear Missiles Were Flown Across America," *Washington Post*, September 23, 2007, p. A1.

5. Robert Norris and Hans M. Kristensen, "U.S. Nuclear Forces, 2008," NDRC Nuclear Notebook, *The Bulleting of the Atomic Scientists,* March/April 2008.

6. Ibid.

7. Warren Strobel, "Cheney at Center of Struggle to Manage N. Korea Talks," Knight-Ridder News Service, December 20, 2003.

8. Blaine Harden, "N. Korea Misses Deadline, but U.S. Response Is Restrained," *Washington Post*, January 1, 2008, p. A7.

9. Glenn Kessler, "Conservatives Assail North Korea Accord: Deal Could Get Nation off Terrorism List," *Washington Post*, February 15, 2007, p. A1.

10. "Agreeing to the Same Framework," *National Review*, February 14, 2007.

11. "Faith-Based Nonproliferation: We'll Believe It When Kim Jong Il Hands Over His Plutonium," *Wall Street Journal*, February 14, 2007.

12. See for example, interview with John Bolton, "Is North Korea Giving Up Nuclear Weapons?" *CNN.com*, February 12, 2007, available at http://transcripts.cnn.com/TRANSCRIPTS/0702/12/sitroom.03 .html; Joshua Muravchik, "Bomb Iran: Diplomacy Is Doing Nothing to Stop the Iranian Nuclear Threat; a Show of Force Is the Only Answer," *Los Angeles Times*, November 19, 2006; William Kristol, "It's Our War: Bush Should Go to Jerusalem—and the U.S. Should Confront Iran," Weekly Standard, July 24, 2006; and Karen De-Young, "U.S. Keeps Pressure on Iran But Decreases Saber Rattling," *Washington Post*, February 11, 2007, p. A18.

13. Harden, "N. Korea Misses Deadline," p. A7.

14. President Bush went beyond the intelligence findings at a news conference in November 2002, claiming that "contrary to an agreement they had with the United States, they're enriching uranium, with the desire of developing a weapon." (quoted in Glenn Kessler, "U.S. Softens Its Claim North Korea Is Enriching Uranium: Some Experts Say Data That Led to Crisis Are Possibly Mistaken," *Washington Post*, March 1, 2007).

15. Joseph DeTrani, testimony before Senate Armed Services Committee, *Hearing on Current and Future Worldwide Threats to the National Security of the United States*, 110th Cong., 1st sess., February 27, 2007.

16. Joseph Cirincione, "We Got Tubed—Again," *Foreign Policy*, March 2007, available at http://www.americanprogress.org/issues/2007/ 03/we_got_tubed.html.

17. George W. Bush, press conference, October 17, 2007, available at http://www.whitehouse.gov/news/releases/2007/10/20071017 .html.

18. National Intelligence Estimate, "Iran: Nuclear Intentions and Capabilities," November 2007, p. 6.

19. Joseph Cirincione, "Controlling Iran's Nuclear Program," *Issues in Science and Technology*, Spring 2006, p. 80.

20. Joseph Cirincione, "The Clock's Ticking: Stopping Iran Before It's Too Late," *Arms Control Today*, November 2006, pp. 18–19.

21. Norman Podhoretz, "The Case for Bombing Iran," *Commentary*, June 2007.

22. Charles Krauthammer, "The Tehran Calculus," *Washington Post*, September 15, 2006.

23. Interview with Deborah Solomon, "The Diplomat," *New York Times Magazine*, November 4, 2007.

24. National Intelligence Estimate, "Iran," p. 8.

25. Joseph Cirincione and Andrew Grotto, "Contain and Engage: A New Strategy for Resolving the Nuclear Crisis with Iran," Center for American Progress, March 2007, p. 26.

26. Ibid., p. 5.

27. Robert Kagan, "Time to Talk to Iran," *Washington Post*, December 5, 2007, p. A21.

28. "Looking at America," *New York Times*, December 31, 2007, p. A17.

29. Moisés Naim, "A Hunger for America," *Washington Post*, January 2, 2008, p. A13.

30. George Perkovich, with Deepti Choubey, Rose Gottemoeller, Jessica T. Mathews, and Sharon Squassoni, "2007 Report Card on Progress," Carnegie Endowment for International Peace, June 2007, p. 5.

31. Laurent Pirot, "French Offer Saudi Nuclear Energy Help," *Los Angeles Times*, January 13, 2008.

32. "French Energy Companies Bag Big Contracts on Sarkozy Trip to Gulf," *Forbes.com*, January 15, 2008, available at http://www.forbes.com/markets/feeds/afx/2008/01/15/afx4531188.html.

33. Ercan Yavuz, "Spent Fuel from Turkey's Future Plants Becoming Hot Commodity," *Today's Zaman*, January 15, 2008; Erdal Saglam, "Ambitious Nuke Plans Revealed," *Turkish Daily News*, January 15, 2008.

34. John McCain, "An Enduring Peace Built on Freedom," *Foreign Affairs* 86, no. 6 (November/December 2007): 31.

35. Hillary Rodham Clinton, "Security and Opportunity for the Twenty-first Century," *Foreign Affairs* 86, no. 6 (November/December 2007): 12–13.

36. The winning argument was that no hearings had been held on the CTBT since 1999, therefore it was impossible to declare that there was a "sense of the Senate" in favor of ratification.

37. Quoted in Jeffrey Laurenti and Carl Robichaud, eds., *Breaking the Nuclear Impasse: New Prospects for Security Against Weapons Threats* (New York: Century Foundation, 2007), p. 9.

38. National Security Advisory Group, "Reducing Nuclear Threats and Preventing Nuclear Terrorism," October 19, 2007, available at http://www.cnas.org/en/cev/?13.

39. Margaret Beckett, Secretary of State for Foreign and Commonwealth Affairs, United Kingdom, remarks at Carnegie International Nonproliferation Conference, June 25, 2007, available at http://www.ProliferationNews.org.

40. Prime Minister Gordon Brown, "Speech at the Chamber of Commerce in Delhi," New Delhi, India, January 21, 2008, available at http://www.number10.gov.uk/output/Page14323.asp.

GLOSSARY

ADVISORY COMMITTEE ON URANIUM Committee established in October 1939 to report to President Franklin Roosevelt on the status of uranium research and make recommendations on the role of the federal government. The committee recognized the explosive potential of nuclear chain reactions and recommended that research funding be increased.

ANTI-BALLISTIC MISSILE SYSTEMS Weapons designed to intercept ballistic missiles, most commonly in midcourse or final reentry phases of their flight. Existing systems are all designed to hit the missile warhead, whether directly or with a spray of pellets, though research continues on possible laser weapons.

ATOMIC BOMB A bomb whose explosive power is generated from the fission of uranium or plutonium.

ATOMIC ENERGY COMMISSION (AEC) Agency established under the Atomic Energy Act of 1946 to regulate and develop the U.S. atomic energy program.

BALLISTIC MISSILE A missile that is propelled upward with a rocket engine in an initial boost phase, after which the engine stops and gravity controls the remaining trajectory as it arcs back to earth.

BIOLOGICAL AND TOXIN WEAPONS CONVENTION (BTWC) Entered into force in March 1975, the BTWC bans the development, production, and stockpiling of any biological agent that has no peaceful use, as well as any weapons or equipment designed to deliver such agents. As of June 2006, 155 of the 171 signatories have ratified the treaty.

CANDU (Canadian deuterium-uranium reactor) A Canadian-designed reactor that uses heavy water as a moderator/coolant and natural uranium for fuel.

CENTRIFUGE A tall, narrow metallic casing with a fast-spinning rotor on the inside. Centrifuges linked together in a cascade are used to enrich uranium. See also GAS CENTRIFUGE ENRICHMENT.

CHAIN REACTION The repetitive process in which neutrons released from an initial fission reaction go on to split other atoms, releasing more neutrons that then trigger more fission reactions and so on. Nuclear weapons have explosive releases of energy because the chain reaction is extremely rapid. Nuclear reactors, on the other hand, control the speed of the chain reaction in order to produce heat (in a power reactor) or large quantities of neutrons (in a research or production reactor).

CHEMICAL WEAPONS CONVENTION (CWC) Bans the development, production, and use of chemical weapons and aims to destroy all chemical weapon stockpiles. The CWC entered into force in April 1997. As of October 2006, there are 180 state parties to the convention.

COMPREHENSIVE TEST-BAN TREATY (CTBT) A treaty banning all nuclear explosions. Opened for signature in September 1996, the treaty will not enter into force until all 44 states listed in Annex 2 of the treaty complete ratification. As of May 2006, 176 states have signed the treaty and 132 have ratified it. However, 10 of the 44 Annex 2 states have not ratified the CTBT, including the United States.

COOPERATIVE THREAT REDUCTION (CTR) A U.S. Department of Defense program started in 1991 to dismantle, secure, or destroy nuclear weapons, their delivery systems, and chemical weapons stockpiles in Russia, Ukraine, Belarus, and Kazakhstan.

CORE The center of a nuclear weapon containing the highly enriched uranium or plutonium. Also, the core can refer to the central area of a nuclear reactor with the fuel elements.

CRITICAL MASS The minimum mass of fissile material needed to sustain a chain reaction. The exact amount varies according to the physical and chemical properties of the material.

CRUISE MISSILE A guided, unmanned device that uses aerodynamic lift to deliver a payload to a target. Cruise missiles are self-propelled and can include some unmanned air vehicles (UAVs).

CUBAN MISSILE CRISIS A confrontation between the United States and the Soviet Union in October 1962. The United States discovered that the Soviets were building nuclear missile installations on Cuba. Tensions eased after thirteen days, when the Soviets agreed to dismantle the installations.

DETERRENCE Nuclear deterrence is the notion that one state must build up a credible and reliable retaliatory nuclear force to deter an enemy state from any preemptive nuclear strike.

ELECTROMAGNETIC SEPARATION A technique to enrich uranium involving the movement of uranium ions through a strong magnetic field. The uranium-238 ions move in a slightly different curve from the uranium-235 ions, thus enabling the two ions to be separated.

ENRICHMENT Refers to uranium enrichment—a process of increasing the concentration of fissionable uranium-235 isotopes in relation to nonfissionable uranium-238.

FAT MAN The implosion-type nuclear weapon with a plutonium core dropped on Nagasaki, Japan, on August 9, 1945. The second nuclear weapon ever used in combat, Fat Man had an explosive yield of about 20 kilotons of TNT.

FISSILE MATERIAL A more restrictive subset of fissionable material, fissile materials include atoms that can be split both by slow neutrons and fast neutrons (thus fissile materials can more easily and consistently sustain a chain reaction). Uranium-235 and plutonium-239 are both fissile materials.

FISSION The splitting of a nucleus by a neutron. The fission of a nucleus releases several neutrons, heat, and radiation.

FISSIONABLE MATERIAL Any material whose atoms can fission. Includes all fissile materials, but also materials that can be split by fast neutrons, such as uranium-238.

FUSION The merging of two lighter nuclei to form a single, heavier nucleus. Fusion of light elements releases an incredible amount of energy.

GAS-CENTRIFUGE PROCESS A method of uranium enrichment in which heavier isotopes are separated from lighter ones through centrifugal force.

GASEOUS DIFFUSION A method of uranium enrichment that separates uranium-235 and uranium-238 by taking advantage of their slight differences in mass and thus their rates of diffusion through a porous barrier.

HAIR-TRIGGER ALERT Alert level at which nuclear weapons can be launched within fifteen minutes.

HEAVY WATER Refers to water molecules that have two heavy hydrogen atoms, known as deuterium (one proton and one neutron), in place of the two hydrogen atoms (just one proton). Heavy water is used in reactors to slow down neutrons without absorbing them, allowing for a controlled, sustained chain reaction.

HEAVY-WATER REACTOR A reactor that uses heavy water to slow down the neutrons and control the chain reaction. Also see CANDU.

HIGHLY ENRICHED URANIUM (HEU) Uranium in which the percentage of uranium-235 nuclei is greater than 20 percent. Weapons-grade uranium is enriched to greater than 90 percent. Natural uranium has only 0.7 percent uranium-235 nuclei. Highly enriched uranium is one of only two materials used for the cores of nuclear weapons, along with plutonium.

HYDROGEN BOMB A nuclear weapon many times more powerful than the atomic bomb and which generates explosive energy from nuclear fusion.

INTERNATIONAL ATOMIC ENERGY AGENCY (IAEA) An institution created by the United Nations to further nuclear safety and security, science and technology, and safeguards and verification.

ISOTOPE Isotopes are forms of an element that have the same atomic number (number of protons) but have different numbers of neutrons, giving each isotope a different atomic weight. Radioactive elements can have fissile and nonfissile isotopes.

KILOGRAM (kg) One kilogram is equivalent to 2.2 pounds.

KILOTON (kt) A nuclear explosion of 1 kiloton is equal to an explosion of 1,000 metric tons of TNT.

LASER ENRICHMENT METHOD A method of enriching uranium by which a laser is tuned to ionize uranium-235 atoms (in this case giving them a positive charge) without affecting other atoms. These positively charged atoms are attracted to a negatively charged plate and separated. This process has yet to be applied commercially.

LIGHT WATER NORMAL WATER (two hydrogen atoms and one oxygen atom). See also HEAVY WATER.

LIGHT-WATER REACTOR A reactor that uses normal water to control the reactor temperature and the speed of the chain reaction. Light-water reactors use low enriched uranium as fuel.

LIMITED TEST BAN TREATY (LTBT) Entered into force in October 1963, the LTBT banned any nuclear test explosions in the atmosphere, in outer space, or underwater. The treaty has 108 signatories, 94 of which have ratified it. Only 23 have acceded to the treaty.

LITTLE BOY The gun-type nuclear weapon using highly enriched uranium dropped on Hiroshima, Japan, on August 6, 1945. The first nuclear weapon ever used in combat, Little Boy had an explosive yield of about 13 kilotons of TNT.

LOW ENRICHED URANIUM (LEU) Uranium in which the percentage of uranium-235 nuclei is less than 20 percent. Low enriched uranium is usually between 2 and 6 percent and is used as fuel in light-water reactors. Natural uranium has only 0.7 percent uranium-235 nuclei.

MANHATTAN PROJECT Top-secret U.S. project initiated in 1942 to build an atomic bomb. General Leslie Groves directed the project, which had facilities in Chicago, Illinois; Hanford, Washington; Oak Ridge, Tennessee; and Los Alamos, New Mexico. J. Robert Oppenheimer directed research at Los Alamos. The effort concluded with the first ever nuclear device, known as Trinity, which was tested in the New Mexico desert on July 16, 1945.

MEGAWATT (MW) A measure of power equal to 1 million watts. When describing a nuclear power plant: 1 million watts of electricity (MWe); when describing a research or production reactor: 1 million watts of thermal energy (MWt).

METRIC TON One metric ton is equal to 1,000 kilograms—equivalent to 2,200 pounds or 1.1 tons.

MILLING A process in which natural uranium ore is crushed into powder and then leached to concentrate the uranium oxide (U_3O_8) to around 80 percent. See also YELLOW-CAKE.

MISSILE TECHNOLOGY CONTROL REGIME (MTCR) Established in 1987, the MTCR is a voluntary association of thirty-four countries that seeks to limit, through export controls, the proliferation of missiles, rocket systems, unmanned air vehicles, and related technology.

MULTIPLE INDEPENDENTLY TARGETABLE REENTRY VEHICLE (MIRV) Refers to land- or sea-based ballistic missiles carrying multiple warheads that, upon reentry, can independently maneuver and strike separate targets. For example, the U.S. MX missile carried ten warheads.

NATIONAL INTELLIGENCE ESTIMATE (NIE) An authoritative report, coordinated with all U.S. intelligence agencies, on a specific national security issue, usually forecasting future events and implications.

NEUTRON An uncharged particle found in atomic nuclei. Neutrons have a slightly greater mass than protons do.

NON-PROLIFERATION TREATY (NPT) Entered into force in 1970, the NPT is intended to prevent the proliferation of nuclear weapons and weapons technology, promote peaceful nuclear energy cooperation, and move toward disarmament. As of March 2005, 188 states adhered to the treaty. North Korea withdrew from the treaty in January 2003. India, Pakistan, and Israel are the only countries never to have signed the NPT.

NUCLEAR ENERGY The energy released by nuclear reactions (fission or fusion) or by spontaneous radioactivity.

NUCLEAR FUEL Any material used to generate nuclear energy. Natural uranium and low enriched uranium are the most commonly used fuels. Some reactors use highly enriched uranium or plutonium.

NUCLEAR FUEL CYCLE A series of steps that processes uranium ore into usable nuclear fuel. The back end of the fuel cycle includes the disposition or recycling of spent nuclear material after its use in a reactor.

NUCLEAR FUEL-FABRICATION PLANT A facility where natural or enriched uranium is manufactured into fuel rods that are used in reactors.

NUCLEAR REACTOR A facility where fissionable material is used to generate heat through a controlled chain reaction. The heat is then used to generate electricity, usually by powering a turbine. Reactors produce plutonium as a by-product and thus can be used to as a source for fissile material for nuclear weapons.

NUCLEAR SUPPLIERS GROUP (NSG) Created in 1974 after India's peaceful nuclear test, the NSG is a group of forty-five nuclear supplier states that aims to control the spread of nuclear and nuclear-related (dual-use items) technology through strong national export control laws.

NUCLEAR WEAPONS Weapons whose explosive energy comes from a nuclear reaction, including both atomic (fission) bombs and hydrogen (fusion) bombs.

PLUTONIUM–239 A fissile isotope of plutonium manufactured in nuclear reactors as uranium-238 is bombarded with neutrons and undergoes radioactive decay. Plutonium-239 is one of only two materials used for the cores of nuclear weapons, along with highly enriched uranium.

POTSDAM CONFERENCE Meeting between U.S., British, and Soviet leaders from July 17 to August 2, 1945, on various subjects including postwar plans for Europe. Also, the leaders of the United States, United Kingdom, and China issued the Potsdam Declaration, calling for the unconditional surrender of Japan.

POWER REACTOR A nuclear reactor built to produce electricity. Other reactors are used for research purposes or for producing plutonium.

PROTON A positively charged particle found in atomic nuclei. Protons have slightly less mass than neutrons do.

RADIOACTIVITY The spontaneous emission of energy from an unstable atomic nucleus.

REPROCESSING The process through which the uranium and plutonium in spent reactor fuel are chemically separated from unwanted by-products.

RESEARCH REACTOR A nuclear reactor designed to provide neutrons for experiments and material testing. Research reactors can also be used for the production of medical isotopes.

STRATEGIC In the context of this book, *strategic* refers to deployed, long-range nuclear capable missiles and aircraft that act as nuclear deterrence against one's enemy.

STRATEGIC ARMS LIMITATION TREATY I AND II (SALT) SALT I (1972) was an agreement between the United States and the Soviet Union to freeze the number of strategic ballistic missiles at the 1972 levels. SALT II (1979) placed ceilings on strategic nuclear delivery vehicles and on MIRVed ballistic missiles (see also MULTIPLE INDEPENDENTLY TARGETABLE REENTRY VEHICLE).

STRATEGIC OFFENSIVE REDUCTIONS TREATY (SORT) A 2002 agreement, also known as the Moscow Treaty, between the United States and Russia in which each country pledged that by 2012 the aggregate number of their nuclear warheads will be between 1700 and 2200.

TACTICAL In the context of this book, *tactical* refers to shorter-range (nonstrategic) nuclear-capable missiles and aircraft.

THERMONUCLEAR BOMB See hydrogen bomb.

TRITIUM A hydrogen isotope with one proton and two neutrons. Tritium can be used in fission weapons to produce extra neutrons that add to the chain reaction. In this way, either less fissile material is required or the yield of the weapon is boosted as much as five times.

UNITED NATIONS MONITORING, VERIFICATION, AND INSPECTION COMMISSION (UNMOVIC) Created in 1999 by the UN Security Council, UNMOVIC was charged with verifying Iraq's obligation to give up all chemical, biological, and nuclear programs as well as missiles with ranges greater than 150 kilometers.

UNITED NATIONS RESOLUTION 1540 An April 2004 resolution adopted by the UN Security Council that requires states to create and enforce strong export controls, to criminalize proliferation of weapons of mass destruction (WMD), and to secure any WMD-related materials in their territories.

URANIUM A naturally occurring radioactive element. There are two common natural isotopes: uranium-235 (0.7 percent of natural uranium) and uranium-238 (99.3 percent of natural uranium).

URANIUM–235 The only fissionable isotope found in nature. Uranium-235 only makes up 0.7 percent of natural uranium. Light-water reactors use uranium that has about 3 percent uranium-235. Weapons-grade highly enriched uranium usually has 90 percent or more.

URANIUM–238 A fertile isotope, meaning that it does not easily fission, but can be converted into fissile material through neutron absorption. Nearly all (99.3 percent) of natural uranium is composed of this isotope.

URANIUM HEXAFLUORIDE (UF_6) Highly toxic gas that is the intermediate stage between yellowcake and enriched uranium. UF_6 is the feedstock for all uranium enrichment processes.

URANIUM OXIDE (U_3O_8) The most common oxide found in natural uranium ore. Uranium oxide is extracted from the crushed ore. Yellowcake is about 80 percent uranium oxide. See also yellowcake.

WEAPONS-GRADE Fissile material ideal for nuclear weapons. This includes uranium enriched to at least 90 percent uranium-235 and plutonium that is approximately 93 percent plutonium-239.

YELLOWCAKE A powdery concentrate of about 80 percent uranium oxide (U_3O_8) that is produced when uranium ore is crushed and leached. Yellowcake is converted to uranium hexafluoride gas (UF_6) in the process of creating enriched uranium.

YIELD The energy released in a nuclear explosion, expressed in equivalent metric tons of TNT. For example, a nuclear yield of 13 kilotons is equivalent to 13,000 tons of TNT.

INDEX